"The American Statesmen Series was a pathbreaking venture in its time; and the best proof of its continuing vitality for our time lies in the testimony of the introductory essays written by eminent scholars for the volumes of the Chelsea House edition–essays that not only explain the abiding value of the texts but in many cases represent significant scholarly contributions on their own.

"Chelsea House is contributing vitally to the scholarly resources of the country–and, at the same time, helping us all to understand and repossess our national heritage."

–Professor Arthur M. Schlesinger, jr.

Lewis Cass

American Statesmen Series

The Home of Lewis Cass

Other titles in this Chelsea House series:

CHARLES FRANCIS ADAMS, *Charles Francis Adams, Jr.*
JOHN ADAMS, *John Quincy Adams and Charles Francis Adams*
JOHN QUINCY ADAMS, *John T. Morse, Jr.*
SAMUEL ADAMS, *James K. Hosmer*
JUDAH P. BENJAMIN, *Pierce Butler*
JOHN C. CALHOUN, *Hermann E. von Holst*
SALMON P. CHASE, *Albert Bushnell Hart*
HENRY CLAY, *Carl Schurz*
ALBERT GALLATIN, *Henry Adams*
ALEXANDER HAMILTON, *Henry Cabot Lodge*
PATRICK HENRY, *Moses Coit Tyler*
ANDREW JACKSON, *William Graham Sumner*
JOHN JAY, *George Pellew*
THOMAS JEFFERSON, *John T. Morse, Jr.*
JAMES MADISON, *Sydney Howard Gay*
JOHN MARSHALL, *Albert J. Beveridge*
JAMES MONROE, *Daniel Coit Gilman*
GOUVERNEUR MORRIS, *Theodore Roosevelt*
JOHN RANDOLPH, *Henry Adams*
CHARLES SUMNER, *Moorfield Storey*
MARTIN VAN BUREN, *Edward M. Shepard*
GEORGE WASHINGTON, *John Marshall*
DANIEL WEBSTER, *Henry Cabot Lodge*

Forthcoming titles in this Chelsea House series:

JOHN P. ALTGELD, *Harry Barnard*
THOMAS HART BENTON, *Theodore Roosevelt*
JAMES G. BLAINE, *Edward Stanwood*
DANIEL BOONE, *Reuben G. Thwaites*
WILLIAM JENNINGS BRYAN, *M. R. Werner*
AARON BURR, *James Parton*
PETER COOPER, *R. W. Raymond*
STEPHEN A. DOUGLAS, *Allen Johnson*
DAVID FARRAGUT, *Alfred Thayer Mahan*
ULYSSES S. GRANT, *Louis A. Coolidge*
NATHANIEL GREENE, *Francis Vinton Greene*
MARCUS ALONZO HANNA, *Herbert D. Croly*
SAM HOUSTON, *Marquis James*
HENRY KNOX, *Noah Brooks*
LUTHER MARTIN, *Paul S. Clarkson and R. Samuel Jett*
ROBERT MORRIS, *Ellis Paxson Oberholtzer*
FRANKLIN PIERCE, *Nathaniel Hawthorne*
WILLIAM H. SEWARD, *Thornton K. Lothrop*
JOHN SHERMAN, *Theodore E. Burton*
WILLIAM T. SHERMAN, *B. H. Liddell Hart*
THADDEUS STEVENS, *Samuel W. McCall*
ROGER B. TANEY, *Carl Swisher*
TECUMSEH, *Glenn Tucker*
THURLOW WEED, *Glyndon G. VanDeusen*

LEWIS CASS

ANDREW C. McLAUGHLIN

INTRODUCTION BY

HOLMAN HAMILTON

American Statesmen Series

GENERAL EDITOR

ARTHUR M. SCHLESINGER, JR.

ALBERT SCHWEITZER PROFESSOR OF THE HUMANITIES

THE CITY UNIVERSITY OF NEW YORK

CHELSEA HOUSE

NEW YORK, LONDON

1980

Cover design by Zimmerman Foyster Design

Printed and bound in the United States of America

Library of Congress Cataloging in Publication Data

McLaughlin, Andrew Cunningham, 1861-1947.
Lewis Cass.

(American statesmen)
Reprint of the 1899 ed. published by Houghton
Mifflin, Boston, issued as v. 24 of American
statesmen.
Includes index.
1. Cass, Lewis, 1782-1866. 2. United States
--Politics and government--1815-1861.
3. Legislators--United States--Biography.
4. United States. Congress. Senate--Biography.
I. Series: American statesmen (New York)
II. Series: American statesmen ; v. 24.
[E340.C3M15 1980] 973.5'092'4 [B] 80-24025
ISBN 0-87754-192-2

Chelsea House Publishers
Harold Steinberg, Chairman & Publisher
Andrew E. Norman, President
Susan Lusk, Vice President
A Division of Chelsea House Educational Communications, Inc.
70 West 40 Street, New York 10018

CONTENTS

ILLUSTRATIONS

FOLLOWING PAGE 196

General Introduction

BLAZING THE WAY

Arthur M. Schlesinger, jr.

THE ORIGINAL AMERICAN STATESMEN SERIES consisted of thirty-four titles published between 1882 and 1916. Handsomely printed and widely read, the Series made a notable contribution to the popular appreciation of American history. Its creator was John Torrey Morse, Jr., born in Boston in 1840, graduated from Harvard in 1860 and for nearly twenty restless years thereafter a Boston lawyer. In his thirties he had begun to dabble in writing and editing; and about 1880, reading a volume in John Morley's English Men of Letters Series, he was seized by the idea of a comparable set of compact, lucid and authoritative lives of American statesmen.

It was an unfashionable thought. The celebrated New York publisher Henry Holt turned the project down, telling Morse, "Who ever wants to read American history?" Houghton, Mifflin in Boston proved more receptive, and Morse plunged ahead. His intention was that the American Statesmen Series, when complete, "should present such a picture of the development of the country that the reader who had faithfully read all the volumes would have a full and fair view of the history of the United States told through the medium of the efforts of the men who had shaped our national career. The actors were to develop the drama."

In choosing his authors, Morse relied heavily on the counsel of his cousin Henry Cabot Lodge. Between them, they enlisted an impressive array of talent. Henry Adams, William Graham Sumner, Moses Coit Tyler, Hermann von Holst, Moorfield Storey and Albert Bushnell Hart were all in their early forties when their volumes were published; Lodge, E. M. Shepard and Andrew C. McLaughlin in their thirties; Theodore Roosevelt in his twenties. Lodge took on Washington, Hamilton and Webster, and Morse himself wrote five volumes. He offered the authors a choice of $500 flat or a royalty of 12.5¢ on each volume sold. Most, luckily for themselves, chose the royalties.

Like many editors, Morse found the experience exasperating. "How I waded among the fragments of broken engagements, shattered pledges! I never really knew when I could count upon getting anything from anybody." Carl Schurz infuriated him by sending in a two-volume life of Henry Clay on a take-it-or-leave-it basis. Morse, who had confined Jefferson,

John Adams, Webster and Calhoun to single volumes, was tempted to leave it. But Schurz threatened to publish his work simultaneously if Morse commissioned another life of Clay for the Series; so Morse reluctantly surrendered.

When a former Confederate colonel, Allan B. Magruder, offered to do John Marshall, Morse, hoping for "a good Virginia atmosphere," gave him a chance. The volume turned out to have been borrowed in embarrassing measure from Henry Flanders's *Lives and Times of the Chief Justices.* For this reason, Magruder's *Marshall* is not included in the Chelsea House reissue of the Series; Albert J. Beveridge's famous biography appears in its stead. Other classic biographies will replace occasional Series volumes: John Marshall's *Life of George Washington* in place of Morse's biography; essays on John Adams by John Quincy Adams and Charles Francis Adams, also substituting for a Morse volume; and Henry Adams's *Life of Albert Gallatin* instead of the Series volume by John Austin Stevens.

"I think that only one real blunder was made," Morse recalled in 1931, "and that was in allotting [John] Randolph to Henry Adams." Half a century earlier, however, Morse had professed himself pleased with Adams's *Randolph.* Adams, responding with characteristic self-deprecation, thought the "acidity" of his account "much too decided" but blamed the "excess of acid" on the acidulous subject. The book was indeed hostile but nonetheless stylish. Adams also wrote a life of Aaron Burr, presumably for the Series. But Morse thought Burr no statesman, and on his advice, to Adams's extreme irritation, Henry Houghton of Houghton, Mifflin rejected the manuscript. "Not bad that for a damned bookseller!" said Adams. "He should live for a while at Washington and know our *real* statesmen." Adams eventually destroyed the work, and a fascinating book was lost to history.

The definition of who was or was not a "statesman" caused recurrent problems. Lodge told Morse one day that their young friend Theodore Roosevelt wanted to do Gouverneur Morris. "But, Cabot," Morse said, "you surely don't expect Morris to be in the Series! He doesn't belong there." Lodge replied, "Theodore . . . *needs the money*," and Morse relented. No one objected to Thomas Hart Benton, Roosevelt's other contribution to the Series. Roosevelt turned out the biography in an astonishing four months while punching cows and chasing horse thieves in the Badlands. Begging Lodge to send more material from Boston, he wrote that he had been "mainly evolving [Benton] from my inner consciousness; but when he leaves the Senate in 1850 I have nothing whatever to go by. . . . I hesitate to give him a wholly fictitious date of death and to invent all the work of his later years." In fact, T.R. had done more research than he pretended; and for all its defects, his *Benton* has valuable qualities of vitality and sympathy.

Morse, who would chat to Lodge about "the aristocratic upper crust in which you & I are imbedded," had a fastidious sense of language. Many years later, in the age of Warren G. Harding, he recommended to Lodge that the new President find someone "who can clothe for him his 'ideas' in the language customarily used by educated men." At dinner in a Boston club, a guest commented on the dilemma of the French ambassador who could not speak English. "Neither can Mr. Harding," Morse said. But if patrician prejudice improved Morse's literary taste, it also impaired his political understanding. He was not altogether kidding when he wrote Lodge as the Series was getting under way, "Let the Jeffersonians & the Jacksonians beware! I will poison the popular mind!!"

Still, for all its fidelity to establishment values, the American Statesmen Series had distinct virtues. The authors were mostly from outside the academy, and they wrote with the confidence of men of affairs. Their books are generally crisp, intelligent, spirited and readable. The Series has long been in demand in secondhand bookstores. Most of its volumes are eminently worth republication today, on their merits as well as for the vigorous expression they give to an influential view of the American past.

Born during the Presidency of Martin Van Buren, John Torrey Morse, Jr., died shortly after the second inauguration of Franklin D. Roosevelt in 1937. A few years before his death he could claim with considerable justice that his Series had done "a little something in blazing the way" for the revival of American historical writing in the years to come.

New York
May, 1980

INTRODUCTION
TO THE
CHELSEA HOUSE EDITION

Holman Hamilton

It may be that a thoroughgoing cynic would describe Lewis Cass as essentially a first-rate second-rate politician and leader. There were times in his life when the use of "second-rate" would surely be unfair; the most obvious of these, of course, came during the eighteen years when Cass served brilliantly as Governor of Michigan Territory. At other periods of his life, however, even a third-rate ranking might be too high. All in all, he was not an impressive figure on the floor of the Senate; in an era of great oratory, his speaking sank far below the norm. And as Secretary of State under James Buchanan there were moments when he seemed little more than a tragic excuse for elevation to Cabinet rank.

It is an intriguing mixture of a man, therefore, whom we appraise in this introduction for the revised American Statesmen Series. Cass's career began flourishingly. Born in Exeter, New

Hampshire, on October 9, 1782, he had the advantage of attending the celebrated academy at Exeter, where Daniel Webster was a schoolmate. Cass went west when young and grew up with the West of his time. Studying law, he was recognized for his legal ability; soon found himself the youngest member of the Ohio General Assembly; and was a general officer during the War of 1812. Although his military career on the whole was less than outstanding, he did distinguish himself at the Battle of the Thames and as a result was forever known as "General Cass."

It is virtually impossible to exaggerate the vigor, variety of interest, and judiciousness demonstrated by the transplanted New Englander throughout his gubernatorial years. Not even William Henry Harrison at a slightly earlier time in Indiana did more commendable work than Cass farther north. Perhaps the expression "cool judgment" best characterizes the leader's record. While he strongly advocated more democracy in Michigan and less dictation from the Governor himself, it may be concluded that to a considerable extent until 1831 Cass was Michigan and Michigan was Cass.

Happily married to Elizabeth Spencer, and the father of a young family, Cass was decidedly a man of private as well as public business. Early during his connection with Michigan, he bought a large tract of land in what became downtown Detroit. Later, he acquired much more land in the same area. The result was that the Governor was rich. Financially independent, he could do what he wanted to do with the remainder of his career—giving little thought to efforts at the bar, mercantile enterprise, or other interests, except as sidelines.

In 1831, Cass proved a logical choice for the post of Secretary of War in Andrew Jackson's second Cabinet. There he remained five years, continuing to the eve of the Van Buren administration and being identified with both the Black Hawk War of 1832 and the notorious Trail of Tears in the American Southwest. By Jacksonian standards, no one could have carried out the duties of the department with greater efficiency than the man from Michigan. Let it be remembered, too, that Cass headed the War Department in the course of South Carolina nullification. Much historical work remains to be done respecting details of his attitudes and contributions in each regard.

Cass's only foreign service took place from 1836 to 1842, when he served as Minister to France under Presidents Jackson, Van Buren, Harrison, and Tyler. Anti-British throughout his life, Cass was no particular favorite of his old chum Secretary of State Webster. The minister's relations with King Louis Philippe, however, were extraordinarily good in every way. Cass and the French appeared to enjoy each other. And Cass was even said to resemble the French monarch, which could hardly have been construed as a compliment either way.

Returning to the United States when the annexation of Texas and the Mexican War loomed as major issues before the country, Cass tried hard to find a viable solution to the question of the Wilmot Proviso. In fact, neither Stephen A. Douglas of Illinois nor even Daniel S. Dickinson of New York had a sounder claim to the authorship of "Popular Sovereignty." Cass ran for President as the Democratic nominee in 1848, using "Popular Sovereignty" as his campaign watchword. This was essentially the same slogan reused by Franklin Pierce in 1852, by James Buchanan in 1856, and by Douglas himself in the dramatic election of 1860. In Cass's case, he almost certainly would have defeated Whig nominee Zachary Taylor had it not been for a split in the Democratic party and the Free Soil candidacy of Martin Van Buren. Cass had served as a United States Senator prior to his presidential race and afterwards was again elected to that post—demonstrating the durability of his support in Michigan.

When Mrs. Cass died, her husband sought the White House no more but did agree to take the ranking appointive post in the Buchanan administration. From 1857 until December 1860, Cass was in general an efficient functionary in the Department of State. His influence on Buchanan, and especially on the domestic side of Buchanan's policies, was in the main minimal. Disagreeing with the President over extremely critical matters of a domestic nature in the late autumn and early winter of 1860, the venerable Cass resigned the secretaryship. It was perhaps reflective of the handicaps of his years and the nature of his weaknesses that he then tried to induce the chief executive to keep him in the State Department after all. But the career of the old gentleman now was at an end. And back he went to Michigan, where death came to him on June 17, 1866.

Many favorable things may be said concerning this political leader, especially in terms of his Michigan governorship, his efficiency as a War Department administrator, and his diplomatic gifts. Something of a scholar, and the author of a number of articles and books, he respected learning and made the most of his contacts with European culture. He had many friends in the Senate, one of the most curious being Henry S. Foote of Mississippi. He also possessed power in that body but as an orator could be one of the greatest bores around. From the point of view of the 1980s it is easy to disparage "Popular Sovereignty" and all its works; my own thinking is that scholars should be more aware of the intricate issues involved and less inclined to criticize congressmen who tried hard to find sensible solutions to a difficult problem. In his prime, there was something perhaps too pompous in Cass's personality—after his prime, perhaps at least a suggestion of the pathetic. Still he remains a significant figure—less colorful certainly than a Clay, a Webster, or a Calhoun, but far worthier of serious study and of scholarly analysis and depiction than most of his contemporaries.

The volume reproduced here came from the pen of one of the most distinguished of American historians. A native of Illinois, Andrew Cunningham McLaughlin moved to Michigan as a small child and grew up there; for many years his education was exclusively associated with that state. Principally recognized as a constitutional historian, McLaughlin is chiefly identified with the University of Chicago. He won the Pulitzer Prize in history, was president of the American Historical Association, and unquestionably ranked among the half-dozen notables of his profession in his era.

McLaughlin's *Lewis Cass* is far from being a great book. He composed it when he was very young, when he had much to learn, and when he was on less than solid ground regarding some of the major issues under consideration. Nevertheless, it is an absorbing volume to study and restudy for those very reasons and because McLaughlin recognized his own defects (chiefly youth and inexperience) and was wonderfully candid in discussing them with his readers. General Cass would have been an extremely difficult subject for any young biographer in the 1890s. Thus, rather than looking down our noses at the occasional limitations of McLaughlin, we have an opportunity to compare in an intelligent way what he did and did not do with what subsequent historians have been able to achieve.

Lexington, Kentucky
June, 1980

BIBLIOGRAPHICAL NOTE

The best book on Cass in many ways is *Lewis Cass, The Last Jeffersonian* (New Brunswick, 1950). Its author, Frank B. Woodford, was a Detroit newspaperman who both knew how to write and was not slovenly in research. The main defect of Woodford's product is that he seems on less secure ground during Cass's post-gubernatorial years than before. In terms of Michigan's territorial period, the volume is one that admirers should come back to year after year for fresh stimulation.

There are several early Cass biographies—not at all bad, and in fact superior to most of the contemporary books published on prominent Americans in the mid-1850s. W. L. G. Smith's *Fifty Years of Public Life: The Life and Times of Lewis Cass* (New York, 1856) should never be compared in the same breath to Woodford and McLaughlin, but it does have its special uses as various valuable Cass letters and other documents can be found there.

Numerous Cass writings are also available in Volumes X and XI of the *Territorial Papers of the United States* (Washington, 1943) and in the *Michigan Pioneer and Historical Collections.* There is an unpublished doctoral dissertation by Richard G. Hewlett, "Lewis Cass in National Politics, 1824-1861," available in the Burton Historical Collection at Detroit. *Messages of the Governors of Michigan,* edited by George N. Fuller, 4 vols. (Lansing, 1925-29); Floyd B. Streeter, *Political Parties in Michigan, 1837-1860* (Lansing, 1918); Elizabeth S. Brown, "Lewis Cass and the American Indian,"

Michigan History, XXXVII (June 1953), 286-98; and especially Francis Paul Prucha, *Lewis Cass and American Indian Policy* (Detroit, 1967) will shed light in a number of otherwise obscure locations.

AUTHOR'S PREFACE TO THE 1899 EDITION

THIS volume does not pretend to give a complete and detailed account of the life of Lewis Cass. Even some of the more important facts in his public career are omitted, or only alluded to in passing. He has been studied as a representative of the old Northwest, and one of the chief purposes of the book is to show the development of that section, to trace the growth of its political life. Evidently this could not be done in detail; all the manifestations of the Western spirit could not be dwelt upon, nor was it possible to estimate exactly the power and influence of Western sentiment in the councils of the nation, or to weigh accurately the Western ingredient in our national character. But students of American history have come to see that the course of events is not explicable if one pays attention to the work and the principles of Eastern men alone, and I am led to believe that, by studying the career of a man who thoroughly embodied for many years the nature of the newer West as it was before the civil war, I may have thrown some light upon the general history of the United States. Whether I have succeeded in this or not, one may say with confidence that a series of American statesmen would not be complete if it did not contain the biography of a typical Northwestern man, and show some appreciation of the fact that one of America's heaviest tasks and greatest achievements was to transform a wilderness into populous, organized communities, and that, as years went by, this Western country, full of eager, active, energetic men, who were made by natural circumstances self-confident and assertive, impressed itself upon the national life, and did something to shape the destinies of the United States. Some of the acts of Cass, which I believed, when preparing the first edition of this book, were due in large measure to personal characteristics or peculiarities, I have come to look upon as somewhat representative. His continuous, unbending opposition to England, for example, seems to have been a part of the exuberant patriotic enthusiasm of the West; and coupled with this was the feeling of "manifest destiny," which undoubtedly influenced him when considering such questions as the annexation of Texas and the "reoccupation" of the whole of Oregon.

In the preparation of this revised edition, I have not thought it best to make many changes. I have added something to the text of the first edition, and have made a few changes that seemed to me to be desirable. I have altered slightly the account of the surrender of Hull, thinking that the statement did not make sufficient allowance for the difficulties with which he was surrounded, and that it did not sufficiently take into consideration the fact that to some extent he was the victim of an incompetent military administration. But on the whole the judgments of the earlier edition must stand as they were first written.

Little material was found ready at hand for writing this biography, and I have been somewhat hampered by not having the correspondence or any considerable quantity of the private papers of Cass. Mr. W. L. G. Smith, while writing "The Life and Times of Lewis Cass," seems to have had access to a diary kept by Cass when on a tour to Greece and the farther East. Of the original I have found no trace, and have felt at liberty to refer to Mr. Smith's excerpts. In other particulars the pages of the public documents and of established authorities have furnished me with materials. I have not attempted to strengthen my assertions by reference to my sources of information; but in a few instances I have indicated by a footnote the material used, when I have consciously taken a suggestion from a secondary writer or borrowed a phrase or statement of fact. Occasionally a novel or important assertion has been supported by a reference to authority.

To those who are unacquainted with the details of the life of Cass, it may seem that I have given him praise where none was due, and at times made forced and unjustifiable excuses. This is the natural failing of a biographer; but I believe now, as I did when preparing the first edition, that on the whole my estimate is not far from right, although I admit, of course, that I may be mistaken, knowing how difficult is the task of forming such a judgment. While preparing the book I conferred with political foes of Cass as well as political friends, and found a remarkable consensus of opinion. I am not ready to believe that, if he was, as is often charged, a time-server and a "dough-face," bartering the approval of his conscience in exchange for political preferment, the men whom I consulted, and whom I knew to be men of probity and sound judgment, who were well acquainted with Cass in his lifetime, and some of whom were his earnest political opponents, would have had unswerving confidence in his sincerity. I may venture here to call the attention of the reader to a fact mentioned in the text and given on the testimony of the late Alpheus Felch, that the Michigan delegation in Congress approved of the Nicholson letter before it was published, which certainly is an indication that it was not a mere political subterfuge, but was the expression of honest opinion.

In the preparation of this book I received valuable suggestions from James V. Campbell, Isaac P. Christiancy, George V. N. Lothrop, and Alpheus Felch. All these persons were well acquainted with the public career of Cass, and three of them knew him intimately. I obtained some material through the kindness of the late Charles H. Bell of Exeter, New Hampshire. Grateful acknowledgments are also due to Professor Isaac N. Demmon, and to Professor Thomas M. Cooley, the learned writer on Michigan history.

ANDREW C. McLAUGHLIN.

UNIVERSITY OF MICHIGAN,
April 18, 1898.

LEWIS CASS

CHAPTER I

THE OLD NORTHWEST

THE five States north of the Ohio River form an historical and a geographical unit. They have their individual peculiarities, but possess common traditions and doubtless a common destiny. Their history does not begin with the Ordinance of 1787. Long before this characteristic American constitution was passed, or the Puritan of New England sought a new home west of the Alleghanies, this portion of our country had its records and its annals. In its later development under American auspices it felt the fashioning influences of the past. Tendencies strengthened by age cannot be counteracted in a moment. Time and trial are necessary elements in such a transformation as that which rejuvenated the old Northwest, filled it with vigor, with energetic American life and modern zeal for industry and political activity. The United States was the third power to occupy it. The earlier tenures by France and England furnished obstacles in the way of later American progress.

The Northwest is the first foster child of the Republic. The principles of Americanism now seem inborn and inbred; but foster child it is, and its growth has been influenced by its parentage and early training. Into parts of the country north of the Ohio the people from the South and East came suddenly and in swarms, which changed the face of nature so quickly that the historian has been content with exclamation. But Michigan was not thus re-clothed and energized in a moment. Wisconsin lagged and shuffled in her progress. Even Illinois and Indiana were slightly retarded by inherited incumbrances. It is true that "north of the Ohio the regular army went first,"[1] and the settler followed in its wake. But the regular army does not transform and renovate or sweep away on its bayonets the customs of a century's growth.

American statesmanship is not confined to waging political warfare or to winning victories of diplomacy. A good portion of the life of Lewis Cass was spent in striving to Americanize Michigan and other portions of the Northwest, to introduce popular government, modern methods of legal procedure, modern habits of life, modern civilization. In the development of Michigan from territorial confusion and uncertainty to the order of statehood, there were constant exertions to overcome inertia and to break away from the sluggish forces of the past. While guiding and directing

[1] Roosevelt, *Winning of the West*, vol. i. p. 24.

these exertions, while inculcating democratic ideas, while holding forth attractions to settlers, while struggling for the independence of the Northwest against British aggressions, Cass was performing the work of a national statesman and his efforts were of national concern.

Popular government was but slowly introduced into a territory which had been long contentedly under the sway of absolutism. Sault de Ste. Marie was established fourteen years before Philadelphia; Detroit but nineteen years after her Quaker sister. And yet, a hundred and twenty-five years after Penn begged his colonists not to be "so governmentish," the inhabitants of Michigan were living without capacity to appreciate or desire to know the delights of political controversies, which were so dear to the Americans of the coast. For more than a century after the exploration of the Northwest its history pertained to that of Canada, and that portion of the country, which was first settled and first came under Canadian influence, was the last to free itself from trammels of Celtic bondage and provincial ignorance.

The French with gracious ease seemed to insinuate themselves into the western country, following the watercourses as great highways to the unexplored interior. Long before the institutional Englishman plodded his way westward to the Alleghanies, the Frenchman had traversed the country of the Great Lakes and the Mississippi valley, and was familiar with the haunts of the beaver. The proselyting spirit of religion and the spirit of trade vied with each other in efforts to lead the way. Early in the seventeenth century, Récollet fathers landed at Quebec, prepared to begin a work of conversion among the Indians. Five years before the founding of Plymouth Champlain knew something of the great West. Gradually, by way of the Ottawa River and Georgian Bay, the Western country was discovered, French soldier or priest boldly entering unexplored rivers or skirting the coasts of unknown lakes with calm courage or with a simple faith which drove out fear. Wisconsin was known before Rhode Island was settled; and the hardy Jesuits began their work in northern Michigan before Puritanism had more than emerged from behind its stockades in a corner of rocky New England.

But the Iroquois could not be charmed by chanted vespers nor softened by Christian influence. The priest endured tortures and prayed without ceasing and without avail. Had he been successful, the Indians of western New York and northern Ohio would have been won over to purposes of French statecraft. They would have become an implacable enemy to Dutch aggression, an impassable barrier to the advance of English traders. As it was, England's enemies were pushed northwest into the upper lake region, and the Ohio valley was kept by the savage, until the English farmer, in response to demands of trade and agriculture, carried with him over the mountains the Penates of a constitutional state. Ohio had no history until the American colonist was ready to enter the country, ready to establish there real nerve centres of English influence, real vital and life-giving homes of English politics and English civilization.

There is nothing more interesting in the course of history. The heathen and savage guarded till the fullness of time a land destined to become the home of American constitutionalism, not to be blighted by imposed governments ordained by Richelieu and the state-absorbing monarchs of France. Long after Illinois and Wisconsin were known and their rivers described with some pretense at accuracy, Ohio was a *terra incognita*, the shores of Lake Erie unknown, the Ohio and the Wabash confused. Not till after the middle of the last century was there anything like an accurate knowledge of that portion of the Northwest which was nearest to English settlements and naturally the most accessible to the French. Even the Connecticut Land Company in 1796 found, by its surveys, that the Connecticut Reserve had a million acres less than geographical ignorance had anticipated.[1] This explains to some extent why the occupancy of Ohio, signalized by the landing of the "new pilgrims," at Marietta, differs from the occupation of many other portions of the Northwest.

[1] Hinsdale, *The Old Northwest.*

Neither the daring voyages of Hennepin, whose lies reveal a glimmer of truth and cloud an enviable reputation, nor the explorations of Joliet and Marquette need be recounted here. The journey of La Salle, who in 1682 floated his canoe down the Mississippi and took possession of the country in the name of King Louis, proclaimed the birth of New France with its two heads, as Parkman has so graphically expressed it, one in the canebrakes of Louisiana and the other amid the snows of Canada. But the task of connecting these two heads, of vitalizing the whole monster, of filling its veins with life-giving blood, was difficult and in the end impossible. Efforts were strenuously made to hold firmly the portions first known to French influence. Jesuits and traders settled in Wisconsin and Michigan. In 1671 Saint-Lusson, in solemn fashion, in presence of Indian braves and Frenchmen at the Sault, took possession of the surrounding country with overawing pomp and splendor. The great historian of French America may well suggest that all that remains of this pompous sovereignty is the "accents of France on the lips of some straggling boatman or vagabond half-breed." Yet this occupancy meant the introduction of French ideas, of French methods and policy of state, of French civilization guarded or retarded by the dictates of an absolute monarch. It meant that a century and a half was to pass before Michigan could cast aside her foreign trappings and take her place as a prosperous American territory with progressive American ideas. Ohio, which hardly knew the face of a white man until the New Englander came over the mountains with school-book and hymnal in his hands, was ready for statehood in fifteen years from that immigration. Michigan had to serve a dreary and necessary tutelage of nearly one hundred and seventy-five years from its first settlement before it struggled irregularly to its place beside the neighboring States. Wisconsin, discovered by the pushing fur trader two hundred and fifty years ago, has seen only within the last half century the beginnings of agricultural and manufacturing life.

The fur trade induced the French to take possession of Michigan and to hold it against all English aggression. Late in the seventeenth century there were efforts on the part of the English of New York to attract the Indians with English goods and rum, but all efforts to turn the fur trade from Montreal to New York were unavailing. If these attempts had been successful, the history of the northern lake region would have been totally different. Michigan would have been an English colony before Georgia, and in all probability would not for a century have lagged behind that State in progress. Nothing but concentrated and patriotic action could win the Northwest to England. For Louis XIV. took thought for the fur trade, and every element of Canadian progress or failure was of interest to him. He "subsidized nearly every branch of trade and industry, and in other instances did for the colonists what they would far better have learned to do for themselves."[1] Whatever revenue he obtained from Canada was derived from the fur trade, and this trade must be supported by the power and cunning of France. He was ready to salve his conscience with the statement that brandy not only secured the trade of Indians but drew them from English Protestantism within the blessed influences of the true religion.[2]

Yet the Northwest was really held for France by those whom Governor Denonville himself described as the damaging element in Canadian life. The fur trade was "hardy, adventurous, fascinating." Every effort was made to keep it under the control of the government, that the king might find remuneration for vast outlays and that the colonists might not feel its fascinations too strongly. Trade was put in a straight-jacket and chained to Montreal; monopoly succeeded monopoly in successive failures. But trade is aggressive if it exists at all, and it broke from its fastenings and flung away restraints. The Indians were intercepted on their way to Montreal, were "drenched with brandy," and their beaver skins bought for a song. Finally the adventurous and reckless among the settlers fled to the western woods, where they might live or trade as they desired. These law-breakers did now for France the work which

[1] Parkman's *Old Régime in Canada*, p. 284.
[2] *Ibid.* p. 327.

she was not quite ready to do for herself. These wandering bush-rangers held the Northwest against the English, and became the first white settlers of the Northern States. The English of New York were feeling their way in the direction of the fur country, and even before the end of the seventeenth century the Northwest might have fallen into the grasping clutches of English trade, to be settled by Englishmen and ruled with English methods, if the hardy, lawless *coureur des bois* had not pushed his way into the coveted country.

The bush-rangers hated England and adored the France whose laws they disregarded. They established trading posts throughout the wilderness some years before they made the attempt at permanent settlement. With an accurate knowledge of the topography of the country they took positions which in later years have been singled out for purposes of trade as well as defensive warfare. Du Lhut established a post on the northern shore of Lake Superior to prevent the possible approach of the Hudson Bay Company from the north. Governor Denonville was obliged to ask this man, who at one time was in danger of attracting all the youths of New France to the woods, to fortify the straits as a barrier to English advance in the South. In spite of restrictive laws and the displeasure of Louis himself, who, with a natural love of order and method, was sorely annoyed at the irregularities of the straggling *coureurs des bois*, who seemed to be destroying his fondest hopes of systematic and concentrated settlement along the St. Lawrence; in spite also of hardships and privations, the reckless bush-rangers increased in numbers, until it was said that every family of quality in Canada could count its friends and relatives among the rollicking outlaws, while the despairing English, longing for the beaver of Michigan, announced that they too must have "bush lopers."

A "picturesque" element were these men in the life of early Canada, picturesque on their return to brawl and gamble in the settlements after a long, successful journey of fur hunting, and "artistic,"[1] as with courage and reckless thoughtlessness they made their way into the western wilderness. But they were more than picturesque and artistic. They early influenced the savages to hate the English, and to look upon the French as their allies, and this was of vast importance in the after efforts for domination. Moreover, with a marvelous adaptability, many assumed Indian habits and ingratiated themselves by becoming Indians. After years of law-breaking or wood-ranging, unused to the amenities of civilization or the restraints of law, they settled through the western country with Indian wives or concubines, raised a brood of half-breed children, and passed their days in worse than savage idleness.

When the time came to change French for Eng-

[1] Parkman's *Old Régime in Canada.*

lish control, the Indians reluctantly consented, and down to the middle of the present century, although the British were generally preferred to the Americans, the French were greatly preferred to either. "Whatever may have been the reason," said Governor Cass, "the fact is certain that there is in the French character peculiar adaptations to the habits and feelings of the Indians, and to this day the period of French domination is the era of all that is happy in Indian reminiscences."[1] At the Sault de Ste. Marie, in 1826, a Chippewa chief, addressing the American agent, thus pathetically referred to the happy days of the French dominion in the West: "When the Frenchmen arrived at these falls they came and kissed us. They called us children and we found them fathers. We lived like brethren in the same lodge, and we had always wherewithal to clothe us. They never mocked at our ceremonies, and they never molested the places of our dead. Seven generations of men have passed away, but we have not forgotten it. Just, very just, were they towards us."[2]

"The French empire in America," says Parkman, "could exhibit among its subjects every shade of color from white to red, every gradation of culture from the highest civilization of Paris to the rudest barbarism of the wigwam."[3] The *savoir vivre* of these people displayed itself. With

[1] *Historical Sketches of Michigan*, p. 24.
[2] Mrs. Jameson, *Winter Studies, etc.* p. 130.
[3] *Conspiracy of Pontiac*, p. 69.

their influence over the Indians and their traditions of inertia, their hatred of innovation and their utter lack of ability to understand constitutional principles or legal procedure, they formed a conditioning element in the development of the West. An experienced observer writing in 1845 assures us that the average French-Canadian voyageur had less perception and general intellectual capacity than his Indian companion.[1] These men, and their fathers before them, living in ignorance, fell to a plane below the ignorant savage with whom they mingled. At the present day the half-breeds form a large shiftless element among the woodsmen of the northern lake region. Many of these bush-rangers, leading Indian lives, were scattered among the western tribes, but besides these a large number of watermen, retired from active employment, formed rude settlements along the streams and bays which open into the great lakes. Here in unambitious content they spent their lives and perpetuated their lazy characteristics in a numerous progeny. Often Indian wives tilled the fields while the gossiping voyageur smoked away the day. In some of the more regular settlements there were French women, and though there was a remarkable ignorance of agricultural methods, the men succeeded in raising enough to keep their families in comfort.

The first settlements in Wisconsin were all of this irregular kind. Retired watermen, in their

[1] H. R. Schoolcraft, *Onéota.*

narrow farms fronting the river, lived in blissful ignorance of any aim in life except to live. The *coureur des bois* settled thus as fancy dictated. Such an irresponsible settlement was the one at Prairie du Chien. And a like settlement gradually grew up at Green Bay, begun near the middle of the last century, and slowly augmented by the advent of unemployed *engagées*. Their small farms were tilled with care sufficient to secure the necessary crops of wheat and peas. At the beginning of this century it was impossible to tell what blood flowed in the veins of the settlers. There was only one woman, we are told, in the latter settlement who pretended to be "all white," and she had been "accidentally" imported. Nevertheless the manners of these simple people were fascinating, for in spite of the admixture of the blood of the red man, who has his own dignity and stately ease, they never lost the graces of old France. Here at Green Bay there were good examples of what these semi-French conceived to be government. Many are the amusing stories of how Justice Reaume, in patriarchal fashion, enforced his own sweet will as the law of the land. Well on in the present century, when Wisconsin was fairly under American government and there was an effort to introduce popular methods, this curious old justice knew much more of *Coutume de Paris* than of the common law. His jackknife in the hands of an extemporized constable performed the functions of a common seal, and he gave his unique decisions in his broad French or broken English without reference to anything but the law of prejudice.

Turning to Michigan, we find there various settlements of this kind, founded under similar conditions; but these did not become centres of growth and development under the French *régime.* Michigan was the home of the beaver, and the French authorities soon realized the importance of securing this portion of the West by responsible settlements. La Motte Cadillac seems first to have entertained the idea of making "the straits" a centre of French control in the West, to defend the fur trade, prevent English encroachments, and assure permanent influence over the neighboring Indian tribes. Already renowned as a faithful officer and soldier, he at last gained the end of his desires, and in 1701 reached Detroit with his company of soldiers and artisans. These early settlers were not lowborn or lawless. Everything was conducted in an orderly and systematic manner, under the auspices of government. The slur passed upon the citizens of Detroit by Governor Hull and Judge Woodward in October, 1805, was a needless one. "When it is remembered," they said, "that the troops of Louis XIV. came without women, the description of persons constituting the second generation will not be difficult to conceive."[1] La Hontan's graphic description of how women were sent over in cargoes to become

[1] *Michigan Pioneer Col.*, vol. viii. p. 404.

the wives of the Canadian settlers is well known. Mother Mary, not entirely pleased with such consignments of mixed goods ("*une marchandaise mêlée*"), complained of "*beaucoup de scandale.*" Doubtless Canada has been feebly blessed by these persons and their descendants. But such were not the early settlers of Detroit. The whole history of that city shows that the residents were of no mean birth, surely not in a demoralized condition, or from a low and depraved ancestry. Into various portions of Canada many respectable and even noble persons immigrated, and the permanent settlements of Michigan were not less favored.

For various reasons Detroit developed but slowly after this auspicious foundation. At times the French authorities were unfriendly to colonization. They were encouraged in their hostility by the missionaries on the one hand, who feared the vices of civilization, and who desired that the Indians should come in contact with none but themselves, and by the fur trader on the other, who was naturally averse to the advance of the homes of men into the midst of the lodges of the beaver. Moreover there was no instinctive appreciation of the fitness of things. Land was granted under the most absurd feudal restrictions, so to be held until American practical sense disposed of the absurdities. The place was, however, a centre of French influence in the West, and gradually assumed permanence and a degree of prosperity. It was not an ill-formed, straggling village, where rough watermen and half-breeds passed their lazy lives. We have reason to believe that from the first there was comfort, and occasionally even an approach to elegance, in the houses that clustered in and around the stockade. For some of the early townsmen were artisans, who desired by work and by a very moderate thrift to establish themselves and their families in comfort. It will not do, however, to banish entirely from the colony the picturesque bush-ranger. The town, which had been placed in the very midst of his hunting grounds, was often visited when savings were to be squandered in merriment and riot; the descendants of these happy trappers and watermen were the boatmen of the earlier part of this century; their frail canoes carried Cass to many a treaty ground, from Detroit to the head of Lake Superior, to Green Bay or Chicago.

Seventy-five years ago Detroit was still a French settlement, and fifteen years ago its French characteristics were evident to the stranger in a casual visit to the city. The few Scotch who came in during the latter years of the English dominion affiliated with the French and appreciated their conservatism. In consequence of this ancestry, there has always been a steadiness and sobriety in business and a caution and reserve in society. It has not felt until recently the stir of American life as has Buffalo, or Cleveland placed in the heart of "New Connecticut." It can scarcely be doubted that conservative French Catholicism has had its influence in giving a peculiar tone and setting a dignified pace. It is true that after Detroit had been ostensibly an American city for forty years, the introduction of New England life gave the town a look of prosperity and activity which was lacking to the Canadian towns across the river. But the comparison rather accentuates than contradicts the previous assertions. Not long ago, easily within the memory of men now living in Detroit, the well-to-do French peasant held his acres and refused twice their value, or demanded perhaps that the city put a rail-fence on each side of the street which eminent domain had forced through his land. In 1818 the people of Michigan refused to take upon themselves the popular privileges offered by the charter of 1787. A number of other examples might be given of how conservatism has influenced Michigan and its chief city in their development into modern American life.

For a long time Detroit was practically Michigan. For French and American tendencies are different. If the Americans had first settled Michigan, the farmer would have pressed into the country in the footsteps of the fur trader, farms would have appeared in secluded places in the forests, and a town would have grown up from natural causes and developed as the needs of the farming community of the back-country dictated. But as the gregarious and social tendencies of the French have made Paris the centre of their life, so in the western woods all roads led to the rude metropolis, and it had an unusual dignity and importance. We are enabled, therefore, to concentrate our attention; and in examining with some care the life of Detroit and its vicinity we shall see the lives of the better element of the French settlers in the northwest. Their habits are the best guide-posts to their characters, and best indicate the peculiar position of these people in northwestern history.

Down to 1763 the city grew slowly by the immigration of discharged soldiers or settlers from Canada. In the time of the English domination there came a few English traders and a few canny Scotch with their habits of thrift and deftness. But the French *habitant* does not allow his ease to be interfered with. Everywhere the world presents the same roseate hue to his contented vision. After 1796 some Americans, making their way into the territory, jostle him about a little, insist on trial by jury, talk to him of popular elections and other incomprehensible problems, suggest the idea that Detroit may become a great commercial centre. He is called upon by an impudent investigating committee to show the title deeds to the farm which his father and father's father held before him. A look of uncertainty and mild inquiry occasionally appears on his placid face. The narrow streets are filled with Indians rushing to exchange their peltries for American goods, and to pay enormous prices for inferior articles. After the war of 1812 a few Marietta settlers find their way to the Straits, and a few educated families from New England form a conspicuous element in the city's life. But the Frenchman passes this all by with a shrug at the curious activity of the energetic "*Bostonais.*" His social life flows smoothly on in the same old channels. Until the people from New England and New York begin to pour into the territory through the newly-opened Erie canal, one can trace few changes in the general characteristics of the place. Detroit in the first quarter of this century has still the tint of a bygone age. One feels, as he looks at her, that he has slipped back into the Middle Ages, long before there was any prophetic consciousness of the dust, din, and uproar of the busy and scientific nineteenth century. He sees a picture of unpretentious comfort and happy listlessness. Without even the knowledge that Protestantism was a religion, the *habitant* clung to his beloved Catholic worship. His daily life was graced with interruptions of picturesque festivals, cheered with merrymakings and adorned with highly-colored ceremonies. Like the neighbors of Goldsmith's good vicar, he "observed festivals and intervals of idleness and pleasure; kept up the Christmas carol, sent true-love knots on Valentine morning, ate pancakes on Shrovetide, and religiously cracked nuts on Michaelmas eve." With the simple joy which comes with the consciousness of irresponsibility, he took part in games and jollities, which are far below the responsible dignity of later American money-making.

The *habitants*, whose farms stretched back from the river, with scarcely a gap between them from Lake Erie to Lake St. Clair, had in general the characteristics of the better class of Canadian farmers.[1] They were honest, hospitable, religious, inoffensive and uninformed, possessed of simplicity and civility. Without ambition and attached to ancient prejudices, they sought no more than the necessaries of life. Many, as a result of happy inaction, were poor without realizing their poverty; some were well-to-do without boasting of their wealth. Strangers were received with unembarrassed politeness, without traces of rusticity in manners or speech. Mrs. Jameson, the delightful critic of Shakespeare, who visited this western country in 1837, writes, in wondering admiration of the polished address of the simple farmer: "If you would see the two extremes of manner brought into near comparison, you should turn from a Yankee store-keeper to a French Canadian." His language, too, betokened his pure descent; for the patois of the French settler of the Northwest is largely a myth created by the reasoning imagination of thoughtless travelers or indiscriminating writers. The bushranger, whose settlements have been described, doubtless often cumbered his speech with Indian words and confused it with half-remembered constructions. But such was not the case with the *habitants* near Detroit or the average farmer of Canada. It was "curious" but not un-

[1] George Heriot, *Travels in Canada*, London, 1807.

usual to find in the western wilderness "a perfect specimen of an old-fashioned Norman peasant — all bows, courtesy, and good humor;" and his speech was not less purely Celtic than were his unalloyed courtesy and grace.

The Frenchman is dependent on companionship. The pioneer life of the American farmer ripens individuality and intensifies salient characteristics, until the word "character" itself is synonymous with person; but nothing is more evident than the utter lack of individuality or aggressive personality among the Western Frenchmen. When one of a class is seen all his fellows are known to us. The Frenchman could not think of going alone into the woods to cut out of the very forest a home for himself and family, a feat of wonderful self-sufficiency so common to the independent American farmer. One farm must be within hailing distance of another, or the French farmer is miserable in his loneliness. Down the Detroit River the farms extended back from the stream, each having its own water frontage. Such "pipe stem" tracts may still be seen in the vicinity of Detroit, like those of the quaint settlements along the St. Lawrence and its tributaries. The social farmers could shout to one another from their doorsteps,[1] and would carry on their gossipy conversations when they ought to have been tilling their fields. The stream-haunting Canadian has been happily compared to the beaver or the muskrat. At times

[1] Bela Hubbard, *Memorials of a Half Century*, p. 116.

he seemed to live in the waters and marshes around him, building his cabin where it was accessible only to a canoe. The miasma which he breathed seemed to furnish him with food rather than engender disease. A century and more after the founding of Detroit the farms still clung lovingly to the river banks, and a mile back from the streams was still seen the untouched forest. The troops, who came from Ohio to Detroit in 1812, found only one muddy road winding along between stream and wood, a situation which offered the lurking savages every opportunity for ambush and attack. What roads there were, the water-loving *habitant* despised; but over his rough highways he jogged merrily to market with a two-wheeled Norman cart and rough dwarfish pony, a curious mongrel animal of unknown pedigree, but with an endurance and possible speed which delighted the simple peasant or his rollicking sons.

Covetousness was the most infrequent vice; for, although they did not know the best arts of husbandry, these simple farmers nevertheless provided from their own resources everything necessary to supply their wants. The arts of the tailor and mason were often added to the clumsy skill of the agriculturist; while tanning and shoemaking were not uncommon acquirements. Their implements were crude, rough, and heavy; their methods of tillage ludicrous to the modern farmer. The cumbersome plough, to which was attached a pony, or mayhap a cow or steer, was used somewhat effectively, but the corn was tilled with the Indian hoe in the simple fashion learned from the red man. In fruit-raising they excelled; beautiful orchards were often crowded into the narrow farms; cherries and peaches furnished by distillation an exhilarating drink, and cider continually provided a mild stimulant. But the French farmer did not succeed in becoming the ruling spirit and progressive citizen of the West, because, as a French traveler gravely suggests, he talked too much and consulted his wife too often, and spent his time in argument rather than in work.

The ordinary *habitant*, however listless and unambitious, did not lack many comforts. Gay and happy with a little, he often indulged even in the pomps and vanities of life. Some of the families had plate and silks and luxuries of various kinds, which, though not paraded, revealed noble descent, and argued the existence of at least the traditions of wealth.[1] The houses were simple, of hewn logs, occasionally covered with clapboards, and lighted in the low upper story with quaint dormer windows, which gave, to those in the town especially, a Dutch appearance, and suggested to the New York immigrant, as he entered the territory, the Knickerbocker region of his own State. Here the people lived in simple and picturesque fashion. Their amusements were many, and their gayeties intense. When Detroit under its American rulers began to take on business airs, many were the

[1] Campbell, *Outlines of Political History of Michigan*, p. 212.

grumblings at the ordinances which prevented horse-racing through the narrow streets, or interfered with the jolly game of ten-pins, for which the street was used as an alley, and a cannon ball as a missile. When winter set in, the people gave themselves up to pleasure-seeking. Their shaggy ponies, which had been allowed all summer long to roam the woods or scamper uncontrolled along the river banks, now became their special pride. The swiftest of the herd was dearly cherished; and the highest ambition of the farmer was to drive the fastest pony. The frozen river was the theatre of delights, or the "Grand Marais"[1] a few miles above the city, swollen with autumn rains, offered its icy attractions. Sunday, as in most Catholic countries, was a day for enjoyment as well as solemn worship, and Saturday was generally an occasion of unrestrained merry-making. Indeed, one need not single out days. Sleigh-riding, dancing, feasting, and uncontrolled levity filled up the passing winter weeks. A summer's providence was easily lost in a winter's mild dissipation.

Such was the life of a simple and illiterate people, and such it long continued to be. Years after the introduction of American farming methods, business enterprise and governmental policy, we find the same unprogressive spirit, unaffected by the serious humor with which the American under-

[1] Sheldon, *Early History of Michigan*, p. 371; *Memorials of a Half Century*, p. 141.

takes both his work and his pleasure. One naturally lingers over this picture of early social simplicity and unrestrained gayety; for, leaving out of consideration the influences on history and development, all that now remains is a "pipe-stem" farm or a huge old pear-tree, to remind us of this mediæval mosaic snugly fitted into modern civilization.

One must not think, however, that all the settlers were of this fortunate, light-hearted, comfortable class, who labored lazily in summer and spent the winter in energetic frivolity. These formed the majority at Detroit and in the eastern portion of Michigan. But two classes can be differentiated. There were some of the lower class who gave up a life of wandering but never became used to the graces and loose restraints of such civilization. A few retired watermen and bush-rangers settled there, in despair over their vanishing profession. The "dark-complexioned imps with high cheek-bones and indescribably mischievous eyes," whom Harriet Martineau described as Flibbertigibbets rowing or diving or playing pranks on the shores of Michigan, were the half-breed progeny of these men, who joined themselves in informal wedlock with the beauties of the forest. There were some of these bronzed watermen, unattractive though picturesque, even in Acadian Detroit; and they formed the most ignorant and the rudest element of early Michigan.

Frenchtown, where Monroe now stands, had a

goodly number of farms nestling up to each other, with their heads on the banks of the River Raisin; and these were mostly inhabited by French Canadians quite inferior to those near Detroit. They exhibited more than the usual density of ignorance and stupidity in tillage. As late as 1816 General Cass, in a letter to the secretary of war, stated that not a pound of wool was manufactured by a person of Canadian descent in the Territory, although four fifths of the inhabitants were of that descent; the fleece of the sheep was thrown away or used to cover up a cellar window. The making of soap for family purposes was an American innovation. Especially the Raisin settlers, it is apparent, were slothful to the point of poverty. In the destruction and desolation left by the war of 1812, they seemed caught in the meshes of ignorance and despair; and the bounties of government were needed to extricate them. In 1807 the farmers of Canada had begun to adopt from the English the idea of fertilizing their exhausted farms;[1] but long after that the French of Michigan dumped all fertilizers into the rivers.[2]

Once more a comparison between Michigan and Ohio will show how different were the American and the earlier French settlers. One of the first acts of the Ohio Company was to provide for the services of a suitable person as a public teacher for the settlement on the Ohio. The directors

[1] *Travels in Canada*, George Heriot.

[2] Cass's Letters, State Archives, Lansing, Michigan.

were "requested to pay as early attention as possible to the education of youth and the promotion of public worship among the settlers," and to employ an instructor "eminent for literary accomplishments." In Michigan, a hundred years after its settlement, general education was unthought of. A few of the more wealthy and worldly of the Detroit townsmen sent their sons to the East. An occasional school was of no influence, no centre of enlightenment. In 1817 the "Gazette," a struggling newspaper of Detroit, thus encouraged the French to effort: "Frenchmen of the Territory of Michigan, you ought to begin immediately to give an education to your children. In a little time there will be in this Territory as many Yankees as French, and if you do not have your children educated the situations will all be given to the Yankees," — a touching utilitarian appeal to come in the very year when curious old Judge Woodward was coining from his inventive brain "Catholepistemiad, or University of Michigania." For just at that time the Yankee minority were beginning to think of the text-book and the ferule. Many a year after this editorial the French seemed fully convinced that it is folly to be wise. Few children learned to read, but the patient priest taught them their catechism and showed them how to tell their beads with devotional regularity.[1] The people were ignorant of the English language, and often did not know of the legislation enacted

[1] Hubbard, *Memorials of a Half Century*, p. 140.

by their new rulers. In 1810 a petition was presented requesting the publication of laws in French as well as English.

The slow method of conducting legal business, coming in with the Americans, was a source of never ending surprise to the ordinary inhabitant, who had rarely come into contact with any but the sharp edge of the law. The proceedings of the new courts puzzled him. Unaccustomed to trial by jury, he could see no advantage in that intricate and tedious method of deciding a suit which would have been disposed of in a moment by the French or the English authorities before the arrival of the technical American. For a long time all legal business, where a Frenchman was concerned, was carried on through the medium of an interpreter — a clumsy method at the best. The attorney was a new species, which seemed, ghoul-like, to fatten on other's misfortunes, and to take a gruesome pleasure in seeking out forgotten titles and undivided interests. The Americans have not unjustly been called a litigious people. Often the enthusiastic Western lawyer encouraged litigation, and there was every temptation at Detroit to peer into neglected corners; for scarcely a landholder in the Territory knew how he held his land. The French, on the other hand, were exasperating to the busy Yankee; for they never did to-day what could be delayed till the morrow.[1]

[1] *Report of Committee of House of Representatives relative to State of Territory of Michigan*, 1807.

The first public building in an American settlement is the court-house, the second the jail, and the third the schoolhouse, where religious services are sometimes held.[1] The first thing the French do is to erect a church under the direction of a fatherly priest, and the village clusters around it, or stretches out from it along the river bank. The noticeable feature to-day in the antique villages of Canada is the little chapel surmounted by a cross. By its side are the priest's tidy dwelling and flower garden, all in a neat and holiday attire in comparison with the houses which crouch in humble penitence near by.

Kaskaskia and Vincennes and other settlements were places of importance in Northwestern history, and there, too, the French influence is discernible. But though more than once French conservatism acted as a brake on the wheels of progress, Illinois and Indiana did not feel the burden of the old occupancy as did Michigan. The old towns of these two States had passed a century of listless existence, not varied by the introduction of new ideas, or bothered by needless civilization, when the pushing American settler came to turn them upside down with his provoking hurry and energy.

Lewis Cass was a statesman of the Northwest. He was for a number of years engaged in the administration of Northwestern affairs; and when he passed to a broader field, he remained for years

[1] Schoolcraft, *Journey in Central Portion of Mississippi Valley*, p. 37.

the most conspicuous representative of the people of the Northwest. In the earlier period he was a leader, and guided rather than obeyed the reins of the popular will. When in later years he ceased to guide, he long represented his constituents. Their progress can be seen in a study of his life. His life can be seen in studying the progress of his section of the country. No adequate portrait of the man can be obtained, unless there is a background, which will throw his characteristics into relief. In the pages which follow there will be no effort to measure exactly French resistance to American civilization and government, or to determine accurately the weight of Cass's influence in making Michigan American. Such tasks are from the nature of things impossible. But there will be an attempt to recount his work, and to exhibit him in proper perspective. It is evident that there were difficulties to be overcome. The Northwest was a natural pendant to the St. Lawrence Valley; but won by the English, and later won from them by the Americans, it became pendant to the country east of the Appalachians. Its political allegiance was thus determined. But its social existence, its real political life, its individuality could not be recreated by force and arms. Perhaps one is not altogether wrong in thinking that as the civil law and French custom remained in Louisiana after its acquisition by the United States, Michigan, too, might in no small measure have retained the permanent impress of French ideas, had it not been for the energy of one of the most American of American statesmen. However that may be, the characteristics of the French settlers have their importance in Northwestern history, and even if we admit that this element in Michigan was submerged by the inflowing tide from the Eastern States as early as 1830 or 1835, a narrative of Northwestern development must take its beginnings in an account of the French occupation, and must consider the nature of French life and habits of thought and action. The *habitants* were not a source of danger; they were not treacherous conspirators; the descendants of the more intelligent and well-to-do became substantial citizens of Detroit and of other cities. And yet one must see that the assimilation of this element was not an unimportant task. Doubtless Judge Schley spoke in exaggerated phrase when he wrote of Detroit, in 1802: "Nothing frightens the Canadians like taxes. They would prefer to be treated like dogs, and kenneled under the whip of a tyrant, than contribute to the support of a free government." But this exaggeration, if such it be, leads one to realize the underlying truth, and to see how different was the situation in no small portion of the Northwest from that obtaining in other parts of the United States in early times.

One other phase of Northwestern history needs to be examined if we are to understand the development of the country, or appreciate the work of its statesmen. The possessors of the St. Lawrence valley had a traditional control over the Indians. Wolfe's victory on the Plains of Abraham has been called the most important date in modern history, and the beginning of the history of the United States. It had its influence on the Northwest. English rum took the place of French brandy. English presents supplanted French tact. For the rest of the century the Indians looked to the English for encouragement and protection. During the Revolution, Detroit was the centre of their dealings. Hamilton, "the hair buyer," paid the bounty on American scalps, and doled out rum in enormous quantities. "I observe with great concern," wrote Governor Haldiman, "the astonishing consumption of rum at Detroit, amounting to the rate of 17,500 gallons per year."[1] By the peace of 1783 the Northwest was ceded to the United States, but the military posts were not given up by the British. The Indians were encouraged[2] to prevent the Americans from entering the country north of the Ohio, and only a corner of that region was occupied before Wayne's victory over the Indians in 1794. As the French

[1] Haldiman Papers, *Michigan Pioneer Collection.*

[2] A full examination of the original material of the period enables one to say with assurance that the English government at no time openly instigated the Indians to hostilities against the United States. But the English officials in this country sympathized with the Indians in their desire to retain all the country north of the Ohio; and some of them at critical juncture gave material aid to the red men in the way of food and blankets, if not ammunition.

fur trader had hindered the encroachments of the British, so now the fur trader of English Montreal sought to prevent the Americans from entering the fur region of the Northwest. Detroit was not given up till July 11, 1796. It is said that, on leaving the fort, the English filled the wells with rubbish, and destroyed the windmills of the vicinity. This is only an ill-humored tradition; but beyond all doubt they left behind them the rubbish of a cruel and unnecessary occupancy, much less easily removed and much more inimical to the advancement of American interests than was any material débris. The Indians long remained dependents of the British and attached to British interests. A great portion of the life of Cass was devoted to winning the Indians to their proper allegiance, and obtaining a proper respect for American authority. All the energies of this Northwestern leader were not absorbed by two tasks, counteracting British influences and introducing American democracy. But these first presented themselves as he entered the field of national statesmanship; these form the starting point, and explain many a circumstance throughout the whole course of his life.

CHAPTER II

EARLY LIFE

One who examines the genealogical records of New England will observe that the name Cass appears not infrequently. One branch of the family is traceable to John Cass, of Hampton, born in 1644. From him descended Jonathan who, in the days before the Revolutionary War, was living in Exeter, N. H. He seems to have been a young man of exceptional vigor and promise. The place of his residence is pointed out with interest, and the local historian finds reason to describe him in a manner likely to enlist sympathy and attention. At the outbreak of the Revolution Jonathan was an energetic young blacksmith,[1] too full of life and eager restlessness to be

[1] William T. Young in his *Life of Lewis Cass*, published at Detroit in 1852, and written doubtless in some measure from information obtained from Cass himself, calls Jonathan a "mechanic." W. L. G. Smith, in his *Life and Times of Lewis Cass*, says that the father was a part of the time engaged in cutting logs and making lumber. The late Charles H. Bell of Exeter, who has written the history of that place, assured me after examining the town records that he was a blacksmith. Probably he was not engaged permanently in any one employment; but I am led to believe that he was not shiftless and did not live in poverty.

wedded to the fiery joys of the forge, and too full of patriotism to await the second call to arms when the battle of Lexington proclaimed that war was actually begun. His comrades afterwards remembered him as an erect handsome man with keen black eyes, and so he appears in the artistic portrait still preserved by his descendants.

He must have been in his twenty-third[1] year when he entered the army, which he is said to have done almost immediately after Lexington. He was present at the battle of Bunker Hill, and seems to have been actively engaged at Princeton, Trenton, Monmouth, and all the other important battles of the war in the central and northern part of the country. His merits won him an ensigncy as early as 1777, and by the close of the war he had secured a captain's commission. At that time he returned to Exeter, to remain till other duties called him once more to a life of greater excitement and activity when the presence of British emissaries in the West demanded a second enlistment.

In 1781 he married Mary Gilman, who belonged to a branch of the Gilman family which traces its ancestry back to Norfolk, England, where, in 1558, were living the forefathers of those who in 1635 landed in Boston, and began life in the New World. In a house which stood on the east side of Cross Street, now Cass Street, Exeter, Lewis Cass was born October 9, 1782. The house was

[1] Niles, vol. xxxix. p. 157; Evarts, *Muskingum County, Ohio*, p. 352. *Contra*, Smith's *Life and Times of Lewis Cass*, p. 15.

not, as Mr. Smith describes it, a "small unpretending wooden dwelling-house," nor is there any reason for crediting the tradition that young Lewis was cradled in "a sap-trough." The building was large for those days, or at least far from small and humble. It was one of the customary pine boxes of New England, with a central chimney and a front hall, on each side of which opened large, square, comfortable rooms. Jonathan no doubt was able to furnish a good cradling for his first-born. Lewis was the eldest of six children, the youngest of whom was only eight years his junior.

His boyhood fell in the uneasy anxious times of the Confederation. The air was full of political clamor, and electric with dreaded disaster. State selfishness and political greed were the accompaniments of personal selfishness. Avarice and dishonesty were the natural effects of a demoralizing war. All, who thought, hoped desperately or foretold the worst. In after years Lewis Cass looked back upon those boyhood years with a memory retentive of their deep impressions. If in later years he had a never-failing love for the Union and the Constitution, he might trace it in part to the relief that came when the Constitution was adopted, and the Union was no longer a shadow. "You remember, young man," he said to James A. Garfield in 1861, "that the Constitution did not take effect until nine States had ratified it. My native State was the ninth. It hung a long time in doubtful scale whether nine would agree;

but when, at last, New Hampshire ratified the Constitution, it was a day of great rejoicing. My mother held me, a little boy of six years, in her arms at a window, and pointed me to the bonfires that were blazing in the streets of Exeter, and told me that the people were celebrating the adoption of the Constitution. So I saw the Constitution born, and I fear I may see it die."

His native State had known, before that joyful ratification, much of turbulence and disorder. The paper-money mob of 1786 was one of those explosions which were only too common throughout the distraught Confederation. Paper money had played many a prank in colonial times, but the favors of an unlimited issue were still eagerly sought by those whom the war had impoverished, and by those who, restless when the war was over, demanded new opportunities, and were dissatisfied because a war for liberty had not brought them wealth, honor, and the golden age which had been preached as the ever-present heaven of democracy. The contest which ensued between the supporters of law and the mob is graphically described by local historians.[1] Jonathan Cass, whose zeal for authority and love of order are apparent throughout life, was so carried away by enthusiasm, tradition tells us, that in his eagerness to charge upon the grumbling mob he leaped his horse over a well. A trivial incident this, no doubt, but it shows what sort of blood was in the family veins.

[1] *History of New Hampshire*, by McClintock, p. 371.

It usually falls to the lot of a biographer to narrate at least a few instances of prophetic precocity. But none are to be told of Lewis Cass. It is clear that in early years he was fond of study, and evinced a capacity which encouraged his father to give him a good education. In 1792, when the boy was scarcely ten years old, he entered the academy in Exeter, and came into the stimulating presence of Benjamin Abbott. The stern discipline and accurate scholarship of the principal had a moulding influence on the minds of his pupils, and the years spent at the academy were important ones in the life of Cass. Nothing especial, however, is known of this period of his career. Presumptions of fine scholarship have been made, perhaps not without warrant. Webster thirty years afterwards remembered him as "a clever fellow, good-natured, kind-hearted, amiable, and obliging." Perhaps he was one of those considerate school-fellows who refrained from laughing at the rustic manners and uncouth appearance of the youthful Daniel, and thus won his grateful remembrance.

Meantime his father, who had been unsuccessfully presented to Washington as a suitable marshal for the State, had accepted a commission in the army raised for the defense of the western frontier, and was with "Mad Anthony" in his cunning and vigorous campaign. Major Cass was left in command of Fort Hamilton, and retained command until the treaty of Greenville. Here he continued to live for some time while Lewis was carrying on his studies in the academy.

There have been many conflicting statements, needlessly inaccurate, concerning the education which Cass received. There is still in existence in Exeter a certificate, supposed to be a copy in the handwriting of Cass himself, which very plainly sets forth the advantages which he secured. It is there stated that he had been a member of the academy for seven years, and had acquired the principles of the English, French, Latin, and Greek languages, geography, arithmetic, and practical geometry; that he had made "valuable progress in the study of rhetoric, history, natural and moral philosophy, logic, astronomy, and natural law." The usual testimony of good moral character follows this enumeration of his acquirements.

The course of Cass's life immediately subsequent to his residence at the academy is not easily discernible. His father had returned from the West some time after the treaty of Greenville, and in 1799 was stationed, probably in some military capacity, at Wilmington, Del. A few months, passed in teaching in an academy at that place, seem to have satisfied young Cass that the uneventful life of the schoolmaster was not to his liking. The major had brought home from his Western sojourn such glowing accounts of opportunities, that pedagogics were laid aside for the hardships and excitement of pioneering. Nothing could be much more incongruous than Lewis Cass in the class-room in those restless days of his young manhood when he was energetic to the very point of wastefulness, and burned with an ardor for trial, activity, combat. The family slowly made their way into the Ohio valley.[1] Lewis, with his bundle on his back, plodded over the mountains into the "Old Northwest," which was yet young enough, and bore the wrinkles of age only where the Frenchman had introduced antiquity and sloth. Major Cass resigned his commission at Pittsburgh, and pushed on into Ohio.

The wilderness which he had left after the treaty of Greenville was a wilderness no longer. Now at the beginning of the new century towns were starting up as apparitions, here and there, with ghost-like quickness. The long stretches of lonely forests, which he had known, were now alive with busy farms and bright with wheat and maize. All down the Ohio valley were the buzz and bustle of industry. The New Englanders were there with their thrift and their parsimony and their shrewd business methods which astonished and annoyed the easy-going Southerner. For the slave owner, too, was there, a slave owner no longer. Many such had moved to the unshackled northwest, now that the fear of the Indians was removed, and with a magnanimity useless on the plantations of the South had given freedom to their slaves. Virginia,

[1] The family seems to have spent a short time at Harper's Ferry and Winchester. See Smith, *Life and Times of Cass*, p. 19.

Kentucky, and North Carolina lost many energetic citizens, who sought the untarnished freedom of that new land, where the curse of slavery could not be bequeathed to their children. Still other immigrants from the South, however, never gave up the hope of introducing the system which the Ordinance of '87 forbade. At Marietta and in its vicinity were the driving sons of Puritanism, who had begun a settlement with much of the same serious purpose and the same sad energy which had marked their ancestors of the rock-bound coast. School and church were there; and much of the puritanic ideal alloyed with modern zeal for material prosperity. But farther to the west, in the direction of Cincinnati, were Southerners full of characteristic hospitality and magnanimity and Jeffersonism, and a few full of ignorance and sloth and the lazy disposition of more sunny and smiling skies. This was no place, one would say, for him who was not ready to make his way with hoe and axe. Yet in southern Ohio there still remains a certain modicum of this unprogressive, indolent element, continually presenting the query, whence came the motive and the energy to move to the northern woods at all.

Major Cass seems to have brought his family to Marietta in October, 1800, and to have gone north to the vicinity of Zanesville the next year. Lewis Cass probably settled in Marietta in the latter part of 1799,[1] and began there his study of

[1] It is almost impossible to determine this date with accu-

the law in the office of Mr. R. J. Meigs, who was afterwards governor of the State of Ohio. The major located forty land warrants, for one hundred acres each, in the vicinity of Zanesville, and Lewis spent at least a portion of his time in the wilderness, helping his father to hew his way to comfort. Solomon Sibley on his way to Detroit found his friend of after years pounding corn in a hollow stump before his father's door, and the traveler was invited to partake of the evening meal, the preparations for which were thus primitively begun. The young man, eager for a career, and fond of study, learned from experience the privations of frontier life. He felt the impulses, generous and strong, which come to the woodsman. The settlers in the West of after years needed to tell him nothing. He knew their needs, he realized their capacities, he sympathized with their longings. All this appreciation of Northwestern characteristics moulded his career and increased his usefulness.

There were various and different elements in the population of Ohio, as already suggested; but everything in frontier life calls for activity and

racy. I have thought best, in spite of strong evidence for the date 1800, to adopt the one given in Young's *Life of Cass*, inasmuch as Mr. Young is supposed to have had the advice of Cass himself in the preparation of the book, and the copy from which I take the statement was the general's own copy. If such an evident mistake had been made, I am inclined to think that it would have been indicated on the margin by the subject of the memoir. There are many other reasons for deciding upon this date.

stimulates to energy. Only those of restless disposition or fearless independent thought were apt to leave their homes in the East to begin life again in the West. There were no prescribed customs, no rut for thought's progress, no smothering upper crust of wealth and aristocracy. Everybody knew what everybody else was worth, and measured with rude exactness the height of the true man without reference to the length of the purse or to the pedestal of inherited position. Intimate acquaintance with Nature suggested to the settler breadth, generosity, and the spirit of sturdy independence. Land was almost his only possession, and from the time of Tacitus land-owning and Anglo-Saxon freedom have been curiously interwoven. Is there no indication of race decay in these latter days when Americans give over to Germans and Swedes the title to their western prairies?

In those days, when the common man, by virtue of his own inherent vigor, was pushing his way to independence, there came a faith in the energy, the sagacity, the proper impulses of this same common man. Though Cass in his study for the bar spent much of his early manhood in Marietta, a town of New England prejudices, he was carried away with enthusiasm for popular sovereignty and faith in the people, the loudly proclaimed doctrines of Jefferson, who with wondrous cunning was shaping for practical political service in America the edge-tools of Rousseau, which, roughly handled, had cut so many grievous wounds in the body of distressed France. Jefferson was to Americanize and make practical the French extravagances. Yet all the antecedents of Lewis Cass were Federalist. Can it be fairly charged, as it was in after years in the heat of party contests, that he became a disciple of the new school only for office and lucre? It would seem not. Meigs was a Jeffersonian. Others of the pushing politicians were Virginians. The Federalists, in the dread of the nightmare Jeffersonism, opposed the entrance of Ohio into the Union, and even Manasseh Cutler himself was in opposition to a policy which the ambition of youth desired. Surely, if prejudice does not blind, one can see other forces than avarice driving the young barrister into the camp of the Democracy. Ohio, in her haste to become a State, and in her hatred of those who hindered her, in her dread of the meddling policy represented by St. Clair, adopted a constitution which ought to have warmed the heart of the loudest advocate of a weak government, and came into the Union as a Jeffersonian State.

The first certificate of admission to the bar under the new constitution of 1802 was given to Lewis Cass, probably in the autumn of 1802. Ebenezer Zane had cut a post-road from Wheeling to Lewiston, perhaps the first piece of "internal improvement" undertaken by the government. "Zane's trace," a winding bridle-path with "corduroy" bridges, earned for its creator three sections of land on the Muskingum, and there in

1799 Zanesville was founded. Soon after his admission to the bar Cass began practice in this little town, which was then struggling up in the wilderness. The "streets," filled with underbrush and lined with blackened stumps, offered but slight æsthetic attractions; but in 1804 Muskingum County was created, and Zanesville assumed the dignity of a county seat. Cass this year was elected prosecuting attorney and began his public career. The reputation of the young lawyer seems to have been already somewhat widely diffused. This was partly due to his influential friends in Marietta and to his acquaintance in other portions of the State.

In those days a young barrister's duties were not confined to hanging out a sign and listening for a client's footsteps. The county seats were widely separated by long stretches of wilderness. Journeys of a hundred or a hundred and fifty miles were not uncommon. Judge and lawyers mounted their horses and started on the circuit. Occasionally an old Indian trail offered unusual facilities for travel. Sometimes eight or ten days were spent on a journey, the travelers finding shelter where they best could, at times thankful for dry ground to lie upon, and again warmly welcomed to a lonely log cabin, where some trustful farmer from over the mountains was endeavoring to subsist with his crop of Indian corn planted at random in a half-cleared field. Danger often added dramatic interest to weariness. Streams swollen with rains[1] must not be regarded as barriers, and the horse which could not swim was of little use to the barrister. Cass in after years merrily recalled "the dripping spectacle of despair" which he exhibited when in crossing Scioto Creek his faithless horse threw him and his luggage into the water. "These, however, were the troubles of the day; but, oh, they were recompensed by the comforts of the evening, when the hospitable cabin and the warm fire greeted the traveler! — when a glorious supper was spread before him, — turkey, venison, bear's meat, fresh butter, hot corn bread, sweet potatoes, apple sauce, and pumpkin butter! — and then the animated conversation, succeeded by a floor and a blanket and a refreshing sleep!"[2]

Courts were held where necessity or convenience dictated, often in a log court-house with generous interstices neither chinked nor daubed; at times in a public house where judge, jury, lawyers, and witnesses were huddled together in perplexing confusion; not infrequently in a settler's cabin where a court-room was quickly improvised, and the judge made use of the bed for his august bench. In these curious journeys there was merriment as well as danger and fatigue; and in these strange court-rooms there was much of legal learning and forensic skill. There was also rare opportunity for sharpening wit and increasing self-reliance. Justice was meted out with a quickness

[1] *Letters from Illinois*, p. 61, London, 1818.

[2] *France, its King, Court, and Government*, by Lewis Cass, p. 121.

and directness often unknown in these artificial days of the dilatory plea. Perhaps it was a result of communion with Nature, but however this may be, certain it is that he who was not ready, direct and keen, fitted into no place in the judicial system of Ohio in those days of itinerant courts and direct justice.

The constitution of Ohio provided that no person should be a representative who had not attained the age of twenty-five years. In October, 1806, Cass completed his twenty-fourth year, and in spite of ineligibility was that month elected to the legislature and took his seat on the first Monday of December. He became at once an influential member. A new country bestows no premium on the experience of age; young men are for counsel as well as for war.

This year Burr began his sinuous operations in the West. The affair was long a puzzling episode in our history. Burr, fallen from his high estate, was prompted by a restless ambition to win new glories in the West. Did he mean to establish a colony on the Washita River? Was he planning an expedition against the Spanish Dons? Did he fancy himself sitting on the throne of the Montezumas? Did he actually so misinterpret Southwestern spirit that he hoped he might detach the Western States from the Union? Only recent investigations[1] have given decided answers to these questions. The first was his ostensible design,

[1] *History of the United States*, Henry Adams.

the last his fondest hope. He possibly dreamed of being able to make his colony, or perchance New Orleans, the basis of other conquests, relying on his stär of destiny to guide him to Mexican wealth and grandeur. But he seems to have sought much fouler fame as the leader of a Western revolution. The plaudits of the Southwestern cities in an earlier visit had kindled his desires and fanned into a blaze his cynical ambitions. He lacked all moral basis for his intellectual judgments. He was unable to appreciate moral enthusiasm as distinct from personal greed. He could not sympathize with the generous patriotism and devotion and the warm love of country in the hearts of an open-hearted people, whose grumblings he would torture into treason. Parton tells us in an adroit paradox that the public mind was prepared to believe anything of Burr, provided only that it was sufficiently incredible. But Burr himself also, in the dark recesses of his bright mind, was curiously credulous of the impossible.

Blennerhassett, a fanciful Irish gentleman, had expended a good portion of a modest fortune in the purchase and adornment of a small island in the Ohio River some twenty miles southwest of Marietta. Peace, tranquillity, innocence, idyllic repose, were said by the eloquent Wirt to be the tutelary deities of this new Eden. Into this garden of primitive bliss or modern folly Burr came with his insinuating manner and winning address. Mrs. Blennerhassett was charmed, and her imaginative husband soon quivered with eagerness for colonization and conquest. It is true he was so near-sighted that on his gunning expeditions a servant aimed his gun for him and told him when to pull the trigger; but he was now ready to hunt for Spanish Dons and to begin with Burr a military expedition, the end of which he must have partly understood.

Blennerhassett's island was taken as a rendezvous for the conspirators. But General Wilkinson, on whom Burr had relied for assistance, concluded that he did not wish to become a "Washington of the West;" and President Jefferson, not loath to suspect, and yet surprisingly blind, dispatched a "confidential agent" to the scene of the incipient expedition. By him Governor Tiffin was informed that there was something of strange purport going on within the limits of the State. A message stating the suspicions of the governor was sent by him to the legislature, and that body was advised to take necessary measures of precaution. Cass was a member of the committee appointed in pursuance of the governor's recommendation. He had often visited the island, and had listened to the eulogies which the giddy Blennerhassett lavished upon Burr, and now that his suspicions were aroused he soon found reason for hardening them into conviction. Young as he was, he seems to have been the influential and active member of the committee. He drafted a bill which the committee reported, and he vigorously supported it before the House. The governor was authorized to use the forces of the State for suppressing the undertaking, and he acted with corresponding promptness and decision. Boats, gathered at Marietta, were seized by the militia, and some companies of young woodsmen and farmers, who were gayly bent on adventure and had been charmed with the novelty and possibly the glory of the enterprise, were intercepted on their way to the place of rendezvous. This was the "first blow" to the conspiracy, as Jefferson confessed. A presidential proclamation was issued shortly before the Ohio law. Burr, meeting on his way down the Mississippi with the news of disaster, resolved to trust the wilderness rather than the courts of law. He was captured, brought to trial at Richmond, but acquitted for lack of evidence of participation in an overt act of treason.

In the mean time, at the instigation of Cass, the Ohio legislature adopted a resolution expressing to President Jefferson its attachment to the government, its confidence in his administration, and its abhorrence of rebellion and insurrection. This won from the President a politic reply, in which with charming adroitness he magnified popular sovereignty and pushed his pet principle of the necessary vigor of state authorities under the Constitution. He was still somewhat fearful of slumbering conspiracies, and is said to have suggested to Governor Tiffin the advisability of removing all postmasters west of the mountains who might be fairly suspected of "being unfriendly to the unity of the nation." Practical civil administration would always teach that postmasters are *ex officio* dangerous conspirators.

President Jefferson did not forget the young advocate who had so effectively supported his government, and in 1807 Cass was tendered a commission as United States marshal. He hesitated to receive it, fearing that it would interfere with the practice of his profession. But he recognized that the appointment, coming as it did, was a distinction and an announcement of the President's confidence and gratitude. So he accepted and retained the office until after the outbreak of the war of 1812.

In 1806 Cass was married to Miss Elizabeth Spencer, a descendant of General Spencer of Revolutionary reputation. The history of his domestic life is the simple one of uneventful happiness. So even and uniform was his private life, so blessed with a paucity of annals, that nothing more than this direct assertion is needed to embrace the whole truth. About the time of his marriage he built on his father's farm what was then considered a handsome "double" house. It was of logs, as all the mansions were in those days, and part of it is still standing. Here his elder children were born, and this was his home for nearly ten years.

The legal profession in Ohio in early days was not a remunerative one, and yet in the first few years of practice, Cass had achieved reputation and accumulated a little property. He was known as one of the foremost men at the bar. His natural capacity for grasping legal distinctions and for mastering details was aided by continuous industry and by a vigor and dignity of speech which were always impressive, often eloquent, and seldom failed to influence. One of his very last acts as a practicing lawyer was the defense of two judges of the State of Ohio, who, in the plenitude of their judicial authority, had ventured to declare an act of the legislature unconstitutional, and were impeached for their presumption. This is an amusing instance of how completely Ohio, framed on the shores and ways of Federalism, once fairly launched, had swung into the current of ultra-democracy. The trial of the judges was sensational. The State was filled with excitement. The speech of Cass on this occasion was masterly and convincing, — an epoch in the judicial and constitutional history of Ohio, possibly an epoch in the judicial history of our country. The acquittal of the judges was a victory for the young lawyer; but it meant also a victory for the dignity of a collateral branch of the state government. It had its influence in counteracting a dangerous tendency in the political thought of the period.

CHAPTER III

THE WAR OF 1812

In many ways the history of our country in the first forty years of its existence as an independent nation does not furnish a story to be read with unmingled delight. The fierce opposition to the adoption of the Constitution perpetuated itself in party opposition and obstruction after 1789. And scarcely had the infant state been given vigorous development by the tender care of the party which had stood sponsor at its birth, when it was turned over to those who had been its opponents and might still prove untrustworthy managers of its affairs. Political feeling ran high in 1801, when the Federalists in their horror of Jefferson plotted seriously to bestow the chief magistracy on Burr. With a sense of strange familiarity one comes into that atmosphere of sectional strife. It is discouraging to see how long there has been "solidity" north and south of Mason and Dixon's line. The British cruiser boarded New England vessels and impressed New England seamen. Napoleon pounced upon our defenseless commerce, and skillfully avoided all consideration of redress. Nor was it because a Boston merchant thought more of his cargo than he did of his countrymen, doomed to fight as Englishmen whether they would or not, that he bore English cruelty with patience, and fumed only at the arrogance of France. It was largely because the southern party, the party of Jefferson, which the New Englander detested, could see no wrong in French aggressions that the New England Federalist saw very clearly the reverse. Nor is the exasperating timidity of Jefferson to be overlooked. In pursuance of the "terrapin policy" of his administration the country had drawn itself within its shell, in the hope of being coaxed out by sweet concessions. But the embargo, which was said at one time to be a measure for the protection of commerce, and at another to be retaliatory, proved destructive of no interests save our own. Instead of building frigates and sloops of war that might protect New England shipping, Congress spent money in constructing the ridiculous gunboats which in the end proved of little or no value. Yet the Eastern States were developing a commerce of no mean proportions, flourishing in stealthy trade in spite of the damage inflicted by the combatants of Europe. But their commerce never entirely recovered from the disastrous effects of non-intercourse and the embargo. By a singular irony of fate, Madison, on whose shoulders had fallen the peaceful robe of Jefferson, was driven into a war of conquest and aggression, a war for which a timorous policy had ill prepared the country. It is not to be wondered at that the war of 1812 was a sectional and party contest, and that, by merely bringing it to a close, the administration won unprecedented popularity.

Our attention in this volume is confined to the progress of events in the West, where from the first hostilities were fathered with a warm affection. Madison and his fellows of the agricultural party had been set in motion by an infusion of young blood from the South, and especially the Southwest, which played strange pranks in the veins of the old Democracy. Vigorous and active was this young Democracy. It made itself felt in Congress in the persons of Clay and Grundy. It was strong in Ohio and in the Territories, which had not yet put on the *toga virilis* of statehood. For the occupation of new territory is an employment analogous to conquest. Only in the more settled portion of Ohio had the rifle as yet been relegated to an ornamental position in the chimney corner; the farmer in the other portions of the Northwest still considered it an implement of husbandry. Moreover, the remembrance of British intrigues, hostile to the safety of the settler, was still fresh in his mind, and his hatred of England had not entirely passed away. He readily attributed the present uneasiness of the Indians to her artful and cunning interference.

The plantation owner of the South might possibly clamor for a war which would in all likelihood damage chiefly the commerce of his political opponent. But the pioneer of the West had not the spirit of sectional prejudice, nor was he hypocritical in his zeal for war; he knew full well that, if hostilities began, the Indian war-whoop would be his *reveillé*. There was a strong national pride in this portion of our country, which had been held as a national domain while the other States were wrangling as selfish members of an impotent confederation. The pride of the Northwestern settler was not narrowed by petty traditions of a neighborhood. He at the very least divided his affections between his old Eastern home and his new Western one. He might believe theoretically in the sovereignty of his new State, but he felt that he had brought over the mountains a portion of the holy fire which was still burning on the altar of the mother Republic. State sovereignty or spiteful sectionalism could not grow in rank luxuriance in the Northwest, as the one did under the fierce heat of slavery, and the other in the equally torrid zone of trade and tariff.

The suspicions of the Western settler were not unfounded; for British interference in the affairs of this country was not confined to impressment of seamen and the seizure of our merchantmen, nor was all hope of the disintegration of the Union relinquished when the frontier posts were at last delivered in 1796. For many years after that, there was an astute surveillance of Western affairs, and an attentive sympathy on the part of the English government for the Indian hunter, who was losing his hunting ground at the advance of the American farmer. As the war cloud in Europe became darker, and the relations with America became more strained, there was renewed interest on the part of England in the welfare of the poor red man. Efforts to attach the Indian to the British interests were evident. There was a feeling of uneasiness in Detroit as early as 1806. In 1807 direct solicitations for the Indian alliance were begun by the English.[1] In 1810 and 1811 presents were handed out at Malden to the visiting Indians with excessive generosity. The value of goods dealt out in the latter year exceeded that of common years by twenty thousand pounds sterling. "All their peltries," said Governor Harrison, "collected on the Wabash in one year, if sold in the London markets, would not pay the freight of the goods which have been given to the Indians."[2] The efforts of Tecumseh and the prophet to form a complete confederation of the tribes of the West may be attributed to lofty Indian patriotism on the part of this red Alexander the Great and the medicine man, his brother. But there is little reason to doubt that much of their energy was due to British instigation,[3] and that the battle of

[1] *American State Papers, Indian Affairs*, vol. i. p. 746.

[2] Farmer's *History of Detroit and Michigan*, p. 273; *American State Papers, Indian Affairs*, vol. ii. pp. 798–802.

[3] *A Chapter of the War of* 1812, by William Stanley Hatch, p. 102; *North American Review*, vol. xxiv. p. 381; *Outlines of Political History of Michigan*, Campbell, p. 257; Eggleston's *Tecumseh*, pp. 91, 92, 126, 127, etc.; Drake's *Life of Black Hawk*, pp. 62, 63.

Tippecanoe, in 1811, where Governor Harrison met and defeated those who had been enticed into the goodly fellowship of the prophet, was the real beginning of the war of 1812 in the West.[1]

Claims have been made that it was because of American greed and cruelty that the English were successful where the Americans desired to be; but such assertions are without basis in the facts. During the Revolution the English government put a bounty on an American scalp as it might on the hide of a wolf; and as the war of 1812 came on, the United States government endeavored to persuade the Indians not to yield to the solicitation of British agents, but did not endeavor until late in the war to procure assistance[2] even from those tribes which could not be brought into the British alliance.

The remembrance of these facts has faded from the memory of those who goad themselves to a pitch of patriotism by recalling the arrogance of Britain on the sea. But these are facts, and there is no desire to heighten animosity by a recoloring of what may very well fade into indistinctness. The judgment of history, however, needs to be

[1] The situation in the West seems to have been much the same as it was twenty years before. The Indians were furnished with ammunition and supplies and were held as firm allies, but there was no attempt to incite them to hostilities before the war with America was begun. See *Report of Canadian Archivist*, 1893, p. 47, etc.

[2] Governor Hull's address to Indians, 1809, *Michigan Pioneer Coll.*, p. 597.

just. So long as such a book as James's "Military Occurrences" is seriously read and referred to in England as history, a plain statement of truth cannot be amiss. The Indians themselves on more than one occasion said that "their Great Father, the President, did not ask them to involve themselves in the quarrels of the white people, but to remain quiet spectators."[1]

All this may seem to have little to do with the young lawyer, whom we left practicing his profession with diligence, and performing his official duties as United States marshal. But it has much to do with him; it is a part of his life. His whole career was changed by the outbreak of the war; a great portion of his life was devoted to counteracting the effect of British influence over the Indians; and an intimate acquaintance with England's ambition and diplomatic stealth made him through his whole life suspicious of her.

Cass himself said in 1827 that the hope of possessing Canada had no more influence upon the declaration of war than the possession of Paris in 1814 by the allies had upon the origin of the Napoleonic war. It is true that the United States would not have begun the war simply for purposes of conquest; she was driven into it by a succession of annoyances which had grown absolutely unbearable. But Cass, when he made this statement, must have forgotten the enthusiasm of his earlier days. Clay's proud boast that with a few

[1] *American State Papers, Indian Affairs*, vol. i., *passim.*

Kentuckians he could conquer poor, oppressed Canada, found an echo in all the country west of the Alleghanies. There was an intense desire to invade the neighboring province, and ask England how she liked to wear the boot on the other foot. A firm belief in the blessings of American liberty persuaded the Western citizen that the Canadian was waiting with impatience the opportunity to make such blessings his own. In no one had this adulation of Americanism developed more strongly than in Cass, and it was coupled with a fierce energy which seemed an augury of success.

On February 6, 1812, Congress authorized the President to accept and organize certain volunteer military corps; and on April 10 he was authorized to require the executives of the several States and Territories to take effectual measures to organize and equip their respective portions of 100,000 militia. Ohio was called upon for her quota of men, and in May twelve hundred volunteers were called together at Dayton. They were divided into three regiments. Colonel McArthur had command of the first, Colonel Findlay of the second, and Lewis Cass was colonel of the third.

Cass here made his first address to his troops: "Fellow-citizens, — The standard of our country is displayed. You have rallied around it to defend her rights and to avenge her injuries. May it wave protection to our friends and defiance to our enemies! And should we ever meet them in the hostile field, I doubt not but that the eagle of

America will be found more than a match for the British lion!" These exclamatory antitheses were said to have been received with "rapturous enthusiasm."

In May Governor Hull, who at that time held the governorship of Michigan Territory, was appointed brigadier-general. He had at first refused appointment partly because he differed from the administration as to the advisability of a land approach to Canada, without support on the lakes, and partly also, doubtless, because he desired to shun responsibility, and dreaded to go back to Detroit as an active commander, where he had miserably failed as a civil governor, because of his pompous vacillation and ponderous indecision. However, he finally accepted, took command of the troops at Dayton, and marched to Urbana, where he was joined by the fourth regiment of regular infantry, about three hundred strong, under the command of Colonel Miller. This regiment had seen service under General Harrison in the Tippecanoe expedition, and was made up of tried men. The march to Detroit was a burdensome one. Part of the way had to be cut through the persistent underbrush, and from the Maumee northward the road in its normal condition was primeval mud and water. On June 26, when he was not far from the Maumee, General Hull received word from Washington, written early on the 18th, the very day on which war was declared, urging him to proceed to Detroit with all possible speed. The same day Colonel McArthur received a letter from Chillicothe stating that before the letter reached him war would be begun. But the actual announcement that war had begun was not received until July 2.

There is no need of covering up the multitude of sins of the Madison administration with any cloak of charitable inferences. It is simply inexcusable that the British at Malden should have received word two days earlier than Hull did, and that every effort was not made to give full information to our army, which was marching practically into the very face of the enemy. In fact the message did not reach Cleveland until the 28th, ten days after the declaration. The administration was creeping like a snail complainingly to war. But that does not entirely excuse Hull for trusting his baggage and papers to a vessel which, sailing on the 1st from the Maumee, was captured by the English off Malden. He seems to have taken very literally the trenchant irony of Randolph, who portrayed a "holiday campaign" in which Canada was to "conquer herself" and "be subdued by the principle of fraternity."

It will be necessary in delineating this portion of Cass's life to enter somewhat fully into this inglorious campaign. For the wisdom of Hull's action is still a subject of discussion, and his descendants, with an amiable regard for his memory, have endeavored to defend his actions as wise, humane, and based on good military principles;

while Cass, who was the chief witness afterwards against the general, has been accused of unworthy motives, as being the tool of an impotent administration, and a vile intriguer for favor.

On July 5 the army reached Detroit. The men were quite ready to rest. Cass himself recalled in after years his feeling of gratification that the long journey was over. The "raw militia" of whom Hull complained had marched over two hundred miles through forest and swamps, building bridges over smaller streams, and enduring hardship and fatigue. They found Detroit a French-American village of quaint aspect, a piece of old France partly inoculated with Americanism. An entirely new stockade had been erected by Governor Hull in 1807, and everything had a well-kept appearance. Cass afterwards stated that he thought some of the embrasures defective and the platform in need of repair. This may have been true, yet Hull is probably not justly chargeable with negligence for not putting the fort into better condition.

There were in the whole of Michigan at that time about five thousand persons, and in Detroit proper not far from a thousand. The Americans in the Territory had used every means to acquaint the government with their dangers. They were a "double frontier," they said, for no farm was protected by another. With a trust that the government would help those who helped themselves, they had raised four companies of militia, which were at this time commanded by Judge Witherell, an experienced Revolutionary officer. They were men accustomed to the privations of frontier life, and had been in continual readiness for war since 1805. Hildreth's estimate[1] that the militia of the Territory raised Hull's force to 1800 is a very low one. Nor will it do to pass over men of this kind with a slur at "militia." The militia of Michigan were no weaklings, and the Ohio troops were of the material which by many a hard fight has given the American volunteer system a glory above a sneer. That Hildreth's estimate, evidently based on Hull's own statement,[2] is too low is quite apparent from the fact that Judge Witherell stated that he received a letter from Hull, dated June 14, announcing that he would soon be at the River Raisin with about 2200 men; and that the general also wrote to the secretary of war that he was confident that his force would be superior to any which would be opposed to it, inasmuch as the "rank and file" exceeded 2000. The roll of troops at Fort Findlay showed 2075 men. Hull's defenders[3] do not deny that this number is substantially correct, but he asserted that there were 392 men more than the President had ordered, and that he had no authority to take any surplus under his command. There were something like four hundred men[4] in the Michigan militia, and there

1 Hildreth, *Hist. of U. S.*, vol. vi. p. 338.

2 Hull's Defense (Appendix to *Trial*), p. 42.

3 *History of the Campaign of* 1812.

4 Hull's *Memoirs*, p. 125; *Hull's Trial*, p. 94.

can be no doubt that Hull's effective army, after liberal deductions because of garrison duty, illness, and other causes, reached over two thousand on July 6.

Now was the time for action. The enemy at Malden had an advantageous position; for they were south of Detroit, and could easily cross the river and intercept supplies. Hull afterwards said that, had he not been ordered to Detroit, he would have begun an attack upon the British from another quarter. This is all *ex post facto* imagination. He knew when he left Dayton that he was bound for Detroit. And now when he was at Detroit he refused to enter Canada until he received authority from Washington. He preferred to leave the enemy their advantage rather than take active measures of hostility.[1]

The morning after the arrival of the army at Detroit, Colonel Cass was sent to Malden with a flag of truce to obtain, if possible, the baggage and prisoners taken from the schooner which Hull had trustfully sent to Detroit from the Maumee. He was led blindfolded into the presence of the commanding officer, and his demands were refused; but before he reached the fort he was able to make a casual survey, which induced him to believe that it was indefensible, and he so declared to General Hull. An examination of it a year

[1] It must be said that Hull realized and stated at the beginning the desirability of controlling the lake if anything effective was to be done in Upper Canada.

later convinced him that his first assumption was well founded, and, inasmuch as Hull in previous years had been at Malden several times, there was no reason why he also should not have appreciated its weakness. On the 9th orders were received from Washington authorizing the army to cross into Canada and begin offensive operations. A council of war was called, and Cass argued eagerly for immediate action. Deserters from Canada acquainted the Americans with the numbers of the British forces, and gave clear indication of the feeling prevailing among the inhabitants of upper Canada. Offensive operations were determined upon in the council, and the young officers were jubilant. But Hull was not hopeful. He advised the secretary of war not to be "too sanguine," as the "water and the savages" were commanded by the enemy. He did not care to burn all argumentative bridges behind him, even when he must have known that his force greatly outnumbered the enemy; and it is to be hoped that in after years, in his peaceful, bucolic existence, he found true satisfaction in the remembrance of his lugubrious reports. In the latest review of this campaign, written with rare judgment and impartiality, the statement is made that Hull from the first "looked on the conquest of Canada as a result of his appearance."[1] The extract just made from his letter to the secretary of war, his hesitation in

[1] *History of the United States of America during the First Administration of James Madison*, by Henry Adams, vol. ii. p. 302.

accepting the commission in the first place, his timid policy and delay, are hardly reconcilable, it seems to me, with this lenient interpretation of his conduct.

Cass, we are told, took his stand in the bow of the first boat in which the troops were conveyed across the river, and was the first American to set his foot on Canadian soil after the declaration of war. This well suggests the ardor of the young colonel, whose zeal for war left no room for indecision and hesitation. He had used every means of obtaining information, and was satisfied that a prompt and bold attack would insure the fall of Malden and the conquest of Upper Canada. The troops reached the Canadian shore just above the present town of Windsor, and the young Ohio colonel, who was always in the lead, hastened to raise the stars and stripes over the sleepy French settlement of Sandwich. A detachment of the enemy had abandoned their position opposite Detroit, and had hastened beyond the Canard River, nearer to the fort, which was twenty miles to the south of Hull's position.

Two hundred copies of a proclamation, in which the fraternity theory was given full vent, were at once distributed. Subsequent events clothed it in a humorous garb, but it was declared able and vigorous by the press of the day, and there can be no doubt of its influence. No less an authority than Judge Campbell, in his "Outlines of the Political History of Michigan," attributes this document to Cass;[1] others whose means of information were good, and who were his personal friends, have made the same assertion. It certainly bears marks of the pomposity and incisiveness of Cass's earlier style. The American army was said to have come to rescue the perishing Canadians from the dragon of tyranny, to pour the balm of liberty and fraternal love into their wounds. They were called upon not to raise their hands against their "brethren." No assistance was required, for a force was at hand which would "look down all opposition," and was a mere "vanguard" of the host which was to follow. Rare sport had the cunning pamphleteers afterwards with this confident announcement of success. The "Wars of the Gulls" represents Madison, the "Great Mogul," soliloquizing as follows: "By proclamation my illustrious predecessor defended this extensive region during a long and warlike reign of eight years, and brought the belligerent powers of Europe to his feet. By proclamation I have commenced this great and perilous war, and by proclamation I will carry victory into the very chimney corner of the enemy."

The inhabitants of Canada were warned, in this circular, that they need expect no quarter if found fighting by the side of an Indian, and that "the first stroke of the tomahawk, the first attempt of the scalping-knife" would be the signal "for an indiscriminate scene of desolation." This clause

[1] See also Smith's *Life and Times of Cass*, p. 38.

was the occasion of some contention between the commissioners at Ghent, where the American representatives attempted to disown the whole proceeding, asserting that it was unauthorized by their government. But such was not the fact. "Your letters, . . . together with your proclamation, have been received," wrote Secretary Eustis on August 1, 1812. "Your operations are approved by the government." The English commissioners shuddered in well counterfeited horror at the idea that an invading army should encourage treason and rebellion among the inhabitants of a neighboring province. But there is no doubt that such was the principle of the "fraternal" conquest of Canada; and it is equally true that England on her own part attempted to stimulate into open enmity the New England Federalists, who grumbled without ceasing at the party war which bade fair to leave nothing more substantial than a remembrance of their commerce, which the embargo had already "protected" into debility.

The effect of this proclamation was immediate. Vaporous as it seems in the light of subsequent events, it was admirably adapted to win the disaffected, and to encourage the French *habitants*, who naturally sympathized with the Americans. The commander at Malden wrote despondently to General Brock, who was governor in Upper Canada, and who, released from his civil duties, soon became the inspiring genius and hero of the war. "Hull's invidious proclamation," wrote Brock to Governor Prevost, "herewith inclosed, has already been productive of considerable effect on the minds of the people. In fact, a general sentiment prevails that, with the present force, resistance is unavailing."[1] So widespread was the despondency that some of the militia in Upper Canada peremptorily refused to march, as many as five hundred settlers in the western district sought the protection of the enemy,[2] and the Indians on the Grand River refused to take up arms. Even Hull was encouraged to hope for success, and continued to "look down" all opposition with a masterly inactivity which never deviated into generalship.

The Ohio colonels were eager for action. Cass urged that the army move immediately upon Malden, to take a position at least as near as the Canard River, which was some five miles distant from the British fort. One cannot say with assurance that Hull should have made an attack at once. And yet if he could not take the place his situation was full of danger from the very beginning. Even the safety of Detroit depended on the ability of the American army either to capture the British position or to hold the enemy completely in check, inasmuch as the line of communication with the south could be easily broken in upon. Whatever was to be done must be done quickly and with energy. But these were just the

[1] Brock to Prevost, July 20, 1812. Tupper's *Life and Correspondence of Sir Isaac Brock*, p. 203.

[2] *Ibid.* p. 204.

qualities that Hull lacked; and if his subordinates were wrong in asking for prompt action, he was unable to impress himself upon them or to bring them to respect his more experienced judgment.

No forward step was now taken. The American army remained quietly at Sandwich, some twenty miles from the enemy, and awaited developments. Colonel Miller, with a few troops, made an expedition into the country, and, returning with provisions, demonstrated the weakness of the enemy. Cass, because of his much asking, was allowed to take two hundred and eighty men and push his way as near as possible to the enemy's stronghold for the purpose of ascertaining its condition. He wanted nothing better. The river Tarontee, as the Indians called it, which has generally figured in history under its French name of the Canard, is a stream of considerable depth, flowing through low, marshy ground into the Detroit. Here a detachment of the enemy was posted, and here was fought the first battle of the war. Cass, to divert the attention of the enemy, left a company of riflemen near the bridge which crossed the stream not far from its mouth. He proceeded with the rest of his troops five miles up the stream to a ford, and came down the left bank. An impetuous charge upon the hostile line threw it into confusion. Three times the British formed, and were as often beaten back. But night was falling. Cass recalled his men to the bridge, and sent word of his success to General Hull.

This first victory of the war was accepted through the country as prophetic of success, and Cass was hailed as the "Hero of the Tarontee."[1] "Hold the bridge, and begin operations at once," was the eager advice of the young officers. But Hull thought the position too exposed, finally saying that Miller and Cass might use their own judgment; they withdrew, for they insisted that the commanding officer ought to have the responsibility. A withdrawal meant a proclamation to all Canada that the American general considered himself as yet too weak to take a stand nearer than twenty miles from the enemy, who were then, undoubtedly, greatly outnumbered. The young officers now openly murmured. They had hardly expected that sluggishness would degenerate into absolute immovability. There is little reason to doubt that from this time the feeling of distrust of their general steadily increased, until McArthur, Findlay, and Cass actually plotted his deposition and the installation of McArthur as the commanding officer. Cass constantly urged movement and action, except on one occasion, when he deferred to the superior technical wisdom of the artillery commanders. In various skirmishes he showed his ardor for the conflict.

General Hull had charge of more than the military operations in Upper Canada; he was, as well, governor of Michigan Territory; yet for some reason, he took no step to announce the outbreak

[1] Lossing's *Field-Book of the War of* 1812, p. 265.

of hostilities to the American garrison at Mackinaw, and the first announcement they received was the summons to surrender, accentuated by the frowning muzzles of British artillery, which had been cleverly placed to command the fort at the weakest point. Of course the island was surrendered, and a post which might have retained a controlling influence over the northern Indians was turned over to the British. This has been attributed to the criminal remissness or imbecility of the secretary of war.[1] But the truth of this assertion is no justification for Governor Hull's failure to put himself into communication with the different portions of his territory. The army in Canada was now distracted, restless, grumbling. The general had no confidence in himself or in others, and the fall of Mackinaw took away even that which he had. Hourly the northern Indians might appear upon the scene, and Hull was borne down with a dread of their barbarous warfare.

Colonel Proctor arrived at Fort Malden with some reinforcements, and an aggressive warfare on the part of the English began. Word was received that the provisions and men for which Hull had been calling had been sent forward by Governor Meigs, and were at the River Raisin. Captain Brush, who was in command of these reinforcements, asked for an escort; for the British could easily cross the river and intercept him on his way to Detroit. Hull hesitated. But the

[1] Lossing's *Pictorial Field-Book of the War of* 1812, p. 271.

Ohio colonels forced him into compliance. An inadequate force was then sent under Major Van Horn. They were repulsed with loss, and Hull's mail fell into the hands of the British authorities. Again Cass and the other colonels said: "Send five hundred men to escort Brush to Detroit." "I can only spare a hundred,"[1] replied Hull from behind his defenses at Sandwich. At length, on August 7, stung into motion by the insistence[2] of his subordinates, he announced a general and immediate attack on the British fort. The army were joyfully engaged in active preparations when Hull summoned his officers and told them that he had decided to recross to Detroit, and on August 8 the army slunk back to its own territory disheartened, mutinous, and surly. The situation was now discouraging, and Hull proposed to give up Detroit and retreat beyond the Maumee. Had he at any time tested properly the strength of the enemy or shown the requisite energy and confidence, there might have been little opposition to this plan; for any one must have been able to see that Detroit could not be permanently held unless the army was strong enough to guard its line of communications. But when Hull suggested the propriety of retreating, Cass informed him that the Ohio militia in a body would refuse to obey such an order.

[1] Lossing, p. 277.

[2] Forbes's *Report of Trial of Brigadier-General William Hull*, p. 57.

Another force, under Colonel Miller, was sent down the river to escort Captain Brush. When they had completed about half the distance to the Raisin, a deadly fire was opened upon them from Indians and English in ambush. The men responded gallantly to Colonel Miller's "Charge! boys, charge!" and one of the most brilliant engagements of the war resulted in a victory for the Americans. But the victory had to be followed up, or Proctor would hurry across from Malden with more troops; for he well knew that Hull had given up all idea of offensive action. Colonel Miller reported his success, and asked for provisions. He had been injured by a fall from his horse, but he did not ask to be recalled. On the way to Detroit his messenger met Colonel Cass, and that officer, learning of Miller's condition, added the following characteristic dispatch: "Sir, Colonel Miller is sick; may I relieve him? L. Cass."[1] But the eagerness of Cass and the bravery of Miller must go for naught. Miller was immediately ordered back to Detroit, while the general contented himself with lamenting that the blood of seventy-five men had been shed in vain.[2]

The colonels now seriously thought of deposing[3] their general; but they finally agreed that Gover-

[1] Lossing's *Field-Book of the War of* 1812, p. 282. The only authority I can find for statement in the text.

[2] Armstrong's *Notices of the War of* 1812, vol. i. p. 30.

[3] *A Chapter of the War of* 1812, William Stanley Hatch, p. 40, and other references; Letter of Cass to Secretary of War, September 10, 1812.

nor Meigs should hasten to Detroit with assistance, and they hoped that he would accept the command. Cass at once wrote a cautious letter to the governor, hinting at Hull's incompetence, and stating that Malden might have fallen, but that the "golden opportunity" had passed. Before the letter was signed the following significant postscript was added: "Believe all the bearer will tell you. Believe it, however it may astonish you, as much as if told by one of us. Even a C—— is talked of by the ——. The bearer will fill the vacancy."[1]

Brock, a general of dash, vigor, and wonderful self-confidence, now arrived at Malden. A few regulars and nearly three hundred militia[2] accompanied him. The numbers of the Indians had lately increased somewhat, although none of the northern Indians appeared at Detroit until some time after the catastrophe of this serio-comic drama. Brock erected a battery where it might effectually play upon the American fort. But no attempt was made to prevent the erection of this work or to drive the enemy from it; General Hull, with admirable sententiousness, replied to Captain Dalliby, who asked permission to open fire upon them: "Mr. Dalliby, I will make an agreement with the enemy that, if they will never fire on me, I will never fire on them. Those who live in glass houses must not throw stones."

Events now hurried to a crisis. On August 14

[1] Niles's *Register*, vol. iii. p. 39. [2] *Life of Brock*, p. 335.

McArthur and Cass with three hundred and fifty men were sent as an escort to Captain Brush, who had determined to find his way to Detroit by a trail which ran some thirty miles back from the river. These young officers were becoming altogether too restless, and might be seriously thinking of mutiny, or, more terrible still, of fighting! On August 15 Brock sent Hull the following letter: "The force at my disposal authorizes me to require of you the immediate surrender of Detroit. It is far from my inclination to join you in a war of extermination; but you must be aware that the numerous body of Indians, who have attached themselves to my troops, will be beyond my control the moment the contest commences. You will find me disposed to enter into such conditions as will satisfy the most scrupulous sense of honor. Lieutenant-Colonel McDonell and Major Glegg are fully authorized to conclude any arrangement that may lead to prevent the unnecessary effusion of blood."[1] Hull detained the messenger some two hours, and then returned an answer fairly bristling with defiance.

HEADQUARTERS, DETROIT, *August* 15, 1812.

I have received your letter of this date. I have no other reply to make than to inform you that I am prepared to meet any force which may be at your disposal, and any consequences which may result from any exertion of it you may think proper to make.[2]

I am, etc., . . . WILLIAM HULL, etc.

[1] Tupper's *Life of Brock*, p. 231; Hull's *Memoirs*, p. 95.

[2] Hull's *Memoirs*, p. 96.

Immediately the British guns opened on Detroit, and the American guns replied. Some damage was done to the frail structures of the town, which was beginning to present a spectacle demoralizing and pitiful. The people of the neighborhood had crowded into the place for protection. Trembling women and bewildered children pleaded by their presence for a bold stand against Indian cruelty and vengeance. All had lost confidence in their obsolete general, and he, tenderhearted and compassionate, was overwhelmed with dread and oppressed with responsibility. Occasionally the old Revolutionary spirit awakened within him, but it was generally smothered by the kindly weakness and hesitancy which prompted to pity and ended in cruel inactivity.[1]

The quiet, beautiful Sabbath morning of August 16 was rudely disturbed by the booming of the British cannon. Again were pictured forth to the general's mind awful scenes of Indian atrocities, the unspeakable horrors of the tomahawk and scalping-knife. His memory of border tales and fables furnished food to his greedy imagination. "My God!" he exclaimed, "what shall I do with these women and children?" He sat on the ground, with his back toward the wall of the fort,

[1] "Desperate the situation seemed to be; yet a good general would have saved Detroit for some weeks. . . . Doubtless his fears were well founded, but a general-in-chief whose mind was paralyzed by such thoughts could not measure himself with Isaac Brock." Adams's *History of the United States during the First Administration of James Madison*, vol. ii. p. 327.

overcome with anxiety and distress. "He apparently unconsciously filled his mouth with tobacco, putting in quid after quid more than he generally did; the spittle colored with tobacco juice ran from his mouth on his neckcloth, beard, cravat, and vest."[1] The enemy cross the river; not a shot from American guns or cannon threatens them. They march toward Detroit along a narrow road, where a well-posted battery can shatter their lines. Not a gun is fired to check them; but a ball from the battery at Sandwich takes effect in the fort; women are carried away senseless; men are killed, and a white flag flutters over the bastions of the American defenses.

That was the end of the "proclamatory" invasion of Canada. Cass and McArthur were hurrying back, hoping to reach the fort before there was any real danger, or to attack the enemy in the rear if he was on the American side of the river. But the white flag had spiked the British guns, and, as they neared Detroit, not a cannon shot awakened the echoes to summon them to action. They soon found that Hull had included them and their force in his capitulation, without giving them a chance to escape. Cass, exasperated beyond endurance, snapped his sword in

[1] *Hull's Trial*, p. 40. Testimony of Major Snelling. There is some testimony to the effect that Hull conducted himself properly; but the overwhelming weight of evidence seems to be that he was at this time utterly unfit for the responsibilities of the moment.

twain, rather than disgrace himself by its surrender. "Basely to surrender without firing a gun!" he moaned in mingled anger and chagrin. "Tamely to submit without raising a bayonet!" Even Brush and his men were included in the surrender at Hull's own instance. For forty years to come Detroit citizens could not remember the occurrence without flushing with mortification. Hull did not have the courage of brave Croghan, who, with his little garrison surrounded by thirty times its numbers, answered a summons to surrender with the reply, "When the fort shall be taken there will be none to massacre." On this sad 16th of August a band of Kentucky volunteers, collected to reinforce Hull, were listening at Georgetown to the eloquence of Clay, who pictured in joyful anticipation the capture of Malden and the conquest of Upper Canada.

It is difficult to ascertain with exactness the number of the men surrendered or of those commanded by Brock. Hull estimated his own effective force at less than 1000,[1] Cass at 1060,[2] not including either the 300 Michigan militia on duty or the detachment sent to meet Brush. Brock, intoxicated with success, reports the capture of 2500 men.[3] This was undoubtedly an exaggera-

[1] Hull's *Memoirs;* Clarke's *History of the Campaign of* 1812, etc., p. 386.

[2] Niles's *Register*, p. 38; Cass's Letter to the Secretary of War; *Hull's Trial*, Appendix No. II. p. 27.

[3] Tupper's *Life of Brock*, p. 247.

tion. His own men, however, aggregated, according to his own report, 1330, including 600 Indians. Possibly he underestimated, for his own glorification, the number of his savage allies. To an inferior besieging force, for the Indians are notoriously useless in attacking a fortress, Hull surrendered with such indecent speed that he made no provision for the Canadians who had deserted to him, nor for the men who were with him and had been eager to fight by his side.

No proper steps had been taken by the government to protect the distant frontier, and Hull had already sent orders for the evacuation of Fort Dearborn, where Chicago now stands; and in spite of the intercession of those who realized the danger, Captain Heald obeyed the order, withdrew his garrison and the families from the fort, and began the long, dreary march to Detroit. They knew that they were marching to their doom, and as they left their fort, their little military band is said to have struck up the Dead March in Saul. It was at least appropriate. Men, women, and children were murdered in a desperate conflict, scarcely any escaping to tell of the event.

One problem remains to be examined: how to account for Brock's rash attack upon a strong fortress defended by a superior force. The answer has been already suggested. He discovered Hull's trepidation, was sure that his opponent was weak, faltering, and despondent. He thus exultingly wrote to his brothers on September 3:—

Some say that nothing could be more desperate than the measure ; but I answer that the state of the province admitted of nothing but desperate remedies. I got possession of the letters of my antagonist addressed to the secretary of war, and also of the sentiments which hundreds of his army uttered to their friends. . . . It is therefore no wonder that envy should attribute to good fortune what, in justice to my own discernment, I must say proceeded from a cool calculation of the *pours* and *contres.*[1]

The soldiers were paroled, and went, shamefaced and angry, to their homes. Hull was taken to Montreal, but was released by his captors, perhaps in hopes that his loud laments over the imbecility of the administration might heighten disaffection.[2] Cass, paroled, under Colonel McArthur's orders, hastened to Washington, and made a report to the secretary of war, which, full of indignation and disgust, was yet a fair statement of the disastrous incompetence of the general. The people were wild with excitement, and poured out abuse on all concerned in the childish totterings of the campaign. The administration and its feeble generals, quite willing to secure a victim for the sacrifice, led Hull, complaining, to the altar. A court-martial met at Albany in January, 1814. Major-General Dearborn, whose considerate and peaceful

[1] Tupper's *Life of Brock.*

[2] A letter from Prevost to Bathurst says, "Hull has been allowed to go to Boston on parole . . . for the purpose of justifying his conduct to his government." *Report of Canadian Archivist,* 1893, p. 73.

mode of warfare had prevented him from making a diversion in Hull's favor, sat as president, and Martin Van Buren appeared as special judge advocate. Cass was the first witness. His testimony was convincing and overwhelming, and was corroborated by that of McArthur and others. Yet his statements have been attributed to sinister motives. He has been charged with duplicity as a tool of the administration, although it is perfectly evident that his enmity towards Hull began in those dreary days in Canada, when Hull's energy was absorbed in summoning councils and discovering excuses for fatal delay. A letter written by Cass to his brother-in-law, Silliman, a few days before the surrender, introduced by Hull to prove the inconsistency of his accuser, has been forced to carry that burden even by later writers. But a fair interpretation will show neither inconsistency nor equivocation.

The court-martial was probably prejudiced against Hull; and yet one cannot say that its findings were altogether unwarranted. Dearborn himself had been inefficient, and was in part to blame for the perilous situation in which the arrival of Brock with reinforcements placed the western army. The war department also had expected too much of Hull, and had not taken prompt and active measures either to keep the enemy occupied in the East, or to give Hull other necessary assistance in his undertakings. And yet any one looking over the evidence will be likely to say that he was not fit for his arduous and difficult task, and that, deficient at first in activity and energy, he showed at the end culpable indecision and a timidity which seemed to many of the onlookers nothing less than cowardice. Perhaps he would have been justified in retiring beyond the Maumee, as soon as he heard of Brock's approach, or saw that he could only with the greatest difficulty, if at all, keep his communication open; but he was not entirely guiltless of producing the state of affairs which provoked the threat that the militia would refuse to obey an order to retreat.

The court found General Hull guilty of cowardice and neglect of duty, and sentenced him to be shot. Madison, tempering justice with mercy, approved the sentence, but remitted its execution, out of respect for the past services of one who, as a boy fresh from college, entered the patriot army immediately after Lexington, fought with cool and fearless energy, endured sufferings and fatigues with noble cheerfulness, and received acknowledgments of faithfulness from Washington himself. His last years were spent in comfort, but not in luxury. Presiding with simple unaffectedness at the "bounteous Thanksgiving dinner," or watching his merry grandchildren dancing in time to the music "of old Tillo's fiddle,"[1] he was much nearer his proper occupation than when commanding a rough, boisterous, backwoods army in a dangerous and important campaign.

[1] *Memorial and Biographical Sketches*, James Freeman Clarke, p. 439.

In December, 1812, Cass was appointed major-general in the Ohio militia, but he was not yet exchanged, and was prevented by his parole from entering into active service. In January the President determined to raise two regiments of regular troops in Ohio, and Cass, instructed to raise one, was appointed a colonel in the army, February 20, 1813.[1] His parole was removed about the middle of January, and he then proceeded with his task. Ohio and Kentucky were furious at the defeat and surrender of Hull. A perfect tidal wave of patriotism and resentment swept over these States, and Cass had no difficulty in obtaining his quota of men. The government, confiding in his fidelity and energy, now made him brigadier-general[2] in the regular army, to act under Major-General Harrison in the West.

In January, 1813, General Winchester had marched toward Detroit with a fine army of stalwart Kentuckians, the foremost young men in the State, who were burning to avenge the surrender of Detroit, and to give a sound whipping to the Indians, whose successful insolence was maddening to a Kentucky pioneer. The massacre at the River Raisin was the sad end of their hopes. Robbing, plundering, murdering, scalping, vile mutilations, barbarities too horrible to mention, followed the fall of the brave Kentuckians, who had come so full of eager pride and bravery.. From

[1] Records of War Department.

[2] March 12, 1813. Records of War Department.

that time to the battle of the Thames the Indians, unrestrained by the infamous Proctor, were a continual menace to the whole territory of Michigan. Their cruelties were constant. Property was wasted or destroyed; everywhere were confusion, misery, and fear.[1]

General Cass was actively engaged in the campaign of 1813. He was, as before, energetic and hopeful, a strong support for General Harrison, who relied upon his advice and trusted in his wisdom. They worked well together. After years found Cass a courageous defender of the "Hero of Tippecanoe," when political scribblers fought the battles over again, and sought to prove the victor a slovenly child of fortune. Some manœuvrings in the neighborhood of Sandusky were without importance to the main body of the army, though rendered famous by Croghan's courageous defense of his fort. On September 10 Commodore Perry sent Harrison his famous laconic, "We have met the enemy, and they are ours." The victorious fleet at once conveyed Harrison to Canada. In spite of the taunts of Tecumseh, who likened the retreating general to a "fat dog that drops his tail between his legs and runs off," Proctor abandoned Malden and retreated to the inte-

[1] *Michigan Pioneer Collection*, vol. iv. p. 320; *Wisconsin's Historical Collection*, vol. iii. p. 318, Witherell's Reminiscences; Niles's *Register*, vol. i. p. 91, giving Judge Woodward's letter to General Proctor; *Barbarities of the Enemy*, A Report of the Committee of the House of Representatives (1813), Troy, 1813.

rior. He was pursued and defeated at the battle of the Thames. "Kentuckians, remember the River Raisin!" was the inspiring battle-cry. Tecumseh, a braver and abler general than his white chief, was there killed by Colonel R. M. Johnson. Only a small portion of Cass's command was present at this fight. He acted, therefore, as aide-de-camp to General Harrison, and was rewarded with a complimentary notice of his services in the general's report to the secretary of war.

CHAPTER IV

GOVERNOR OF MICHIGAN TERRITORY

THE battle of the Thames secured the Northwest to the Americans. General Harrison, desiring to coöperate with our army in eastern Canada and New York, left the command of Detroit and the subjugated portion of western Canada to General Cass. The situation was not a simple one. The Indians, excited by the bloodshed and pillage of the preceding winter and spring, were restless and a constant menace to the little village and the people of the whole region, which was already desolated by the war. On October 29 the President appointed Cass governor of Michigan Territory. He prepared at once to assume the arduous duties of his new office. During a portion of the succeeding winter he attended the trial of Hull at Albany, where he was the chief witness. With the exception of some such temporary absences as this, he was continually resident in the Territory for the next eighteen years, giving to its people the energy of his young manhood and vigorous middle age, and inseparably connecting his name with the foundation and progress of Michigan and the development of the Northwest.

Life at the frontier post was occasionally romantic, but never free from grave responsibility and anxiety. At the outset duties pressed upon him in battalions. Although General Harrison had concluded an armistice with the greater portion of tribes, many hostile Indians were still in the neighborhood, and must be kept in subjection. The homeless fugitives, robbed of their all by the hirelings of Proctor, needed protection and support. Detroit, itself in confusion and anarchy, demanded the careful, firm, and kind hand of friendly authority. Through the whole winter of 1813–14 Michigan Territory was in a pitiful condition. The poor people from the Raisin district, whose houses had been burned or left in desolation, without food or means to obtain it, hovered, clamoring, in the village where the young governor was expected to turn the stones into bread. The lives of the French people had been spared by the Indians because of the general friendliness between the two races, but the hungry savages had killed their cattle, carried off the fruit from the orchards, burnt the fences and the floors of the houses, and left the *habitant* in the direst destitution. Above all, many Indians, no longer supplied from the train-bands of the British army, were themselves thrown on the mercy and humanity of the Americans. The public stores were used to drive away actual starvation; but so great was the want and poverty that a petition for help was sent to Washington; in response to which the

President asked Congress for a special appropriation.

Nothing can be said in exaggeration of the desolate state of Michigan for about two years after its recovery by the Americans. The French at the River Raisin, who, with all their ignorance of farming, had had comfortable cabins, as well as fields and orchards which supplied their humble wants, were reduced to such penury on their return to their farms that even very meagre food was obtained with difficulty. They lacked the nervous tension and vigor which tones up the American pioneer to resist expected danger and surmount difficulties. Light-hearted and cheerful in all ordinary trials, their easy-going dispositions, their unfamiliarity with the common devices which necessity begets in the frontier life of the inventive Yankee, their content with the past, and faith in the unearned blessings of the future, kept them penniless and breadless when keener intelligence might have lifted them above want. The settlers near Detroit were in woeful straits, but everything seems to show that the French of the River Raisin were more ignorant and less thrifty than the *habitant* to the north, and upon them had come the extreme cruelty and destruction of the war. Cass worked for his hungry Territory with untiring vigilance, distributing largesses from the public stores, calling upon the government for aid, organizing and instructing with zeal and energy. No portion of his career is more worthy of admiration than this, when his direst enemies were anarchy and hunger. A true picture of the governorship of Cass and the early history of the reclaimed Territory will be shaded into its proper depth of color by a remembrance of the peculiar trials attending them.

Besides the general poverty and distress of the Territory, other dangers confronted the people of the "double frontier." When the Indians, threatened by starvation, were not praying for sustenance at the hands of the authorities, they seem to have been satisfying their hatred of the "big knives," as they called the Americans, by unexpected attacks upon them and their property. They beleaguered the little village, pillaging, murdering, and scalping in the ruthless fashion which they had adopted under Proctor's tender instruction. Cass felt that his great task was to restore confidence to the cowering people, to induce them to return to their homes, and to begin again their peaceful lives. As a first step to this end, he decided that these annoyances from the savages must cease. A bold attack upon the Indians seemed the most satisfactory method of procedure; and, successful in that, a stockade might be built and blockhouses reared at the expense of the general government, to protect the frontier and overawe the red men. In September, 1814, the settlement was in especial danger from these marauding bands, and the young men of the village organized for an attack. General Cass led the little company into a bloody skirmish, in which the Indians were beaten. During the whole affair Cass displayed that calm ignoring of danger which was so characteristic of him, and which powerfully influenced the impressionable savage. Riding at the head of his men, he was advised by one of his company, Major Whipple, to fall back to the centre, as, should he be killed, it might create confusion; but he answered, "Oh, major, I am pretty well off here; let us push on." Various sallies of this character upon the Indians skulking along the river soon freed the people of their more abject fear. All had confidence in their young governor, and willingly followed him into any danger. "His constant, unremitting vigilance and energetic conduct saved our people from many of the horrors of war, and he was sustained by our *habitants*."[1]

The savages had rendered the British such efficient service that in 1814 our government strove to obtain like aid. Possibly we can plead in justification that this was merely a defensive measure, but we cannot deny the fact. July 22, 1814, General Harrison and Governor Cass met in council with a number of Indians at Greenville, Ohio, and there entered into an agreement in which the Indians promised assistance, and the commissioners pledged protection. Cass returned to Detroit, accompanied by a band which became personally attached to him. Fortunately his influence over

[1] Witherell's Reminiscences, *Wisconsin Hist. Col.* vol. iii. p. 324.

them was so great that the disgraceful scenes of Proctor's occupation were not repeated. The use of savages in civilized warfare is inexcusable; but in this case the disastrous consequences were reduced to a minimum.

In spite of the successful vigor of Cass, his situation was perilous and anxious until the close of the war. Having resigned his military commission April 6, 1814,[1] he found himself in the anomalous position of bearing responsibility unassisted by the requisite authority. The few United States troops that had been left at Detroit objected to receiving commands from a civil officer; the constant presence of threatening Indians, and the disordered condition of the defenses of the town called for action in preparation for a possible recurrence of the events of 1812. Should our army prove ineffective in the East, or should affairs in Europe suddenly take a different turn, Detroit might again, in an instant, become a salient point and a position of great strategic importance. A letter of August 13, from the secretary of war, authorized the governor, in the absence of a general officer, to take command of all the forces at Detroit in case of attack. But with such half-hearted trust he was not content. All save a very few troops were bravely sent to the East to assist the movement of our army on the Niagara frontier, and he was obliged to rely mainly on the volunteer services of the weary and pillaged in-

[1] Records of War Department.

habitants of the Territory. Even in these straits he did not stand all the day idle, complaining of his helplessness; but with his "pet Indians" he gave material aid in the progress of the war by making feints against the Canadian inhabitants and property in the eastern portion of Upper Canada. He asserted, however, in his communications to the War Department, that should a general attack be made by the British forces, he should retire from the Territory, unaided as he was by the militia from the south, which he had had every reason to expect. Amid all these troubles and anxieties, the work of bringing order and tranquillity into the disordered Territory went bravely on.

Peace came to a jubilant country before another campaign brought its load of mingled victory and defeat. Men wept in each other's arms in joy that the war was over, — a war conducted with neither energy nor skill, and concluded by a treaty that was little more than an armistice, settling none of the questions for which we had blustered into the war, with our armor rusty and our flintlocks out of repair. Our victories on the sea had, however, beaten into our opponents a modicum of respect for us. Now, at last, to the happy people the sky seemed spanned by a bow of promise, — no more impressments, no more highway robbery of men and goods from well-behaving neutrals. The pot of gold at the foot of this rainbow did not, however, lie in the neighborhood of Detroit.

Peace for a moment shed its warming rays into that desolate country; but it served only to render more visible the havoc of the war, and to show the immensity of the task of restoring prosperity and confidence and of raising the Territory into a self-sustaining portion of the country.

The work of General Cass's governorship naturally divides itself into a series of undertakings, which clearly present themselves as one glances back over the period, and the importance of which he, at the time, fully realized. By his appreciation of the peculiar duties laid upon him, he made them more distinct, and gave to his administration a singular completeness and unity. His greatest problem, embracing or touching all the rest, was to convert the French settlement, at present tortured by actual want and, at its best, defenseless, foreign, and slow, into an active American community, prosperous and progressive in peace, capable of self-defense in war, a real buckler to that Northwest which never ceased to tempt the covetous eyes of the English. Michigan must be Americanized and colonized; its strategic value must be estimated aright and its physical charms displayed; the whole Northwest must be so protected and guided that the tide of immigration which had set in over its southeastern border would encounter no wall in its onward sweep, until it had carried the schoolhouse and the newspaper into the farthest corner of that land where the Jesuit had, a century before, planted his cross and sung his *ave*.

In 1846–47, thirty years after the first trials of his governorship, Cass was struggling in the Senate for the possession of the far Northwest above the line of 49°; that contest was the afterglow of the fire of his younger life, which had been devoted to the extension of his country's civilization into its remote and seemingly unattractive corners.

The distress consequent upon the British and Indian occupation of Michigan was, as has been said, partly relieved before the war was finished. But through the whole summer of 1815 many of the inhabitants needed assistance. In May, 1815, the War Department authorized Governor Cass to distribute $1500 among the poor of the Territory. This trifling sum, which would hardly keep starvation at bay, much less provide for making the people self-supporting, he was directed to spend with care and economy, and to draw for more if necessary.[1] The national government was not so freighted with a surplus after the war that it could afford to do more than dribble out its dollars. This money, spent in flour to be given to the Raisin settlers, was a temporary relief, but not a remedy for the ills of the Territory.[2] So many of the people were without the fundamental ideas of sensible farming that thrift and prosperity could not be purchased by occasional alms. The happy French farmers near Detroit were content with their big orchards and shaggy ponies. The poorer

[1] Archives in State Department of Michigan.

[2] *Ibid.*

ones, brought for the time being out of actual suffering, began again their careless farming, making no attempt to push back into the unbroken forests which hemmed them in to the river's brink. Cass proclaimed the need of American enterprise and skill. If a few Eastern farmers could display before the astonished eyes of the French Canadian their habitual providence and energy, the old wooden ploughshare and clumsy hoe might give place to more modern implements. With this idea in mind, Governor Cass proceeded to make its necessity evident by direct statement of his desires. But the indirect method seemed, on the whole, more efficacious. If lands were offered freely for sale, and their attractions and value demonstrated by successful tillage, Americans from the older States might be attracted into the Territory. His efforts towards the accomplishment of this purpose furnish in detail an interesting study. The following outlines are suggestive.

By an act of Congress, passed at the beginning of the war, 2,000,000 acres were to be selected in Michigan, to be given as bounty lands to volunteers. Cass desired that these surveys should be quickly made in order that at least a few settlers, taking advantage of the gift, might make their homes in the Territory, and introduce a larger American element on which and with which to work. But disappointing delays awaited him. The surveyors, to whom had been given the task of running the proposed meridian line from the

Au Glaize River due north, beginning their task in the early winter, returned to Ohio after a short absence with a most lugubrious account of the cheerless territory. Cass had been in communication with the Indians, and was able to assure the surveyors that there was no reason to fear; but either hardship and fatigue, or dread of attack, had so perverted their judgment of the country that they described the interior of Michigan as one vast morass, its monotony occasionally broken by sandhills without the covering of attractive vegetation. The President, assured by the commissioner of the land office that scarcely one acre in a thousand was fit for cultivation, advised Congress, in February, 1816, that the quota of bounty lands assigned to Michigan might better be located in other parts of the Northwest.

The people of the Eastern States, receiving this official condemnation of the country, believed for years that the rich, rolling lands of the southern peninsula of Michigan were a barren waste. The great American desert has been a very movable spot in our geography. Cass was never entirely successful in relieving the Territory of the weight of this truthless description. For years it lay like a millstone on the shoulders of the struggling young province. Disappointed and discomfited, the governor did not despair. Insisting upon the good character of the soil and climate, he finally secured, in 1818, the location of a public land office; lands were offered for sale, and the history of Michigan, as an American settlement, began. Slowly it rose to a position of dignity and power, as its resources and beauties were made known. Some twenty years later Harriet Martineau, riding through the Territory, charmed by the luxuriant woods, with their beautiful openings, and the wild flowers scattered in profusion by the roadside, exclaimed: "Milton must have traveled in Michigan before he wrote the garden parts of 'Paradise Lost.'"[1] The progress of the State was slow, but its advance was due to the tireless devotion of its second territorial governor.

The work of Governor Cass in bringing Michigan out from its Gallic sloth was coupled with the task of asserting Northwestern independence and our national dignity in opposition to British interference. In its more evident form this arrogant intermeddling with our concerns ended about two years after the war. But the insidious efforts of the English authorities to render insecure the American occupation of the Northwest continued with more or less heartiness through the whole of Cass's governorship, and, indeed, can be detected until within two or three years of the Ashburton treaty of 1842. In case of another war with America, the Great Lakes and the States bordering upon them would offer special inducement for naval and military movements. An idea of the mighty growth of the young republic permeated the English mind but slowly. It was only during

[1] *Society in America*, vol. i. p. 325.

the Rebellion that a sense of our power was first conveyed to the average Englishman by our enormous armies and our naval enterprises. In consequence of this long ignorance and contempt, for years after the Northwest was a vigorous and well-settled region, the English cultivated its scattered tribes of Indians with remembrance (indistinct, it is to be hoped) of the character of their services in the war of 1812. As we can now look back on the fruitlessness of such efforts and notice the steady advance of the pioneer into the forests and over the plains of the West, we can pass the fact by with a shrug, half of amusement at the persistence of our fond mother country, who so long yearned for her wayward child. But for at least ten years after the treaty of Ghent, these efforts were far from amusing, and, while the "era of good feeling" was casting its genial warmth upon the Eastern partisans, the Northwest was in danger of having its progress retarded by hostile Indians, whom British presents incited to animosity against the Americans and won to loyalty and respect for the Union Jack. Had a war with England broken out before 1840, in all likelihood a great portion of the Indians would have gone where British presents and brilliant tinsel called them. These dangers Cass fully appreciated; and the insult to American independence and American humanity he deeply resented. So keenly did he feel the injustice and perversity of England that he never recovered from his suspicions of her. His dislike of her aggrandizement was natural, and, under the circumstances, justifiable; it colored his whole public career. With annoying frequency, through the whole of his governorship, arose these evidences of British influence. Nothing but his own good sense, promptness, and bravery, checked the insolence of the red man thus encouraged and abetted, and rendered the Northwest habitable and peaceful.

It has been suggested by our general historians that England entered into the treaty of peace of 1783 with the hope that our loose-knit confederacy would soon burst its bonds and give her a chance to absorb the repentant, disconsolate States singly; but our people have perhaps not realized the longevity of that hope. A series of incidents, which I shall not attempt to give in chronological connection with the other events of Cass's governorship, will substantiate the general statements already made.

The bold, ill-concealed interference with our affairs and the projecting of British authority into our territory are partly attributable to the recklessness of local authority, partly, it must be thought, to that widespread feeling of our helplessness, which prompted adherence to the search and impressment doctrine long after the war of 1812. Vessels were stopped and searched on their way to Detroit as late as the middle of 1816. Governor Cass collected sworn testimony, and transmitted it to Washington. Expostulating with the

British authorities, he insisted that the conduct of the boarding officers was arrogant and imperious, and that such actions were contrary to the law of nations and destructive of friendly relations between the two governments. His remonstrances apparently stopped these open violations of our rights upon the Lakes.

Before this, there were various troubles with the soldiers in Canada. A series of letters[1] which passed between Governor Cass and Colonel James, in command of the forces across the river, discloses these difficulties and the unwarranted attitude assumed by the English. The ill feeling and lawlessness of the Indians, some of whom still remained in Canada and received sustenance from the public stores, were continually exhibited in petty acts of annoyance and in deeds of violence, for which there was no excuse. The agent of our government, left temporarily in charge of stores at Amherstburg, was insulted and assaulted by these lawless braves. There was no strong reason for not sending them away and ceasing to recognize them as allies; but the English authorities, in excuse, pleaded the force of compassion and the difficulty of controlling them. On the other side, it cannot truthfully be asserted that the Americans were always courteous and honest. The stragglers in a disorganized country, demoralized by war, are apt to cause annoyances to a hated enemy so temptingly near as were the troops and people in

[1] In the Archives of the State Department at Lansing.

Canada. But while the Indians were still kept in idleness and mischief by the presents from the British, Cass was authorized,[1] May 25, 1815, not to give the Indians presents, inasmuch as the reason for doing so had passed away. To our former enemies the necessities appeared quite different.

In September, 1815, nine months after the close of the war, a robbery and desertion from a British man-of-war gave an opportunity for an offensive violation of our sovereignty. A lieutenant and boat's crew, sent out to arrest the culprit, sought him on American soil. They prosecuted the search arrogantly, entering and examining several houses, and evidently conducting themselves in such a domineering spirit that the citizens were aroused to resistance. One resident of Detroit at the time related that the English "placed sentinels on our highway, one of which fired at a citizen."[2] The deserter for whom they were searching was seized; but meanwhile the behavior of the invading party had so exasperated the citizens that they flew to arms, and turned the tables upon the intruders by arresting the lieutenant and conducting him with due pomp to the fort, while the boat's crew hurried their captive on board their vessel. Colonel Miller gave up jurisdiction in the matter to Governor Cass, as the head of the civil authority.

[1] Letter to Cass from War Department, Archives, Lansing.

[2] Niles, vol. ix. p. 104. Also *ibid.* p. 187. Letters in State Department, Lansing.

Commodore Owen demanded the return of the lieutenant. Cass answered at some length. With only a half-starved Territory at his back he knew how to resent contempt and neglect for well-known principles of law.

Lieutenant Vidal was arrested and brought to me for apprehending forcibly a person in the Territory and conveying him on board a British armed vessel. In so doing he has violated the laws of the country, and subjected himself to the penalty it prescribes for such conduct. Permit me to observe that your demand for Lieutenant Vidal, without offering to restore the person seized and transported by him, was not to have been expected. There are no treaty stipulations between the United States and Great Britain for the restoration of persons deserting from the service of the one and seeking refuge in the territory of the other. Such an arrangement was proposed by our commissioners, but not acceded to. The subject, therefore, rests upon the general principles of international law, and I need not remind you, sir, that that law gives no right to a British officer to enter the territory of the United States and forcibly transport thence any person, whatever may be his description or of whatever crime he may be accused. . . . But, sir, the subject involves considerations of greater interest than those personally affecting the offender. An armed force in the service of her Britannic majesty has apprehended a person within this Territory. . . . It becomes, therefore, my duty to request of you his immediate return.[1]

The circumstances under which this intrusion had taken place partly extenuated it; but it was

[1] Letters in Archives of State Department of Michigan.

a transference to land of that abominated claim, that deserters from English ships could be seized and forced back to their allegiance, a claim which, when carried out with exasperating additions, had inflamed our country, and driven us into a war for the defense of our self-respect. Cass was determined to take a bold stand upon principle. Vidal was imprisoned, tried, convicted, and fined. An appeal for his release was sent to Washington by the English authorities. Our government expressly ratified the action of Governor Cass; but, in order to avoid possible complications and ill-feeling, advised the return of the money received as a fine, if it had not been covered into the treasury. The advice came too late. The hungry coffers of the Territory had quickly absorbed such an unexpected addition to their store.[1]

Another instance, occurring in October, 1815, illustrates more clearly the desires and the assumption of the British. Colonel James, in command at Sandwich, wrote to Cass, complaining that an Indian had been "murdered under most aggravating circumstances, in a canoe close to Grosse Isle, by a shot fired from an American boat." "I need not point out to you," said the choleric colonel, "the line of conduct necessary on this occasion. I shall direct an inquest to be held to-morrow morning, and I beg leave to remind you that the murder has been committed on the body of an unoffending Indian, and my pointing out the cus-

[1] Letters in Archives of State Department of Michigan.

tom of the savages would be unnecessary in the present instance."

The last allusion, a petty threat, awakened the ever-watchful dignity of the young governor. He informed Colonel James that he would make inquiries. "If a murder has been committed by American citizens, and the perpetrators can be detected, they will suffer the punishment which the laws of civilized nations provide for the offense. In an application of this kind it was unnecessary to allude to the Indian custom of retaliating upon innocent individuals injuries which any of their tribe may have received. The laws of the country operate with rigid impartiality upon all offenders, and confident I am that no dread of the consequences will ever induce the courts of justice to punish the innocent or screen the guilty."[1] An examination speedily proved that the Indian had been killed not only in self-defense, but on American territory. "The event," wrote Cass to James, "was connected with the predatory system pursued by Indians on the islands at the mouth of the river, and which, if not checked, will be attended with still more disastrous consequences. The Indian was killed within territorial jurisdiction of the United States, and a British officer has, therefore, no right to ask, nor ought an American to give an explanation."[2]

In connection with the same event came a letter

[1] Letters in Archives of State Department of Michigan.
[2] *Ibid.*

from James, inclosing one from a British Indian agent, which set up claims made by the Indians for some horses stolen from them by the Americans. Cass answered in a trenchant letter quietly, but sharply, asking that questions which did not concern Canadian authority or jurisdiction might be left out of consideration by over-zealous officials. "We do not acknowledge in principle, nor shall we ever admit in practice, the right of any foreign authority to interfere in any arrangement or discussion between us and the Indians living within our territory." That statement was the basis for the work of his whole governorship. His rights and duties were logically presented, — should horses be stolen in Upper Canada and brought upon American soil, all reasonable efforts would be made to return them. But in this instance such was not the case. "In application of these principles, I have only to observe that Stony Island, whence these horses were stated to have been taken, is in this Territory, that the horses were not taken from there to Canada, and that a British officer has consequently no right to make a claim in behalf of the Indians on the subject."[1] This application, of no special importance in itself, was part of a general programme for retaining the affection and dependence of the Indian, for perpetuating his distrust of the Americans, for rendering his presence in the Northwest a menace to American settlement, and for giving

[1] Niles's *Register*, vol. ix. p. 242.

him an exalted idea of the friendship, dignity, and power of the British government. On October 18 there issued from the magistrate of the western district of Canada a circular announcing that a Kickapoo Indian had been "willfully murdered," and offering a reward of five hundred dollars for the capture of the perpetrators of the deed. This insidious announcement, shrewdly calculated to attract the Indians and possibly intended to induce some avaricious Americans to transport their fellow-citizens to Canada for punishment, was deeply resented by Governor Cass. He at once published a stirring counter-proclamation, stating that the Indian was killed on American soil, that the affair was entirely without the jurisdiction of the officious magistrates, and that such pretensions were unfounded and unjustifiable. He called upon the citizens of the Territory to repel by force any attempt "to apprehend any person on the west side of the middle water communication" between Lakes Huron and Erie.

A letter to Secretary Monroe from Cass, in explanation of this affair, charges that such difficulties were due to the "ungovernable temper of James and to designs, which every day more fully discloses, of using every incident which occurs as a means of acquiring and strengthening their influence over the Indians. . . . On the other side of the river the design is avowed of serving their process upon any part of the river or upon any islands of it. The tenor and the object of their measures is to teach the Indians to look to themselves for protection. Much sensation is thereby excited, and it is surprising with what eagerness they gave credit to the report that the British would punish the man who killed their countryman."[1]

In this letter he called attention to the fact that dollars, the American currency, instead of pounds, were offered in the circular as a reward, with the intent, evidently, of influencing persons in American territory. Even more explicitly were the pretensions of England stated by Colonel James a few days after this controversy. He acknowledged the receipt of the stolen horses, which had been returned through the generous efforts of Cass, and added a few telling words. The treaty of Ghent, he asserted, amply provided for the Indians who had been in alliance with Great Britain; all the tribes, even those whose country extended as far as the Mississippi and who were included in the treaty, looked to the English for a fulfillment of an "agreement which insured to them ingress and egress through all parts of America, the same as previous to the year 1811."[2] The acts of the British Indian agents for many years after this speak more loudly than words of a design to protect their past allies and to keep a guardian hand on all, as far west as the Mississippi.

[1] Letter in Archives of State Department of Michigan.

[2] Letters in Archives of State Department of Michigan.

The patriotic zeal of General Cass was applauded in the East as his deeds of bold opposition were recounted in the papers. But few have gathered any idea of the continuance of this trouble, which presented itself in its most virulent form in the first three years of his administration. A study of the Indian treaties which he negotiated shows him continually trying to win the affection and respect of many who were inclined to believe in the power and generosity of the British government. The radius of his influence was constantly lengthening, and the fear and respect for the power which he represented increased. When he began his governorship, he strove to overcome Indian antipathy in the very neighborhood of Detroit. Twelve years later in northern Wisconsin and Minnesota he relieved the Indians from want, and with gentle reproof took from the necks of their chieftains their British medals, and placed in their stead a miniature of their great and mighty "Father at Washington." But in spite of the widening circle of successful management, he cannot be said to have been entirely relieved of his task until he left the Territory. In June, 1819, George Boyd, the Indian agent at Mackinaw, wrote to Cass: "A large body of Indians took their departure hence three days ago for Drummond's Island for the purpose of receiving, it is said, large disbursements of Indian presents at the hand of the Duke of Richmond, and perhaps with a view to influence their attendance on the treaty about to be held by your excellency the ensuing fall at Saginah."[1] In May, 1822, the same agent wrote again on this interesting question: "At all events, I trust that the stand now taken by the government . . . will not be lightly abandoned. To temporize with them, as regards their intercourse with the British posts, will, in the end, prove as injurious to them as it will be disgraceful to us, and I see no better time to draw the strong line between American and British Indians than the present. Whenever I shall have met them fully in council, the result shall be immediately communicated to your excellency."[2] Other words in this letter suggest the present fear of English influence, and the danger that, should another war occur, the Indians would be attracted to our open-handed enemies.

One or two other facts will add to the evidence of British intrigue and intrusion. December 4, 1823, nearly ten years after Cass had been ordered to cease furnishing presents to the tribes lingering around Detroit, we find him writing to Calhoun, the secretary of war, in a tone not of the utmost confidence, and as if the troubles were well known and discouraging, that he will use every effort which prudence dictates to prevent the Indians from passing through the country to Malden to receive gifts, and that a celebrated half-breed has just gone through for the purpose of extending

[1] *Boyd Papers*, in the Library of Wisconsin Historical Society.
[2] *Ibid.*

British influence among the Indians.[1] In September, 1829, Niles quoted from the Canadian "Colonial Advocate" the statement that "about sixty tons of Indian presents are on their way to Amherstburg and Drummond's Island; they are chiefly distributed among British Indians, but great numbers of Indians from the United States territories also partake. Fifty or sixty tons more of presents are on their way up the Alciope. There is no doubt but that they cost the British government an immense sum annually." A large body of Indians at that time passed through northern Ohio on their way to the field of tinsel and brass. The sage Niles remarks mildly that this "policy of the British government should be checked by prompt measures." One of the scenes familiar to the people of Detroit, the remembrance of which has not yet passed away, is that of the tippling, carousing red men, who, loaded with knickknacks and gewgaws in Canada, came across the river, and, exchanging what of their treasures they might to obtain some beloved firewater, held their maudlin encampment on the attractive camping ground below the city.

In the north, near the head of Lake Huron, these gifts were made to American Indians as late as 1839. Had the Caroline affair brought on the war which at one time seemed imminent, the tomahawk and scalping-knife might have done their execution; or, had the northeastern boundary

[1] Archives, Governor's Office, Lansing, Michigan.

trouble been more sanguinary than the "battle of the maps," the war-whoop might again have been heard through northern Michigan and Wisconsin. Without presuming to cast the horoscope of a hypothetical past, one may insist that these assertions have more than a visionary foundation. Mrs. Jameson, in her "Winter Studies and Summer Rambles in Canada," has left us a graphic, artless, and interesting picture of a great Indian council held upon Great Manitoulin Island, in which the policy of the English government is well presented. She prefaces her description by a confession that the assembling of all Indians within British territory "who are our allies and receive our annual presents seems reasonable and politic." By this time it was the policy of Great Britain to gather the Indians together from the northern part of the United States, to settle them in British territory, and bind them to British allegiance by annual bestowal of gifts. Can this be charged to sheer philanthropy, to a desire to take the poor red man from our jurisdiction, and to lay the burden of his sustenance upon the grumbling taxpayer at home, to a willingness to increase the weight of the great Indian problem to the British and Canadian governments?

In the council of 1837, as described by Mrs. Jameson, the Indians were informed that their "Great Father the King" would continue to give presents to the Indians of Canada, but that only "for three years, including the present delivery," should the tribes within the limits of the United States be so treated; the United States, the agent said, justly complained against this policy, which gave "arms and ammunition to Indians of the United States, who are fighting against the government under which they live;" the people of England grumbled at the great expense. "But, children!" he continued, "let it be distinctly understood that the British government has not come to the determination to cease to give presents to the Indians of the United States. On the contrary, the government of your Great Father will be most happy to do so, provided they live in the British empire;"[1] the giving of presents to those residing without the jurisdiction of England would "bring on war between your Great Father and the Long Knives." This needs no interpretation. At least as late as the Ashburton treaty England had on our northern frontier a body of dependent allies, a band of savage mercenaries bought by beads and calico, ready at her word to collect in war-paint and feathers, and to enter upon the dastardly horrors which Michigan had learned to fear. It was due to the efforts of Governor Cass that many were brought to fear and respect him, and that so many were turned from their devotion to the implacable mother of our country.

Observing this work of Governor Cass with the Indians, we find a career of monotonous responsi-

[1] Mrs. Jameson's *Winter Studies and Summer Rambles in Canada*, vol. ii. p. 289.

bility broken at intervals by romantic and picturesque incidents. Until April, 1816, Michigan included all the land east of a line drawn through the middle of Lake Michigan and north of a line drawn from the southern end of that lake eastward until it intersected Lake Erie. In 1816 Indiana was admitted to the Union with a slice pared from the southwestern portion of Michigan. After April, 1818, all land east of the Mississippi and north of the northern line of Illinois was under the supervision of Governor Cass. For the remaining years of his governorship he had control of this vast region. He was *ex officio* superintendent of Indian affairs in the territory. He had, in addition, for a great portion of the time, charge of agencies at Chicago, Fort Wayne, Piqua, and other sub-agencies. In the capacity of special agent and commissioner he came into contact with the Indians of the whole Northwest. He entered into a score of treaties of such importance, and his personal influence was so great, that there is little exaggeration in claiming that the actual possession of the Northwest was due to his exertions. He traveled through the wilderness, enduring hardship and fatigue, everywhere and always studying how he might open up all the vast region for peaceful settlement, how he might win the red man to civilization and comfort. He was the first white man to ride over the Indian trail which became the great highway between Detroit and Chicago. The merry *voyageurs* carried him in their bark canoes over the lake and stream until the Northwest, with its resources and splendid possibilities, was familiar to him. For weeks at a time he was absent from home on long voyages, accompanied by one or two companions of his liking and by the hardy boatmen whose steady, swinging stroke carried him over the waves of the Great Lakes. It is still remembered how the ringing boat-song would awaken the little village on his return, as the long canoe came flying down the river, and the cheery boatmen, bending to their work, lifted their voices in measured cadences of weird and fascinating music.

Duncan McArthur was appointed in 1817 to coöperate with Cass in obtaining land in northern Ohio and Indiana. By a successful treaty this commission acquired for settlement a great deal of land, and obtained the grant of three sections for the "College at Detroit," a gift of value, afterward, for higher education in Michigan. The following year Cass met the Indians at St. Mary's, in Ohio, and entered into a fruitful negotiation for a vast stretch of territory. At Saginaw, in 1819, a large portion of Michigan was secured, and at Chicago, in 1821, he obtained all the southwestern part of the State of Michigan, south of the Grand River. In the latter part of November, 1819, he wrote to Secretary Calhoun for authority to make an extended tour along the southern shore of Lake Superior, thence to the source of the Mississippi, and home by way of Prairie du

Chien and Green Bay. He desired to investigate the Indian tribes, to induce them no longer to go to Canada for presents, to obtain plots of ground at Sault de Ste. Marie and other places, and to investigate the mineral resources of the country, with special reference to copper, which was reported to exist in abundance. "All that will be required," he said, "is an ordinary birch bark canoe, and permission to employ a competent number of Canadian boatmen." He suggested, in addition, an "officer of engineers to make a correct chart," and "some person acquainted with zoölogy, botany, and mineralogy." The plan was received favorably at Washington. A topographical engineer was attached to the expedition. Mr. Henry R. Schoolcraft was selected to conduct the scientific researches, and has left an account of the incidents and discoveries of the journey in his book entitled "Discovery of the Sources of the Mississippi River."

The voyagers, in three birch canoes, left Detroit, May 24, amid the shouts and acclamations of the people, who were deeply interested in the efforts of Governor Cass. Schoolcraft gives a vivid description of the strange scene. The Indians, who had been secured as the hunters of the expedition, were in one canoe, vainly striving to pass by the hardy Canadians, who, in their turn, starting their familiar boat-song, began their steady strokes, and soon gave evidence of their firmer muscle and more enduring nerve. The large orchards and windmills, and the quaint houses lining the river for miles, added a foreign flavor. Skirting the storm-battered shores and long-winding beaches of Lake Huron, the expedition, after a journey of more than three hundred miles, came to Mackinaw on June 6. A few days later they reached the Sault de Ste. Marie, where it was Cass's intent to obtain possession of a piece of ground formerly conveyed to the French, our right to which the Indians had acknowledged in various treaties.

The braves, evidently restless and out of humor, assembled to meet the Americans. Arrayed in their best attire, and many of them adorned with British medals, they seated themselves with even more than their wonted solemnity and dignity, and prepared to hear what Governor Cass desired. At first pretending not to know of any French grants, they finally intimated that our government might be permitted to occupy the place if we did not use it as a military station. The governor, perceiving that their independence and boldness verged on impudence and menace, answered decisively that as surely as the "rising sun would set, so surely would there be an American garrison sent to that point, whether they received the grant or not." The excitement which had been ready to break forth now displayed itself. The chiefs disputed among themselves, some evidently counseling moderation, others favoring hostilities. A tall and stately-looking chieftain, dressed in a

British uniform with epaulets, lost patience with moderation and delay. Striking his spear into the ground, he drew it forth again, and, kicking away the presents that lay scattered about, strode in high dudgeon out of the assembly.

The Indian camp was on a small hill a few hundred yards from that of the Americans. The dissatisfied chiefs went directly to their lodges, and in a moment a British flag was flying in the very faces of the little company of white men. The soldiers were at once ordered under arms. Every one expected an immediate attack, for the Indians, greatly outnumbering the Americans, had not disguised their insolence and contempt. In an instant Governor Cass took his resolution. Rejecting the offers of those who volunteered to accompany him, with no weapon in his hands and only his interpreter beside him, he walked straight to the middle of the Indian camp, tore down the British flag, and trampled it under his feet.[1] Then addressing the astonished and even panic-stricken braves, he warned them that two flags of different nations could not fly over the same territory, and should they raise any but the American flag, the United States would put its strong foot upon them and crush them. He then turned upon his heel and walked back to his own tent, carrying the British ensign with him. An hour of indecision among the Indians ensued. Their camp was quickly cleared of women and children, an indica-

[1] Trowbridge's account, *Wisconsin Historical Collection.*

tion that a battle was in immediate prospect. The Americans, looking to their guns, listened for the war-whoop and awaited attack. But the intrepidity of Governor Cass had struck the Indians with amazement. It showed a rare knowledge of Indian character, of which his own companions had not dreamed.[1] Subdued by the boldness and decision of this action, the hostile chiefs forgot their swaggering confidence, and in a few hours signed the treaty which had been offered them. The friends of Governor Cass who witnessed the scene never wearied of describing it and of commenting on his bravery. One whose knowledge of Indian character was almost equal to that of the governor was wont to remark that for fair, frank courage in the face of danger this action surpassed all others he had ever known.[2] The habitual courage and dignity of Governor Cass, coupled with honesty and mercy, won from the Indians a respect and even love for their "Great Father at Detroit," and gradually forced westward and northward allegiance to Britain and undue respect for her power.

From the Sault de Ste. Marie the party skirted the southern shores of Lake Superior to its western end. By way of the Fond du Lac or St. Louis River, and by means of various portages, they reached the Mississippi, and proceeded up it a

[1] Schoolcraft's *Summary Narrative*, etc., p. 80.

[2] Mr. C. C. Trowbridge, companion and secretary of the governor.

distance estimated at three hundred and fifty miles to what was known as Red Cedar Lake, but which Schoolcraft on his map and in his report named Cass Lake, in token of the "energy and enlightened zeal of the gentleman who led the expedition." Had it not been for the low state of the water, General Cass would in all probability have discovered the true source of the Mississippi as early as 1820. From this point the company paddled between the beautiful banks of the mighty river to Prairie du Chien, and thence made their way across Wisconsin to Green Bay. Here General Cass caused a series of investigations to be conducted for the purpose of discovering the truth or falsity of the theory that there were tides in the Great Lakes as in the ocean. Experiments seemed to prove complete irregularity in the rise and fall of the water-fluctuations, which were in all probability due to the wind and the currents of the lakes. In later years Cass made more extended tests, and published the results of his studies. At Green Bay the company divided, one part going north, the other, including the governor, to Chicago, whence he proceeded overland to Detroit by the old Indian trail. The expedition had been a most successful and profitable one. Mr. Schoolcraft, in his report to the secretary of war, affirmed that the mineral resources of the country were great, and called special attention to the indications of wonderful copper and iron deposits. The Indians were visited, and given an object lesson in the daring and resolution of the Americans. The topography of the country, described with some detail, furnished basis for further explorations and induced greater immigrations.

During these years the internal political affairs of the Territory were not neglected by Governor Cass. When he came into office, the first system of government established under the Ordinance of 1787 was in vogue. The governor and judges were omnipotent, save as they were restrained by the general terms of their fundamental charter. The citizens had taken no interest in the management of the Territory. The *habitant* could not conceive of the necessity or the pleasure of interference with the divine right of government. But their new governor intended that democratic principles should hold sway as widely as possible under his guidance. The people were tempted into self-government. The laws were codified and published, and, so arranged, have since been known as the "Cass Code." Counties were laid out as rapidly as convenience directed. As the Americans came into the Territory in greater numbers, the governor allowed the settlers of each locality to suggest names of persons to be appointed to local offices, and thus practically deprived himself of a prerogative which he might have used for his own ends. He adhered with tenacity to the doctrine that the people should have a direct voice in appointments and in other political affairs in the

Territory. In the spring of 1818, the people were invited to decide by a general vote whether or not to proceed to the semi-representative government permitted by the Ordinance. But the lethargic French and others, who appreciated the good they had, voted against change. For five years the governor and judges retained their autocratic position, at the end of which time the second form was established; a council of nine came into existence, the members of which were selected by the President and confirmed by the Senate from eighteen names presented as the choice of the people. In 1819 the right to elect a delegate to Congress was granted. In 1825 thirteen councilmen were allowed, and in 1827 the people chose the whole number. The judicial system was gradually elaborated to meet the growing needs of the Territory.

The industrial condition of the Territory rapidly improved after 1818. Cass, appreciating the needs of the people, urged upon Congress the building of a road around the end of Lake Erie, as a highway for commerce and an actual necessity for military movements in case of war. National aid was secured. A portion of the small resources of the Territory was appropriated for making a suitable wagon road to Chicago. The stagnant province, even before 1820, took new life, showing by the census a marked increase in population. Before 1830 the barren waste, Michigan, was actually exporting flour to the East, and there was an air of comfort on her borders and an appearance of thrift along her inland roads, which spoke of the success of Governor Cass's efforts to attract eastern knowledge and energy. By the third census of the century Michigan was shown to have over 30,000 people, and to have just claims for speedy admittance as a State. The little frontier settlements which Governor Cass was summoned to defend in 1813 "had extended and spread to the dimensions of a commonwealth under his judicious and statesmanlike care and nurture."[1] The settlers in Michigan were from New York and Massachusetts. Many of those from the former State had previously lived in New England. In consequence, the political spirit which was being breathed into the nostrils of Michigan was the spirit of local self-government in church and state, and in many crises of our history she has given evidence of her parentage. Cass encouraged in every way the growth of political feeling among the people. He was a "democrat by conviction, and not merely in a party sense."[2] "In proportion as all governments recede from the people, they become liable to abuse. Whatever authority can be conveniently exercised in primary assemblies may be deposited there with safety."[3] This was his published creed.

Intellectually and socially the Territory made advances. Governor Cass extended his democracy from politics to learning. Appreciating that reli-

[1] *Michigan*, by Thomas McIntyre Cooley, p. 203.
[2] *Ibid.*, p. 205.
[3] Journal of the Legislative Council of Michigan, 1826.

gion, morality, and knowledge were "necessary to good government and the happiness of mankind," he assisted the church and gave his public encouragement to the school. The percentage of illiteracy in Michigan was very large in its early years as an American province; but in accordance with the comprehensive suggestion of Governor Cass, a broad and generous basis for public education was established, on which has been reared a school system which has become the model for the newer States of the West, and stands to-day as the most perfect embodiment of popular American education in our country. The foundation for this structure bears marks of the broad sympathetic democracy of General Cass. He was a Jeffersonian in all that related to education, and used his influence for popularizing the school-book and the ballot.

"Of all purposes," he declared, "to which a revenue derived from the people can be applied under a government emanating from the people, there is none more interesting in itself, nor more important in its effects, than the maintenance of a public and general course of moral and mental discipline. . . . Many republics have preceded us in the progress of human society; but they have disappeared, leaving behind them little besides the history of their follies and dissensions to serve as a warning to their successors in the career of self-government. Unless the foundation of such governments is laid in the virtue and intelligence of the community, they must be swept away by the first commotion to which political circumstances may give birth. Whenever education is diffused among the people generally, they will appreciate the value of free institutions; and as they have the power, so must they have the will to maintain them. It appears to me that a plan may be devised which will not press too heavily upon the means of the country, and which will insure a competent portion of education to all youth in the Territory."[1] Such views as these were in advance of the thinking of the time. Platitudes upon enlightenment and liberty grew in plenty; but these practical propositions of Governor Cass mark an era in the history of Michigan and of popular education in the United States.

In Indian affairs Cass was not idle in the decade between 1820 and 1830. The treaty of Chicago has already been mentioned and its importance suggested. Other negotiations were soon undertaken. For a long time the constant warfare between the Sacs, Foxes, Sioux, and other tribes in the West, had given vexation to the general government and endangered the peace of the frontier. In company with Governor Clark of Missouri, Cass met the Indians at Prairie du Chien in August, 1825, and secured a treaty determining boundaries and promising peace. The following year, accompanied by Colonel Thomas L. Mc-

[1] Journal of Legislative Council of the Territory of Michigan, 1826.

Kenney, he journeyed to Fond du Lac, and entered there into negotiations with the Chippewas for peace with the other tribes. The Indians were encouraged by direct aid to lead civilized lives, money was promised them for a school, and the United States was granted permission to search for minerals throughout the North. Colonel McKenney's "Tour to the Lakes"[1] contains the incidents of the journey, related in the charming, romantic, personal style of fifty years ago. Other treaties were obtained this year by the governor in the more southern portion of the Northwest.

It was necessary to make still further arrangements for determining definite boundaries between the tribes in the West. In the summer of 1827 General Cass was absent from Detroit for two months, engaged in one of the most important and perilous of his undertakings. Proceeding to Green Bay, with Colonel McKenney as associate commissioner, he found that the Winnebagoes, whom he had expected to meet with the other tribes, were not there. Rumors that they had put on the war paint were in the air, and Cass determined as usual upon crushing out hostilities by prompt and decisive action. He neither delayed nor sent a messenger. He manned his canoe, and made his way up the Fox and down the Wisconsin rivers, for the purpose of discovering the actual condition of things and of communicating with the forces at St. Louis by the quickest

[1] Baltimore, 1827.

possible method. On his way down the Wisconsin he landed boldly at a Winnebago village. There were indications of hostile movements. He remonstrated with the chiefs and warned them of the results of war. As he turned to leave, a young brave aimed his gun at him and pulled the trigger. The gun missed fire, however, and his life was saved. The older chiefs, realizing what the death of Governor Cass would involve, seized the offender and soundly upbraided him; but smouldering discontent was evident. The canoe hurried on its journey to the south and west. Evidences of war became more clear. The citizens of Prairie du Chien, in momentary dread of attack, had crowded together and hastily thrown up some rude defenses. Alarm, consternation, and confusion appeared throughout the mining district of northern Illinois; the roads were lined with the frantic and fleeing people who had dared to enter the wilderness in the delirium of the lead fever of 1826–27. The little village of Galena was filled with the settlers of the outlying districts, and overwhelmed by disorder and panic. Governor Cass quickly organized the people for defense at Prairie du Chien; brought confidence to Galena by his energy and decision; collected volunteers at the latter place, and sent troops immediately up the river where there was more actual danger. He then hastened on to St. Louis to confer with General Atkinson, who at once moved northward with a force sufficient to overawe the Indians, who, finding themselves overtaken in their designs, abandoned their hostile purposes with ill-concealed chagrin. The promptness of the governor's action prevented a devastating war over the whole northwestern frontier. He returned to Green Bay, by way of Chicago, and completed the negotiations he had intended to conduct. The incidents of his flying trip to St. Louis, the light canoe flitting through the dark night down the Mississippi, the silence, the wildness of the scenery, the intense excitement and anxiety lest his efforts should be too late, made the deepest impression upon his own imagination and memory. Years after, in the palace of St. Cloud, the scene came back to him with all its vividness, and he compared the timid Seine with the mighty Mississippi and the even more mighty Missouri, remembering how he was whirled along through the night on a race for peace and the lives of his people.[1]

During these latter years he had opportunity for literary work and for a more general interest in politics. He was summoned to coöperate with Governor Clark in outlining for the government a plan for the treatment of the Indians and for the rearrangement of the concerns of the Indian department. The Territory, now independent and eager for advancement, appreciated his work and honored him. In 1831 he was called to leave his tasks in the Northwest and to take his part in the broader fields of national politics and administration.

[1] *Three Hours at St. Cloud, by an American* (L. Cass).

The great factor in his successful administration was honesty. That there was scrupulous honesty in the business of the Territory needs no proof. But fair, honorable dealing with the Indians was a rarer virtue, and in this he never faltered. He was wont to say in after years that he never broke his word to an Indian and never expected to find that the red man had broken his. Every exertion was made to have the funds and the allowances ready on the day upon which they had been promised. Promptness and boldness in action, a firm self-reliance, a presumption that the power of the United States was mighty and would be obeyed, appealed to the Indian sense of awe and reverence. Treaties were negotiated with fairness, and he warned the general government that if benignant peace was to smile upon the Northwest, the letter of the agreement must be fulfilled. He did not seek to secure the greatest possible advantage in the present without looking to the future or without considering the equities of the case. He informed the department at Washington that neither justice nor the policy of far-seeing wisdom would prompt him or them to take advantage of temporary wants and sufferings. He not only strove to carry out every promise or understanding with an Indian in the most liberal fashion, but he included in his treaties plans for the betterment of the race and for attracting them to peace and civilization. Their beloved fire-water was the Indians' curse. He took every available opportunity to induce them to give up its use. At Prairie du Chien he addressed the assembled braves on the sin and folly of drunkenness, and to point his moral by showing that stinginess was not actuating him, he broke in the heads of several casks and allowed the liquor to rush out upon the ground amid the despairing cries of the thirsty warriors. His keen eye was ever on the watch for those who were seeking to violate the law, cheat the childish red man, and give him the cursed drink.

The respect and even affection which the Indians had for their "Great Father at Detroit" was often manifested, and once felt was not forgotten. Twenty-five years after his governorship was ended, he came unexpectedly into a meeting of Indian chiefs in Detroit; in a moment, forgetting the object of their conference and losing their stoical dignity, they crowded around him to grasp the hand from which they had received so many favors.[1] For he had always stood ready to help them and to treat them with kindness. During many years after the war, when they had once been brought into subjection, they were continually in Detroit, often with frank curiosity or open friendship making their way unannounced into his house, and expecting to be met with courtesy. They made large and unexpected demands upon a generous hospitality; for the British across the river would often welcome the chiefs to their tables, and it would not do for the governor, who appreci-

[1] Smith, *Life and Times of Lewis Cass*, p. 115.

ated their sensitive natures, to rebuff them openly. His tact, careful study of Indian nature, his punctilious respect for his word, his dignity, his kindness, all display themselves in brilliant contrast with many of the brutal dishonesties which have given "Ramona" and such sentimentality more than a fanciful foundation.

CHAPTER V

SECRETARY OF WAR

THE dissolution of President Jackson's first cabinet occasioned great excitement throughout the country. It was considered high-handed and autocratic. Former presidents had retained their cabinet officers, except when necessity dictated a change, and only in the case of the elder Adams had there been anything like a sudden reorganization after the administration had fairly begun. This reconstruction, however, was arranged with some skill, with something of the deftness that might be expected where the shrewd Van Buren was concerned — so deftly, indeed, that it was not at first evident why the resignations were given or what was the animus of the whole affair. In fact, two causes coöperated. The President discovered, by a disclosure from the piqued Crawford, that Calhoun, to whose interests part of the cabinet was devoted, had some twelve years before been in favor of punishing him for his conduct in the Seminole difficulty, and for his unwarranted proceedings in Florida. Jackson never forgave. From this time forth Calhoun was his enemy. The general's mind was so constituted that no one could occupy middle ground; whoever was not for him was against him. Those in the cabinet who could consider with any degree of complacency the probable succession of the Carolinian to the presidency were, in his view, unfit to be his advisers, and absolutely incapable of fair and honorable service. The warrior President was in a continual contest with persons. Persons' principles, not principles *per se*, always filled the lens of his vision. The cabinet ministers devoted to Calhoun were therefore regarded by Jackson not only as personal enemies, but as hostile to his administration.

But, possibly, a much more trivial and absurd reason had even greater influence in bringing about the transformation. The President, with all the energy of an old Indian fighter, espoused the cause of Mrs. Eaton, the wife of his secretary of war, and insisted that she should be received within the charmed circle of Washington society. The victor of New Orleans discovered, however, that mere forcible denunciation would not penetrate into the holy precincts or break down the strong barriers of social prejudice. Mrs. Calhoun, with quiet determination, refused to meet Mrs. Eaton or to recognize her as an equal, and declined to be commanded in her social intercourse by mandates from the White House. The wives of several members of the cabinet as quietly and firmly upheld their independence, while Van Buren, the courtly widower, ingratiated himself with the

President by bestowing on the social outcast his sweetest smiles and studied attentions. It is a curious commentary on the dignity of free government that, by careful politeness to a woman, to whose skirts still clung the dust of an ambiguous past, the secretary of state was enabled to become the recognized heir-apparent of a great popular hero, who, as the "tribune" of the common people, had begun a "reign" of arrogance and anger.

Jackson was incapable of discerning the relative importance of things. He lived on a dead level of intensity; every matter which enlisted his sympathies or aroused his attention was of tragic import. He fought "Peggy" Eaton's battles with the same burning vigor he had used against the British at New Orleans or the Spaniards and Indians of Florida. He threatened to send home the minister from Holland "and his wife," because the Dutch dame had treated his secretary's wife with scant courtesy, by refusing to sit by her at the ball given by the Russian minister. He swore that justice must be done, acted the "roaring lion," and intimated, through the medium of Colonel Johnson, that at least when large parties were given, Mrs. Eaton must be invited, if the cabinet was to retain its present composition; he would "be cut into inch pieces on the rack" before he would allow either Major Eaton or his wife to be injured by vile calumnies; for the woman was pure and innocent as a babe, and he would show foreign ministers and cabinet officers that persecution and conspiracy would not be tolerated.[1]

Early in 1831 a reorganization of the cabinet was determined upon; for the Eaton difficulty was much too stimulating to the presidential temper, and Calhoun's hopes of the succession must be crushed by depriving of public office and influence those who might favor him. As early as 1829 the canny ones among the politicians had begun intrigues in favor of the secretary of state, and he himself had by this time taken Jackson's heart by storm. His assiduous attentions to Mrs. Eaton, his deference and continual kindness were of much more value than even his considerable ability in statesmanship. His coolness and calmness, his quiet and affable manners, the unruffled composure with which he smiled at the important trivialities which vexed the irritable general, endeared him to the old warrior, whose nerves were quieted by the secretary's soothing presence. It was impossible to rave and pace the floor and invoke anything "eternal" or transient while this placid gentleman was sitting by in serene silence. Eaton resigned April 7, 1831. Van Buren followed on April 11, with a letter admirably adapted to conceal the real reason for his withdrawal, while it set forth modestly the fact of his own future candidacy for the presidency, which "disturbing topic" he had in vain attempted to "discountenance."[2] Barry,

[1] Niles's *Register*, vol. xl. p. 377 ff.

[2] *Ibid.*, vol. xl. p. 43.

the postmaster-general, was asked to remain. The other three, who were known as "Calhoun men," were not in the best of humor, and did not appreciate Van Buren's suggestion that the cabinet should be a unit. Ingham, the secretary of the treasury, and Branch, the secretary of the navy, tendered their resignations on the 19th, but they made at the same time the distinct statement that they understood at last that their presence in the cabinet was no longer desired. Berrien retired from the office of attorney-general on June 15 with a similar announcement. The newspapers of the day teemed with abuse and recrimination. Ingham asserted that Eaton had formed a conspiracy to murder him. Eaton accused Ingham of wanton insult, and finally demanded "satisfaction." The affairs of the Eaton family were presented for general inspection, and a most savory ragbag of old scandal was opened for the gratification of a keen-scented public.

The new cabinet was a very able one. It could be counted on as opposed to Calhoun and devoted to Jackson and his heir-apparent. Undoubtedly the President profited by the change. Edward Livingston of Louisiana became secretary of state; Louis McLane of Delaware, secretary of the treasury; Levi Woodbury of New Hampshire, secretary of the navy; Roger B. Taney of Maryland, attorney-general. Barry retained his position as postmaster-general until 1835, when he became minister to Spain, and was succeeded by Amos

Kendall, who, holding the position of fourth auditor, had been an adviser in the "kitchen cabinet" from the beginning of the administration. It was intended that Judge White, senator from Tennessee, should become secretary of war, and give Eaton a chance to fill the vacancy in the Senate. But White refused, and Cass was offered the portfolio. Rumor assigned the ex-secretary to Michigan to take Cass's place, but he was finally appointed governor of Florida, and went to seek consolation for abuse and insult in the everglades of that wild Territory. In August, 1831, therefore, Cass assumed the duties of secretary of war.

National politics were in a peculiar condition. Though he had lost no opportunity to keep himself informed of what was going on in the higher governmental circles, he could not have anticipated the conditions which he discovered. We are but just coming to an appreciation of what this period signifies in our development as a constitutional state. It meant that national politics and methods were mob politics and methods. The trickster politicians who had been turning thumb-screws and pulling wires for thirty years in the States now transferred their machinery to a broader field. Jackson was not a demagogue. He sincerely believed in the doctrines he preached and in the sentiments which he put into practice. But he was the conduit pipe through which flowed into the field of national administration the tide of political proscription, intrigue, and legerdemain which had been long triumphantly deluging the States. Van Buren has been charged with introducing the "spoils system" from New York, where from the beginning of the century removal from office followed change in party control, as night follows day. But the fact is that the virus was well on its festering way in the national system before Van Buren's responsibility began. Although the "Little Magician" must have aided by his counsel and given the benefit of his experience, no one man can be charged with the establishment of the practice of spoils distribution. It came by natural evolution. The scrambling, punch-drinking mob which invaded Washington at Jackson's inauguration, besieging his hotel, crowding and pushing their way into the White House, tipping over tubs of punch and buckets of ices, standing with muddy hob-nailed shoes on the damask furniture, thrusting themselves into the nooks and corners of the executive mansion with the air of copartners, who had at last an opportunity to take account of the assets of the firm, — these were the people who demanded that aristocratic incumbents be deprived of their offices by him who was elected as the representative of "the people," the soldier, the rough and ready statesman who despised the borrowed conventionalities of so-called good society. Such was the inauguration of the spoils system. The offices of trust were handed over to the men who brought the greatest pressure to bear, and could make plain their political influence to the scullions of the "kitchen cabinet." If the student of American politics is to understand the place which the spoils system holds he must see that its introduction was a natural phase in our national development, not a mere incident without antecedent causes rooted in the past. It was when Jackson was installed that "the people" first realized their power and demanded that the divinity of *vox populi* be recognized. There was great talk about "the people" in those canting years, as if our social or political system gave place for classes or privilege. On that notable fourth of March the crowds invaded Washington to shout for a new-found liberty; a Bastille of respectability had fallen, and the guillotine soon lopped off the heads of the office-holding nobility, who had too long lived in aristocratic ease above "the people."

The new cabinet had a dignity of its own. Now that the line of succession was determined upon and the wires laid for eight years to come, there was not so much room for the back-stairs influence. In all the more important matters of state, the real cabinet worked its will and had its proper influence. Only where cunning manipulation was necessary for political prosperity did the spirits of the "kitchen cabinet" introduce their sinister methods. Jackson himself was the presiding genius of his own administration and its mastering spirit. He came to his conclusions swiftly and by instinct, and although they were often tenable only by the help of the blindest obstinacy, his obstinacy was always as blind as the occasion required. But a word of flattery or the right insinuation at the nick of time would start the wheels of his prejudice in the direction desired by a cunning politician. Thus he was often influenced and guided by men of less real ability and strength of character than his own.

The only Indian war in the Northwest after 1815 occurred almost immediately after Cass accepted the war portfolio. Black Hawk, a Sac chief, refused to remain in the reservation beyond the Mississippi. Early in the spring of 1832 he entered Wisconsin and Illinois, and spread alarm and consternation through the West. United States troops were hurried to the spot. Volunteers were called from Michigan and Illinois, and a border war was soon devastating the country. The War Department seems to have been managed with alertness. Cass had been too long acquainted with Indian characteristics not to realize the importance of rapidity and the prompt exhibition of authority. But the terrible ravages of the cholera were added to the horrors of war. The troops died in such numbers that panic and disease seemed likely to do much greater damage than any human enemy. The dreadful summer of 1832 was long remembered by the citizens of the Northwest. A portion of its perils was over when the Indians were nearly annihilated in a battle on August 2. Black Hawk escaped death, but was imprisoned, and the next year was shown around the country as a triumphal captive. The successful administration of Indian affairs during Cass's governorship, and the peace which prevailed during that time, lead one to believe that had he still been governor and superintendent he would have quieted the Indians without all the fuss and flourish of war.

The actual conduct of the affairs of the War Department involved, of course, in the main a great deal of routine work. But the details of that work scarcely need to be given here. In the great questions of Jackson's administration Cass was more than an interested spectator. His position brought him into active coöperation with the President, whose influence had a great effect on his later political life.

An affair more important to the country than an Indian war occupied the attention of his department in the autumn of 1832. Calhoun's dampened ambitions sought encouraging warmth from the fires of state jealousies. The reorganization of the cabinet in opposition to him, the known hostility of the President, the evident drift of political favor in the direction of Jackson and his cajolers, quenched his burning hope, and left him but the ashes of disappointment. His native State was uneasy under a tariff which seemed to be all for the manufacturers of New England, and his zeal for national glory gave place to sectional jealousy, which now blazed brightly forth. His whole life henceforth was given to the support of what he thought were the interests of his State. His elaborate arguments, woven with greatest care, furnished a protecting garment for slavery. His keen eyes were always endeavoring to pierce the veil of the future, and he endeavored to show in prophetic vision before his countrymen the weal and woe which he fancied that he himself discerned. Although he seemed to see farther than his contemporaries, the truths of the future were perverted by his diseased imagination into falsehood, and though he was a seer he did not become a soothsayer. When slave labor comes into competition with free labor, it shows an economical and therefore an incurable weakness. It is interesting to notice that the first practical application of the doctrine of nullification, the sister of secession, came as the result of industrial differences between the North and the South. The most earnest advocates of nullification tilted at the tariff windmill as the cause of their woes, and would not confess, or did not see, the deadening influence of slavery. The tariff of 1828 was so absurd in its provisions that it fairly won the epithet "abominable," but this act did not drive the South to extreme measures. It was left for the more moderate and sensible measure of 1832, which decreased the revenue by several millions, to induce South Carolina to bluster forth in nullification. Calhoun had already begun to print his finely wrought treatises. McDuffie, on the floor of the House, gave utterance to the opinion of his State, when he proclaimed that, if she failed in the struggle she was waging, the brief days of American liberty would be numbered.

South Carolina was frantic because her threats were simply neglected, and during the summer and autumn of 1832 meetings were held, fiercely denouncing protection to Yankee industries, and proclaiming that for the cause of liberty and honor a stand must be made against the tyranny of trading New England. The legislature, which was summoned in October, issued a call for a state convention, and on November 19 the delegates met at Columbia. The practical workings of the nullification theory were now to be exhibited. Calhoun saw more clearly than Jefferson had seen the logical relationship between the federal government and the States of our Union, if it was the result of a compact between sovereignties. He saw that in the State, and not the legislature of the State, must reside this extraordinary power of nullification and resistance. Jefferson, in the angry haste of politics, propounded a half-formed illogical doctrine, based on falsehood and carried to an absurd conclusion. Calhoun selected his course to suit the prejudices of "King Cotton," but when once he had turned the historical compass to a false pole he followed its direction with patient regard for the stern laws of logic. Nullification, as it showed itself in South Carolina, was a legitimate expression of state-sovereignty, and the method of its actual application was an illuminating lesson to those who had not followed argument or appreciated the ends of theory.

A committee of twenty-one, appointed by Governor Hamilton, who was president of the popular convention, drew up an "Ordinance," "To provide for arresting the operation of certain acts of the Congress of the United States, purporting to be laws laying duties and imposts on the importation of foreign commodities." The obnoxious laws were declared null and void, and the legislature was authorized to adopt such measures as might be necessary to give full effect to the views of the convention. All appeals to the Supreme Court of the United States were forbidden, and all officers and jurors were to be bound by oath to observe the ordinance and the laws of the legislature passed in pursuance of it. If there was an attempt on the part of the central government to enforce the tariff laws, the people of the State, it was announced, would consider themselves absolved from all further political obligation as a member of the confederacy, and would prepare to do all the acts of a sovereign and independent community. An address to the people of the United States abounded in mathematical and rhetorical figures, whose services were invoked to prove the injustice of the tariff and to portray the position of the State. "We would infinitely prefer," proclaimed these inconsistent slave barons, forming a political and social oligarchy, "that the territory of the State should be the cemetery of freemen than the habitation of slaves."[1] Not till February 1, however, was there to be a resistance to the laws of the United States.

It was boldly done. But "Old Hickory" at Washington was prompt and energetic. In the heat of the presidential campaign, when the people were shouting themselves hoarse for their hero, and raising tall hickory poles as party emblems, the old general had turned uneasily toward South Carolina, and listened for premonitory rumblings of the earthquake. He did not waste his energy in wringing his hands, as did Buchanan in another fateful crisis in our history. On October 6 the collector of customs was given explicit directions what to do in case there was any attempt to avoid payment of duties. As early as October 29 Major-General Macomb sent word to Major Heileman, commanding the troops of the United States in Charleston, that information received by the executive suggested the possibility of an attempt to seize the forts, and the commander was warned to be on his guard.[2] Additional troops were sent to Fort Moultrie, November 7, and on the 18th Cass wrote to General Scott, directing him to proceed at once to Charleston for the purpose of examining the defenses, and to hold himself in readiness to assist the civil officers of the United States, if

[1] Full proceedings of convention, Niles, vol. xliii. pp. 219, 230, etc.

[2] *American State Papers, Military Affairs*, vol. v. p. 158.

occasion should make it necessary and the President should so direct. A fortnight later a confidential letter from the War Department complimented General Scott on the discretion and good judgment he had manifested. The following sentences from Cass's letter very succinctly state the attitude of the general government toward the whole conspiracy: "I cannot but hope that the good sense and patriotism of the citizens of South Carolina will still prevent the occurrence of those consequences which must result from the attempt to enforce the ordinance recently passed by the convention of that State. In any event, the President will perform his duty, and only his duty, under the Constitution of the United States."[1] Reinforcements were sent to Charleston on the 4th.

Congress assembled on December 3, and read a very quiet and restrained message from the President, in which there was no blare from the trumpet of war. Yet Jackson was excited enough. If his annual message was calm, the storm was to follow. His practical sense pierced the bubble arguments of the nullifiers, and in homely phrase he summed up the dire results of state sovereignty. "If this thing goes on," he said to his friend Dale, "our country will be like a bag of meal with both ends open. Pick it up in the middle or endwise, and it will run out. I must tie the bag and save the country." When South Carolina adopted the

[1] *American State Papers, Military Affairs*, vol. v. p. 159.

ordinance, and nullification was fairly in view, he was prepared to strike. It was generally believed that he had made up his mind to seize Calhoun on the charge of treason, the instant force was used against the officers of the United States, and many believed that the fear of such consequences influenced the final settlement of the controversy. On December 11 appeared his celebrated proclamation, full of earnest, pathetic pleading, strong assertion, and profound argument. Verbally it belongs to Livingston, but it is filled with the spirit of Jackson. On that hang his claims to grateful remembrance. That he was instrumental in infecting the body politic with the loathsome disease of spoils distribution, that his blundering financial management hastened and aggravated a disastrous panic, that under the fostering wings of his administration a whole brood of evil political fledglings matured, — all these faults will be forgotten by the people who remember that the hero of New Orleans bruised with his heel the hissing head of nullification.

Vessels were sent to Charleston by the Navy Department in December, and as February 1 approached every precaution was taken by the War Department to prepare for forcible resistance. Cass wrote to General Scott, ordering him again to Charleston (January 26) to repel with force any attempt to seize the forts, but throughout all to use the utmost discretion and self-restraint. This letter, in some unknown way, reached the public press, and the contents of the last clause, which suggested that two places be examined as possible strategic points for the federal army, caused considerable excitement in the angered State. General Scott assures us, in his eulogistic autobiography, that if a spade had been put into the ground at this time for a new work beyond Sullivan's Island, civil war would have been inaugurated on the spot. The popular imagination pictures Jackson raving for war and aching to crush Calhoun and his fellow plotters. There is no doubt that he occasionally gave way to wrath, and expressed his opinion with more vehemence than grace; it is perfectly clear that he made every preparation against forcible resistance to federal authority; but it is just as clear that he was anxious to avoid a conflict if possible. The letters of Cass at this period show very distinctly the extreme solicitude which tempered the stern decision of the administration. There is good reason to believe that a letter, purporting to come "from one of the ablest men in the country," which appeared in the "Richmond Enquirer" under date of December 13, 1832, was written by Cass himself at the request of the President. Artfully suggesting the importance of Virginia, this letter proposes that the Old Dominion, "in one of those forcible appeals she so well knows how to make," should urge upon Congress a great reduction of the tariff, and "plead as a suffering sister with wayward South Carolina."[1]

[1] Smith's *Life and Times of Lewis Cass*, p. 274.

The suggestion was followed. Virginia, whether influenced by this appeal "from one of the ablest men," or not, prepared to play the rôle of umpire, sending B. W. Leigh as envoy to Charleston. He was there received with honor, and though his pleadings probably had little direct influence, Virginia's intercession gave another excuse for backing down from the high ground of the ordinance. Such was unquestionably Jackson's attitude. While presenting a bold front and making every preparation to defend federal property and execute federal law, while angry with all the heat of his choleric nature at the nullifying conspirators, while every warlike impulse was opposed to capitulation with a State in arms, he nevertheless had a fervent love for the Union, of which even his own unreasoning wrath could not deprive him.

The end of the controversy can be stated in a word. Pending conciliatory measures on the part of the general government, the time for putting the nullifying laws into practical operation was postponed. The President, in a message issued January 16, asked Congress to make certain regulations with regard to the customs districts, and to authorize the use of the military force for the purpose of protecting and assisting the civil officers in the discharge of their duties. A bill drafted to meet these suggestions was introduced into Congress. Perfectly right on every constitutional and political ground, such a proposition was received with some dismay by conservative lovers of peace, and the bill as drafted soon labored under unpopular epithets, and was commonly known as the "force bill" or "bloody bill." Verplanck, a representative from New York, had already introduced into the House a measure for the reduction of the tariff. This was so sweeping in its provisions that it meant practically an abandonment of the protective policy and a complete surrender to South Carolina. Clay, the great compromiser, now came forward, February 12, with a plan for a gradual reduction of the revenue. Great was the consternation at the North when the father of the "American system" was beheld preparing to murder his own child by slow poison. Manufacturers hastened to Washington to prevent such action; but some saw their danger, and remained to advocate the passage of the measure. It was passed side by side with the "force bill." Both were signed by the President on March 2, and thus with mingled threats and coaxings the petulant State was won back to obedience. On the whole, it was a shameful victory for state impudence. Although the "force bill" was passed, and Jackson upheld the national dignity, nullification accomplished its purpose, — the reduction of the tariff. The objectionable ordinance was repealed by South Carolina, but at the same time she proclaimed the "force bill" null and void within her limits.

This was an instructive period in the life of Cass. He completed his fiftieth year in the midst of the controversy, and as yet he had seen very little of national politics. The long years of his governorship had been spent in active management of local concerns, or in long journeys through the wilderness. His constant reading had made him more familiar with questions of national politics than most men would have been had they spent a score of years in a frontier settlement, where for a considerable period even newspapers, with their stale news, came late and irregularly through the mails. His first practical training in national politics he received in the stern Jacksonian school, a school whose cardinal regulations possessed a mischievous inconsistency. Love for the Union, hatred of foreign aggression, championship of popular rights, spoils distribution, machine politics, were badly mingled; strict construction of the Constitution struggled in equal conflict with a reckless abuse of power; and high-handed interference was supported by appeals to the "people," who are unknown in our political system except as they express their will by constitutional and prescribed methods. Cass did not forget the stand taken against nullification. From this time he was a radical Jacksonian Democrat. The success of the administration in its foreign relations also met with his approbation, and increased the feeling which he already had, that our country should present a bold front to other nations. Jackson won his deepest admiration, and inspired him with the love which the peremptory old general seemed often to force upon those about him by his indefinable grace, and by an unexpected and curiously vigorous sweetness in-the-rough.

In 1833 Jackson went North on a tour for recreation and applause. Cass accompanied him. Crowds cheered the tough old general who had just put down nullification. Cities tendered him their freedom and the mob went wild. The aristocrats averted their faces, but the popular enthusiasm was undoubted. Harvard, to the disgust of the learned, dubbed his illiterate excellency Doctor of Laws. From these scenes of merry-making and exultation, and before the exhausting itinerary was finished, the President hurried home, on the plea of illness, to strike another blow at the Bank of the United States. It is possible that he was moved by proper motives. But sheer malice against Nicholas Biddle and his moneyed monster was probably the chief cause. With a reckless indifference to the effect on the business of the country, an indifference which arose from a complete ignorance of the laws of finance and the sensitive nature of capital, he dashed into a contest with the national bank as if he were hunting Indians in the swamps of Florida. By law, the public funds were to be deposited in the bank, subject to removal by the secretary of the treasury, who was to give his reasons to Congress in case of removal. Jackson determined upon a removal of the deposits and a distribution of the money among the various state banks. He had difficulty in getting his cabinet to agree to this. Duane, the secretary of the treasury, was determined to stand on what he considered his prerogative, and refused to remove the deposits at the President's request. He was dismissed, and Taney was transferred to the Treasury, ready to do Jackson's bidding and elaborately to defend his action. McLane, who in the early part of the year had been transferred from the Treasury Department to that of State, and had all along been averse to a removal of the deposits, was still strongly opposed to the measure. He wished to resign, but was dissuaded. On September 23 Cass made an appointment with Lewis to discuss the matter. Lewis was the head of the "kitchen cabinet," the familiar of Jackson. "He commenced the conversation,"[1] wrote Lewis, "by remarking that his object in desiring to see me before I left was to inform me that he had determined to resign his seat in the cabinet, and wished to converse with me upon the subject before he handed his letter of resignation to the President. He said he differed with the President with regard to the measures which were about to be adopted for the removal of the public deposits from the United States Bank, and as his remaining in the cabinet might embarrass his operations, he owed it, he thought, both to himself and the President, to withdraw." Lewis urged him to acquaint Jackson with his intention before he actually resigned, and

[1] Parton's *Jackson*, vol. iii. p. 501.

the result of the interview between the secretary and his chief was that Cass was asked to remain, with the understanding that the responsibility for the act should rest, not with the cabinet, but with the President alone. In a later cabinet meeting, when asked his opinion of the measure, Cass simply and frankly said: "You know, sir, I have always thought that the matter rests entirely with the secretary of the treasury."

The political affiliations of the new West during these years are evident. Michigan was a Territory struggling vehemently until 1837 for admission. Her last successful efforts were stimulated, perhaps, by a hope that if she was admitted to the Union a small rill from the plethoric national treasury would trickle into her ready coffers. Party organization on national lines was hardly known as yet. On all great questions the people naturally belonged with their brethren of New York and New England; but of course there was great admiration among the poor settlers for the "man of the people," and Michigan may be counted in the line of Democratic States until the slavery question offered a great moral issue. There were occasional backslidings from the true Democratic faith. The hard times which followed the financial disasters of 1837 turned people against "the Little Magician," whose magic wand had lost its cunning. The people of Michigan shouted themselves hoarse for Harrison and "hard cider" in 1840, and the State was carried by the Whigs by some 2000 as against a majority of 3000 for Van Buren in 1836, when the vote of the quasi State was only about one fourth of what it was four years later. But it will be noticed that in 1840 Harrison was the popular hero, the stalwart "Old Tip;" "Matty" Van Buren was the aristocrat of the White House, who was rolling in wealth and supping from golden spoons, while the people who had elected him were starving. The students of our politics have not fully confessed the efficiency of poverty as a political motor. Our practical politicians in these latter days have carefully conned the lessons of the past, and cover up most dexterously any advantage their candidate may have by reason of superior education or the ability inherited from good ancestry.

In the other States of the Northwest somewhat similar courses can be traced, varied by the peculiarities of their settlement. Ohio, with her strong Eastern flavor, inclined with some constancy to whiggery. Of the Northwestern States, Illinois alone in 1840 clung by a small majority to the failing cause of Jacksonism, and cast its electoral votes for Van Buren. But that State had all along been peculiarly Democratic. It had a large Southern element. Many of the poor whites pushed their way north over the prairies of Illinois. From 1826 every general election resulted in favor of Jackson and his party until the old general went into restless retirement at the Hermitage. Doubtless the persistency of Illinois in her political course can be attributed largely to this strong Southern element. But it would be anticipating later political divisions to attribute such Democratic affiliation entirely to the Southern settlers. Jacksonian Democracy was the political faith of the masses, of those most easily influenced by the tricks of the politician and the wire-puller. "The people" were Democrats, from whatever part of the country they came. Cook County, which was settled by Yankees, pushing and vigorous men, did not fall behind the settlers of southern Illinois in zeal for Democracy. This county was Democratic even in 1844, casting 2027 votes for Polk and only 1117 for Clay. Democracy was firmly planted and unbending. Party lines at first were not closely drawn, but there was no hope for the man who was opposed to the "man of the people." The campaigns were conducted in that new Western country in a manner which leads us to look with more equanimity upon the vices of modern politics. The saloons in the county seats were chartered by the candidates for popular favors; whiskey in vast quantities heightened the fervor of the people, whose voice was to be the voice of God. Governor Ford, who was an interested spectator on these occasions, tells us of a minister of the gospel whose "morality was not of the pinched kind which prevented him from using all the common arts of a candidate for office." He went forth to election with a Bible in one pocket and a bottle of whiskey in the other, prepared to make himself agreeable to all. So fully had the people adopted the creed of "Old Hickory" that we are told that Democrats were divided in that pork-packing State into "whole hog" Jackson men and nominal Jackson men.[1] The people had come into the West in order to better their condition, and politics were considered by many a legitimate road to bodily comfort. Few seemed to realize that they were laying the foundations of a great commonwealth; but the race of politicians developed, as in the East. The politician "for revenue only" practiced his clever tactics, and early in the history of these frontier States wires were laid as skillfully as in the more populous States of the coast. The people, on the whole, took far more interest in politics than in political principles.

The Western States developed rapidly during these years. The craze for internal improvement left some good behind, and the wild speculation in land drew immigrants into the country by thousands. Steamers on the lakes were crowded with families on their way to Michigan and the West. Ninety steamers arrived at Detroit in May, 1836, crowded with new settlers and with those who were anxious to speculate in the Western lands. Land sales were enormous. The roads in the interior of Michigan were thronged with wagons. The immigrants of this period were, as before, principally from New York and New England.

[1] Ford's *History of Illinois*, p. 105.

Others, from Ireland and Germany, however, began about 1832 to find their way in small numbers into the West.

One other matter of importance remains to be discussed in this period of Cass's life. The removal of the Florida Indians to reservations west of the Mississippi was carefully considered by Cass as soon as he became secretary. He had long contemplated the desirability of such a plan. No one better understood the condition of the red man in the Northwest, or more keenly appreciated the difficulties of the Indian problem. His work in Michigan amply proves his fairness and honesty, his humanity and sympathy. In 1830 he wrote for the "North American Review" a long article on the subject of removal. It is candid in its tone and exhaustive in treatment, pointing out the woeful condition of the Indians in their present situation, picturing their degradation as victims to the vices of Christian civilization. He contended that they must be removed, and that speedily, if a remnant was to be saved. He showed no sympathy for the maudlin sentimentality which would weep over the sorrows of the noble warrior and suggest no remedy for evident evils.

Later animosity has declared that the whole plan of removing the southern Indians was one of the satanic wiles of the slaveholder. But it will not do to antedate political motive. The planters did wish to get possession of the land held by the Creeks and Seminoles, and the planter was a slaveholder. But there is no need of attributing the desire to the political greed of the slavocracy. This error is more plainly illustrated by an earlier instance. Calhoun's plan, when secretary of war under Monroe, to remove the Indians of New York into the western part of Michigan Territory, now Wisconsin, has been seriously referred, not to a desire to release New York, but to a wish to burden the free Northwest and retard its development. It is true that the contradictory interests of North and South came out pretty clearly in the Missouri compromise discussion; but it is anticipating later politics and entirely misconstruing the growth of Calhoun as a statesman and a slavocrat to think that he or any one foresaw in 1820 the whole drift of Southern efforts to obtain room for slavery extension. It is just as much the part of folly to announce that Cass was a "doughface" in 1831, pandering to Southern prejudices and bending a pliable conscience, as it is to state that his good sense in 1820 concerning the removal of the New York Indians was due to a desire to circumvent a plan of a plotting slaveholder. He was a Western man, not a Southerner, and his action was a Western action, based on Western appreciation of the Indian character and of the relation of the tribes to the general government.

The idea of removing the Indians was, as Benton says, as old as Jefferson. It had been discussed at various times. Monroe, in his annual message in 1824, set forth the desirability of transporting them into the West. Cass elaborated a plan in his first report in 1831. He believed that the Indians would be better off if freed from the influence of the whites. He feared the practical application of the doctrine announced by the Supreme Court, that a tribe within the limits of the State was exempt from state control; he realized that the executive and the court were at variance on the subject, and that a uniform basis of management ought to be determined upon if possible. It is apparent that he sided with the President in maintaining the authority of the executive as a "coördinate branch of the government," and perhaps thought that, as far as it affected a present practical question, Jackson was right in his famous opposition to the judiciary: "John Marshall has given his judgment, let him enforce it if he can." Indeed, Cass the next year, March, 1832, seems to have printed an exhaustive argument in the "Globe," attempting to prove that the Supreme Court was wrong and Jackson was right in the Cherokee matter. "When a solemn and final decision was pronounced, and Georgia refused to obey the decree of the court, no reproof for her refractory spirit was heard; on the contrary, a learned review of the decision came out, attributed to executive countenance and favor."[1] When one of the cabinet spent his time in writing a long refutation of a judicial decision of the Supreme Court, affairs of state were assuredly in a badly

[1] From a speech by Mr. Miller, in Senate, 1833.

mixed condition. But the Jacksonian party was a creature more curious than any curiosity of mythology; although its body and legs were popular sovereignty and mob democracy, the head and arms were monarchical arrogance and the invincible obstinacy of self-reliance.

We need not go into the woeful scenes which resulted from the effort to remove the Creeks and Seminoles. As in other difficulties of this kind, the wrong was not all on one side. Sentimental ignorance alone represents the cruel Oceola as a noble brave, fighting with generous patriotism for the lands of his family and the graves of his sires. On the other hand, no one can look upon this scene from the history of a slave-owning country without feelings of shame and indignation. Before there was any excuse for war, the slave dealers were too anxious to get control of the negroes of the Seminoles. Actual hostilities were begun by a wanton outrage; the wife of Oceola was seized as the daughter of a slave, and was carried away into slavery. Oceola's vengeance was felt, and he was captured by treachery. One who respects his country shrinks from poking into the slime of the disgraceful contest, where our government became a trafficker in human flesh, and used its power in behalf of the lowest passions of man. Had it not been for the shameful greed of the slave dealer, who longed to get possession of the negroes who were either held in slavery by the Seminoles or lived with them on terms of equality, the course of the war would have been different and the contest more honorable. But these human vampires respected no treaties and regarded no rights. In the end, the war was not successful. After the expenditure of not less than $30,000,000 and the loss of many lives, after eight years of slave chasing and Indian hunting in the miasmic swamps and everglades, under the torrid sun of Florida, the government was obliged to take the advice which Cass had given when war had fairly begun — obtain peace by giving Florida to the possession of armed settlers.[1]

Many charges and recriminations were the fruits of this shameful affair. Scott was charged with inefficiency. Cass was accused of negligence. Abuse was heaped on all interested. Jackson, as usual, lost himself in a paroxysm of rage because all went not well. "Let the damned scoundrels defend their country," he exclaimed; "he could take fifty women, and whip every Indian that ever crossed the Suwanee."[2] A fair examination absolves the secretary of war from the charge of carelessness or neglect. He apparently acted on the knowledge sent him, and supplied the generals at the front with all the troops they asked for or suggested the need of. The truth is, that it was no easy task to drive a handful of determined men from retreats which were almost inaccessible, and the deeds of the army, as such, were by no means

[1] Schouler's *History of the United States*, vol. iv. p. 319.
[2] Niles, vol. lii. p. 98.

without honor. But Cass cannot be relieved of the charge that negro slavery did not appeal to him in its awfulness, and that he could see no harm in returning the fugitive slaves to bondage. Who in those days did see the institution in its proper light? The war was nearly finished before even Giddings of Ohio branded it as a slave chase and pointed the finger of shame. This war, indeed, marks the lowest depth to which Northern apathy sank. After 1841, not a step could be taken by the government that suspicious abolitionists did not peer about for a possible proslavery motive.

The War Department, at the period of which we are speaking, had charge of many matters which are now cared for by the Department of the Interior. The details of the office demanded constant attention, and it is apparent from the long reports which General Cass made that he studied with care all portions of his duties. He entered into an elaborate discussion of the necessity for coast defenses. Arguing that a navy was the best fortification, he advised the building of a navy which would be at least nearly adequate for purposes of defense. He examined with care the condition of the army, and it may be said, to his honor, that he advocated that the practice of giving whiskey rations to the soldiers should be stopped.

Until Cass took the war portfolio, his life had been spent in active employment. During his governorship he had passed months at a time traveling over the Western country, and now incessant sedentary labor and constant attention to the details of his office were impairing his health, and it soon became evident that he must have change and diversion. The President therefore offered to appoint him minister to France, and Cass accepted the offer, with the understanding that he should be allowed to leave Paris on a tour for recreation and pleasure. James Buchanan has left us the improbable story that Cass was transported because Jackson desired to get rid of him and to employ some one possessed of more alertness and business ability. According to this account, the President used the following language: "I can no longer consent to do the duties both of the President and secretary of war. General Cass will decide nothing for himself, but comes to me constantly with great bundles of papers, to decide questions for him which he ought to decide himself."[1] The light of events to be recorded hereafter will properly illumine this statement made by Buchanan, whose indecision and vacillation cannot be reasoned out of the memory of the American people. Every circumstance refutes it. Jackson admired Cass; Cass loved Jackson. The visitor at the Hermitage in later years saw in the hall the bust of the Northwestern statesman. Their whole intercourse is the best proof of mutual consideration and respect. That a man who had

[1] Curtis's *Life of Buchanan*, vol. ii. p. 399.

continuously acted with promptitude and boldness from the battle at the River Canard until he became secretary of war should suddenly become timid and hesitating is beyond belief. Twice during Jackson's administration Cass offered to resign, and twice was persuaded to keep his office. At the end Jackson accepted the resignation with reluctance. After the return of Cass from France, the venerable ex-President, praising him for his services abroad, referred to their pleasant official relations and to the efficiency with which the affairs of the War Department had been conducted.[1] If the secretary had been grossly incapable, Jackson would not have waited until the closing months of his administration before he put the department into more competent hands. In June, 1836, the appointment as minister to Paris was sent in to the Senate, and immediately received the unanimous consent of that body — no slight compliment, if we consider the height of political animosity in those bitter days.

[1] Private Papers of Lewis Cass.

CHAPTER VI

MINISTER TO FRANCE

THE diplomatic relations between France and the United States were not altogether harmonious between 1833 and the date of the appointment of Cass. A successful treaty, negotiated in 1831, had won from France a promise to pay for the Napoleonic spoliations of American commerce. The United States had long awaited the time when their rights in this matter would be fairly considered, until patience, long continued, was in danger of being construed as timidity. Under Jackson's sway, however, a new system was adopted; when our dignified demands for the fulfillment of the treaty of 1831 were disregarded, and the Chamber of Deputies refused to pass the appropriation bill, the President stormed in the White House, and the shrill voice of John Quincy Adams was heard in Congress calling upon the people to resent a wanton insult and prepare the country for war. In January, 1835, the French minister at Washington was recalled, and in April Livingston left Paris. But judicious and expressive threats had the proper effect. The money was paid. Louis Philippe sat on a tottering throne, and he knew that a war with America would deprive him of popular support. He had, moreover, a real affection for the republic, and an admiration for the vigorous old warrior of the White House, who so fully represented self-confident democracy. The "bourgeois king" had visited America in his earlier days, and had become personally acquainted with men and manners. A tour through the backwoods of Pennsylvania and Ohio brought to him a knowledge of the roughness, heartiness, and good fellowship of the democratic West, and he retained a kingly sympathy and a generous enthusiasm for whole-souled Western uncouthness and the virile Americanism which Jackson personified.

Cass continued to perform the duties of secretary of war through the summer of 1836, and in October sailed for England, there to remain until assured that an American minister would be received in France. After a brief delay on this account, he repaired to Paris and entered upon his duties. The ordinary affairs of the legation occupied his attention for some time. Business had accumulated during the suspension of diplomatic relations, and it now demanded immediate settlement. But a minister's chief function in peaceful times is to be the representative of his country at court, and to care for the social as well as the more material interests of itinerant fellow-countrymen. Even in those days this was no slight task. Sometimes in a single evening he presented as many as fifty of his countrymen to the "citizen king." American visitors in Paris at this time spoke of the respectful attention they received from the legation. The plain, straightforward diplomat from the wilds of the Northwest, whose victories in the crooked and narrow art had hitherto been won over the red savage of the Western woods, quickly assumed a prominent and influential position at the gay capital. It looked as if the days when Franklin received the admiration of the gaudy court, or when Gouverneur Morris practiced his charms, had returned. The minister became the personal friend of the king, and was treated as an intimate.

Actual business of the embassy was not so confining that no opportunity was left for other pursuits. The peculiarities of European life and politics possessed a unique interest for one whose general reading had never been supplemented by travel or a wide experience. Nothing seemed to escape him. His pen was at work a good portion of the time, making his impressions permanent. The ineffectual uneasiness of the French people as he now saw them, and the misunderstandings between governors and governed, were unceasingly curious to one who had never known classes, and whose whole political theory and practice had been based on the principle of equality and the rights of self-government. In a real scientific spirit he traveled through France, noticing the condition of the people and learning continual lessons. He visited England, but a nearer acquaintance did not deprive him of that deep-rooted suspicion and distrust which are so evident in all his public career. He saw Victoria crowned as queen. But all the splendor of court seemed only to harden and sharpen his democratic loyalty. He carried his criticism of English aristocratic life to an absurd extent. He belonged to the school of triumphant democracy. The crass ignorance of the English concerning American life, and the unfriendly criticism of their captious travelers, filled him with an indignation which now is quite amusing.

In accordance with the understanding at the time of his appointment, he left his post at Paris for his vacation. In May, 1837, he set sail with his family from Marseilles on board the old frigate, The Constitution, commanded by Commodore Elliot. A description of his itinerary would now be uninteresting, but to him the journey gave the greatest pleasure. Naturally of a philosophic and scholarly turn, he experienced the delight of the philosopher and scholar in visiting places of historical and archæological interest. On the other hand, his strong practical sense and his sympathy for humanity prevented him from losing himself in the admiration of past glories, when political wrongs and social evils and stagnation everywhere met his eyes. He admired the beauties of Italy and Greece, but they taught him a lesson for America. Everything possessed for him a present and a human interest: no palace or hovel or beautiful landscape won his attention because of mere picturesqueness, or lost for him its peculiar place in the life and history of man. Greece and Italy furnished him an opportunity for studying the real humanities, — not their dead languages, but the places these nations had actually held and were holding in the great drama of the world's history, whose *dénouement* he believed would be the complete freedom, the ideal liberty. He saw in the Parthenon more than a relic and a ruin; he mused over Salamis and Marathon without shadowy romanticism, for he saw before him spots where the destiny of Europe was decided. Delphi itself appealed to no shallow imagination, but awakened thoughts of the eternal power of God, and the shifting, transient nature of the works of man. "Parnassus indeed is there, with the clouds resting on its snowy summit, and the blue waves of the Gulf of Corinth rolling at its feet, in a stream as bright and clear as when its waters purified the persons of the ministers and votaries of the temple, but could not cleanse their hearts from a debasing superstition. But these are the works of God which mock the pride of man and bid defiance to his power, witnesses of change themselves unchangeable."

By special permission from the Sultan the American frigate sailed to Constantinople and on into the Black Sea. The travelers stood in the shadow of St. Sophia; and here again the teachings of sacred and profane history were emphasized and illustrated. A sail through the Ægean recalled the beauties and the grandeur of the "inland seas," and there came vividly to the mind of Cass another scene, when through the islands at the north of Michigan wound a fleet of three hundred Indian canoes. There is something pathetic in the way in which, amid scenes of unbroken interest or magnificence, his mind continually reverted to the rough picturesqueness and daring life of the frontier. The Ægean suggested similarities, the palace at St. Cloud contrasts. At the age of fifty-five he was becoming acquainted with a broader world; with a wider retrospect he was preparing for twenty years of political conflict. Egypt and Palestine were included in the journey, and the Pyramids and the Jordan encouraged more monologue; which, it must be confessed, partook somewhat extravagantly of the stilted grandiloquence common to the rhetoric of fifty years ago. A visit to the islands of Candia and Cyprus called out two interesting articles, which were sent to the "Southern Literary Messenger," published at Richmond. These are full of historic information and of practical philosophy, for after all Cass was a scholar to the end rather than a political trickster, and nothing shows his scholarly inclinations more than the trip to the old East.

In November, 1837, the general returned to Paris, invigorated in body and mind. For some time no very important diplomatic problems were presented for solution, and the time was employed in a study of French manners and political conditions. As has already been said, the king became a close friend of the American minister, so intimate, indeed, that the other ambassadors are reported to have been jealous of the undue influence of the republican representative. Louis Philippe was an affable and courteous man, possessed of a wonderful store of knowledge, and he won the admiration and even affection of Cass. There is no doubt that the citizen king had many noble qualities. His shabby treatment of Gouverneur Morris, who furnished him with funds for his travels in America, and gave him unlimited credit with his own New York banker, is not a complete index to his character. There was much in him that merited admiration, though he had some bourgeois propensities and certain tendencies to smallness where a greater breadth was to be expected. And yet he was a real king, and his grasp of affairs often belied the maxim of the doctrinaires, that the king reigns but does not rule. Thiers served him with his brilliance and Guizot with his philosophic wisdom, but the constitutional "King of the French" did not always give himself up to their guidance. Physical courage he did not lack, but he seems to have needed political energy, promptness, and decision. This weakness afterward showed itself in the evil days of February, 1848, when too complacently he yielded to insurrection, and gave up his crown, soon to be seized by one with more cunning and with more relentless ambition.

The happiness of the domestic life of the king and his personal attractions blinded Cass to political faults. He had begun to take notes of his impressions of France and Europe when he came to Paris, and he now published in an American periodical an account of the life of King Louis Philippe, with a commentary on French government and the conditions of the people. In 1840 these articles were published in New York in book form, with the title "France, its King, Court, and Government. By an American." The book has many merits. It recounts the life of Louis Philippe in his early days of adversity, when he fled from revolutionary France; it relates his travels in an easy flowing narrative, and gives an attractive picture of his wanderings in America and his visit to the Western country with which the writer was so well acquainted. There is a vein of pleasantry and humor in this portion of the story, though Cass by mental construction was ill adapted to light and vivacious description; nevertheless certain aspects of Western life are presented with vividness, and there is the charm which always comes with the tale of one who writes of what he knows and loves. The later life of the king and his character are set forth in an interesting fashion. The description of political France of fifty years ago gives the book lasting historic value. It is apparent that he had peered with no careless glance into the woeful depths of seething Paris; that he appreciated the uneasiness and discontent of its hidden life, that from the standpoint of happy democracy he could judge with peculiar advantage the fruitless longings and insensate clamorings of the people who did not know the good they had, and sought what they could not use. "God be praised!" wrote Cass, "we have no Paris, with its powerful influence and its inflammable materials. He who occupies the lowliest cabin upon the very verge of civilization has just as important a part to play in the fate of our country as the denizen of the proudest city in the land."

From such observations and studies as these, Cass was called to important diplomatic duties. For some time England and the United States had been giving each other the retort courteous, from which the next step is the cut direct. The northeastern boundary question had become an active stimulant to disorder. Maine would not be robbed, and Canada would not be cheated. Even more serious complications had arisen, growing out of the Canadian rebellion of 1837 and the turbulence in western New York consequent upon it. At that time an invasion of the province was threatened by some fugitives and by American sympathizers. A small steamer, the Caroline, was to be used for this purpose, but when lying at the American shore in the Niagara River she was seized by an expedition from Canada and sent over the falls. A citizen of the United States was killed in the affray, and the excitement did not die out in a moment. Three years later Alexander McLeod came from Canada to New York, and openly claimed the honor of having killed the American. He was at once arrested on the charge of murder, and held for trial. His detention immediately became a serious diplomatic difficulty. Lord Palmerston demanded McLeod's release. Our government had not charge of the prisoner and could not surrender him, for Governor Seward positively refused to renounce the jurisdiction of the State of New York. The English now acknowledged the Caroline affair as an international one, and assumed the position that not McLeod, but the British government was responsible, if any breach of law had been committed. It looked in the early part of 1841 as if war with Great Britain was imminent. "If he should be condemned we must throw away the scabbard," wrote Mr. Harcourt, in March. Upon Webster, who had been called to the foreign office by Harrison, and retained in his position when Tyler became President, devolved the task of guiding the country through the difficulties which now beset it.

Cass had a point of vantage from which to view European affairs and to watch the shifting clouds of war and politics. Even Stevenson at the Court of St. James did not have such extra-official means of discovering the popular sentiment of England as were furnished to Cass by the English colony at Paris. On March 5, 1841, Cass wrote to Webster that he had reliable information that the English fleet was preparing for the order to sail to Halifax. "Of one thing I am sure: there is a bad feeling against us in England, and this feeling is daily and manifestly augmenting." The terrible efficiency of the steam frigates, with their heavy guns "carrying balls weighing from sixty to a hundred pounds,"[1] warned defenseless America to forge her coat of mail. Ten days after this first warning another letter was sent relating in confidence the substance of several interviews with the king, who asserted that the French antipathy to England would implicate France in the war if it were once begun. The hostility to England entertained by our minister to France was beginning to affect his speech a little. There was no need of his announcing to Webster, in a strident missive, that the English were the "most credulous people upon the face of the earth in all that concerns their own wishes or pretensions;" that they were "always right and everybody else wrong." He added advice: "Bend all your effort to *steam*. Equip all the steam vessels you can." Webster already appreciated the danger, and such peremptory language was a little beyond the margin of good taste and discretion. There is no evidence that Webster resented it at the time, but when an opportunity for retaliation offered itself he seized

[1] Curtis, *Life of Daniel Webster*, vol. ii. p. 63.

upon it in a manner which suggests the energy of accumulated resentment.

In good season all danger of war from this affair disappeared, when McLeod was acquitted by a jury in New York, in October, 1841.

The winter of 1842 was the beginning of the end of Cass's diplomatic career; it was also the beginning of a new period in his life, the interpretation of which requires patient discrimination. Did he from this time on consciously endeavor to reach the presidential chair by any and all means? Are his acts all to be read in the light of a consuming ambition? Did he henceforth stifle his conscience and give up his principles in exchange for the political support of the slaveholder? The slavery question was fairly in politics. The slave-baron had catechised Van Buren when he came before the people for election. The nefarious gag laws had aroused Northern indignation. The extreme abolitionists were continuing their crusade with wonted vehemence and fanatical vigor. But the day had gone by when Garrison could be dragged through the streets of Boston at the end of a halter, or Prudence Crandall insulted and impoverished in puritanic Connecticut. In the wavering North the ultra-abolitionist was allowed in peace to denounce the Constitution as "a covenant with death and an agreement with hell." The moderate abolitionists, at the same time, prepared to fight with the ballot in accordance with rule and reason. In the midst of all the sound and nonsense of the "hard cider" campaign of 1840 little attention was paid to the nominees of the Liberty party. For them a vote was cast so trifling that it scarcely caused a ripple on the placid satisfaction with which the country welcomed the election of plain "Old Tip." But the slavery question was fairly in politics. Henceforth a candidate for favors must run the gauntlet for Southern inspection, and soon for Northern investigation as well.

In December, 1841, the representatives of England, France, Prussia, Russia, and Austria, high contracting parties at London, entered into a treaty for the suppression of the slave trade. The cruisers of each nation were accorded the right to detain and search vessels belonging to any one of the others, if such vessel should "on reasonable grounds be suspected of being engaged in the traffic in slaves." Inasmuch as English ships of war outnumbered those of the other countries, this gave to England special facilities for checking this traffic, against which she had proclaimed a war to the knife. Moreover the treaty was a pretentious and suspicious formality, for the Mediterranean was specially excluded, and no ship belonging to Russia, Austria, or Prussia had ever been engaged in the slave trade, or been interfered with, on that charge, by British vessels. That England had the motive of bolstering up her claims to search and visitation seems, therefore, undeniable. Cass was uneasy. The people whom he hated had gained possession of a leverage. Stimulated by his antipathy his imagination conjured up evils to come. On February 1, 1842, a pamphlet from his pen was published in Paris, inveighing against the treaty and attempting to infer the purpose of England from her past assumption of right. It bore the title, "An Examination of the Question, now in Discussion, between the American and British Governments, concerning the Right of Search, by an American," and had for a motto, "'When we doubted, we took the trick.' London Times, January, 1842." The pamphlet contained a discussion of the whole question of the right of search, showing the insolence of Britain in the past, her steady progress toward dominion on the sea, and the reasons for fearing that the quintuple treaty was simply another step toward a consummation she so devoutly wished. The suspicions of the design of England were perhaps partly unfounded; but she had no right to complain because she was suspected. Lord Brougham, in the House of Lords (February 21, 1842), announced that the sole wish of England was "to see the infernal slave traffic put down," and that "any general right of search," or any object except the prevention of slave trade in Africa was not sought or contemplated.[1] We now may do England more justice than Cass could then do her. But in view of all her conduct, then fresh in men's minds, the United States was bound to

[1] Hansard's *Parliamentary Debates*, vol. lx. p. 718.

object to such apparent justification by the other four great nations of Europe.

The pamphlet was received with approbation in America. Niles printed the document in full, to the exclusion of "other matter," remarking that it was "attributed to the pen of our vigilant and talented minister at the French court."

On February 13 a protest against the concurrence of the French government in the quintuple treaty was written at the American legation at Paris and transmitted to M. Guizot, minister of foreign affairs. This asserted that England had recently been vigorously claiming the right to enter and examine American vessels for the purpose of ascertaining their nationality; the ratification of the treaty under consideration might seem to sanction this right claimed by one of the contracting parties. "The United States," it continued, "do not fear that any such united attempts will be made upon their independence. What, however, they may reasonably fear is that in the execution of this treaty measures will be taken which they must resist." The appeal to French jealousy of England, the covert intimation that war might ensue, — "one of those desperate struggles which have sometimes occurred in the history of the world," — sufficed to turn France into opposition, and she refused to ratify the treaty. The sensitive French people felt that England was far too condescending; and, moreover, France had her own sweet sins; for many of her southern ports had more than a vicarious interest in the remunerative traffic. Not till 1845 did the two countries agree to keep an effective double fleet on the coast of Africa to crush the trade, a plan which, it will be seen, was an imitation of the one adopted by America in 1842. England was greatly annoyed at the withdrawal of France. Lord Brougham attacked Cass as a leader of low American democracy pandering to mob jealousy of England. Wheaton, however, asserted that the treaty of Washington was the determining influence which brought about the rejection of the treaty by France, and Webster and Cass afterwards had a spirited controversy on the subject in the Senate,[1] in April, 1846.

The American government sanctioned the protest which Cass had sent Guizot on his own authority, and accepted its doctrines. "Tyler too," the quasi-Whig, who had been borne into office with Democratic luggage in the whirlwind of popular enthusiasm for Harrison, and was now ruling in solitary state, a president without a party, was not the man to object because of too much zeal for slavery. Webster, although he publicly approved, looked somewhat askance at the pamphlet and protest, and privately commented severely on the conduct of both Cass and Stevenson. "They thought," he said, "to make great political headway upon a popular gale."[2] Even the pamphlet

[1] *Congressional Globe*, 1st Session, 29th Congress, p. 627.

[2] *Memoirs of John Quincy Adams*, vol. xi. p. 243.

he declared "quite inconclusive" as a "piece of law logic," however distinguished it might be for ardent American feeling.[1] History, however, has proved the reverse. All flat denunciations of search and visitation were unsuccessful, while the inconclusive "law logic" of Cass has become a recognized rule in international law. He plainly propounded a principle which Mr. Webster seemingly failed to grasp, although it is the only reasonable and sensible ground for determining such difficulties. It would not do to declare: "If you touch our vessels we will fight." Were we to protect every piratical slaver which insolently raised our flag? The principle, as laid down in the pamphlet, and years afterward, through the efforts of Cass, acknowledged by England to be correct, was simply this: you have no right to touch our vessels on the high seas; if you suspect that a vessel carrying our flag is not entitled to it, you examine her papers at your peril; if you are mistaken, you must answer to the American government. This reasoning underlies the whole common law, and Mr. Webster ought to have been wiser than to sneer at it.

In political circles in America the action was widely discussed. Adams called Cass's protest "absurd," and finally poured out upon it one of those pieces of venomous resentment which sometimes issued from him when the thought of the iniquity of slavery caused the old man's blood to

[1] Curtis's *Life of Daniel Webster*, vol. ii. p. 118.

boil. He wrote: "Cass's Protest of the 13th of February, 1842, against the ratification by France of the treaty signed and sealed by her own ambassador, is a compound of Yankee cunning, of Italian perfidy, and of French *legèreté*, cemented by shameless profligacy, unparalleled in American diplomacy. Tyler's approval of it is at once dishonest, mean, insincere, and hollow-hearted."[1]

There was, however, great diplomatic wisdom in the movement. Tyler wrote to Webster that he had "risen from the perusal of the foreign newspapers with a feeling essentially in favor of General Cass's course." "The message has been the basis of his movements, and the refusal of France to ratify the treaty of the five powers gives us more sea-room with Lord Ashburton. . . . The 'Times' of London assumed a tone which looked confoundedly as if the ratification by the five powers was afterward to be proclaimed as equivalent to the establishment of a new rule of national law."[2] There was exultation in more than one quarter. "For the first time in our history," wrote Wheaton from Berlin, "could it be said that the American government had exerted an influence on the policy of Europe."[3] The wisdom of the action can be determined only by a consideration of the circumstances of the case. It is easy enough now to hurl invectives because our

[1] *Memoirs*, vol. xi. p. 338.
[2] *Letters and Times of the Tylers*, vol. ii. p. 233.
[3] Quoted *ibid.*

foreign minister interfered with a treaty, the ostensible intent of which was to check the slave trade. It is easy enough to attribute it all to the craving ambition of a crafty "log roller," as does Von Holst.[1] "The scheming political 'log roller,' with a high aim at the object of his own personal ambition, and the hot temperament of the would-be great man of mediocre endowments and mediocre education, coöperated to give such a form to the effusions of the ardent patriot that Adams's hard judgment upon them seems scarcely exaggerated." This keen German critic of our country's history, who has so shrewdly interpreted and so skillfully arranged his facts, has frequently failed to pierce into American popular feeling and emotion; moreover, an affectionate regard for Adams has often blinded him to the faults of the noble old man, and a bitter entry in a diary replete with denunciation has been taken as temperate criticism. No one can estimate too highly the life and work of that last of the Puritans; but he who writes history by the fitful light of such comment will see but darkly.

The prime motive for the action of Cass in this affair was his inveterate dislike and distrust of England, sentiments which he had good cause to entertain. It will be remembered that not until 1839 (less than three years before the date of his pamphlet) did the English give up their efforts in the Northwest, as already described, and that his

[1] *History of the United States*, vol. ii. p. 489.

whole life preceding his admission to Jackson's cabinet had brought him into antagonism with British aggression. Filled with pride for America and her institutions, he had met in Europe the sneers and condescensions of English travelers, who looked pityingly upon his country and with qualified approbation upon France. His writings in the early years of his ministry shadow forth the same suspicion. Yet no one can say decisively that the slavery question did not also move him. The pamphlet announced that the writer was no slaveholder, that he never had been, and never should be; but he found his way to the beaten track of biblical justification, and pointed to Joseph in the bondage of Egypt. A few months before his objection to the treaty he had been proposed as a candidate for the presidency by a meeting in Philadelphia, and had published in the "Philadelphia Sentinel" a carefully worded reply. "He certainly does not in his letter," says Niles, "court a nomination to that office; but yet admits that in the contingency of being called upon by the general voice of the Democratic party he would not withhold his assent."[1] But even on the supposition that the presidential bee had begun its buzzing, it is anticipating later political tactics to suppose that, as the prime condition of Democratic support, he threw himself into the arms of the slavocracy. "The favoring gale," which would waft him on his way, was bold opposition

[1] Niles, lxi. p. 80, October 2, 1841.

to England, ardent Americanism, and evident disapproval of forcible abolition.

Admitting as possible the play of various motives, it is still true that the pamphlet and protest were entirely justifiable. England had been asserting with renewed vigor her right of visitation, which she now cleverly distinguished from search, and had carried her principles into exasperating practice. Mr. Eugene Schuyler, in speaking of the treaty, has left the weight of his undoubted authority in favor of General Cass's action. "Fortunately," he writes, "our minister to Paris at that time was General Lewis Cass, a man of great experience, of decided views, and who had succeeded in obtaining a very intimate and friendly footing with the French government."[1] This author shows more plainly than any one else has done, how the defense of American rights on the seas is coupled with the name of Cass.

The Ashburton treaty was signed at Washington August 9, 1842. It was ratified by the Senate August 26, by a vote of thirty-nine to nine. Webster could fairly pride himself upon the result of the negotiations; and the approval of the Senate seems very complimentary to his efforts, if one considers his anomalous condition. Even before a treaty was signed, there were clamorous demands for his resignation by the Whig newspapers; for it was hard to bear with equanimity that their own giant should be used to sustain the renegade

[1] *American Diplomacy and the Furtherance of Commerce*, p. 252.

Whig who occupied the presidential chair. Yet Tyler's own self-satisfied suavity, it may be said, had aided not a little in smoothing out the "wrinkles of negotiation."[1] Virginian though he was, he first suggested that each nation should keep a squadron on the coast of Africa to suppress the slave trade,[2] a stipulation which forms article eight of the treaty. The squadrons were to be independent of each other, but the two governments agreed, nevertheless, to give such orders to the officers commanding the respective forces as should enable them "most effectually to act in concert and coöperation, upon mutual consultation," as exigencies might arise, for the execution of all such orders.

A copy of the treaty, and the news of its ratification, reached Paris September 17, and Cass immediately sent word to his government that he could no longer be useful in his position, and that his private affairs demanded his attention at home. When later he had received letters and dispatches from Mr. Webster in relation to the matter, he sent a long communication in which he complained because there was no renunciation by Great Britain of her right of search. The pretensions of the English in this regard had of late been productive of some injury. American traders had been stopped and searched with a view to ascertaining their real nationality, and whether or not

[1] Schouler's *History of the United States*, vol. iv. p. 403.

[2] *Letters and Times of the Tylers*, vol. ii. p. 219.

they were slavers. Cass by his pamphlet and protest had identified himself with the controversy, and now that a treaty had been made and ratified he felt piqued that England was not forced to forego her assumption; his government had not gone so far as he had expected, or as his protest had promised. He was in an awkward position, and he tried to extricate himself by criticising Webster and by objecting to the treaty after it had been signed and ratified. His own enthusiasm and sense had prompted him to oppose Great Britain, and the President had approved his conduct. But now affairs had taken a different turn. Resignation was open to him, and a dignified withdrawal would have been sufficient. A bitter correspondence, however, which attracted a great deal of attention, was begun between Cass and Webster. Adams wrote about it in that bitter diary: "The controversy between Lewis Cass and Daniel Webster about the Ashburton Treaty, the rights of visitation and of search, and the Quintuple treaty, still, with the comet, the zodiacal light, and the Millerite prediction of the second advent of Christ and the end of the world within five weeks from this day, continue to absorb much of the public and of my attention." He compared the "rumpus" to the complaints of Silas Deane and to Monroe's famous attack upon the Washington administration.

The letters which passed between the ex-minister and the secretary of state have been published in the public documents, and do not need presentation here. The President reported them in answer to a request from the Senate. Cass insisted that he was thrown into an embarrassing position by Webster's action, and charged that the country, through the secretary of state, had stultified itself in not making a renunciation of the right of visitation and search a condition precedent to the consideration of the matters which were treated of in the eighth article. He did not directly criticise the President and Senate, but announced his belief that the ratification of the treaty ought to have been coupled with an express denunciation of the right of search. Webster, on the other hand, asserted that no such stand was needed on our part, that the Ashburton treaty reaffirmed and made stronger America's opposition to English assumption on the seas, that the government of the United States relied on its own power and not upon statements in treaties or conventions. Again Mr. Webster ought to have been wiser. Our vessels were being visited and searched in spite of our "power" and our denial of such a right. Short of war, negotiation was the only means of obtaining cessation of such annoyances. He himself found it necessary to protest in later years. The odious right was claimed, and occasionally exercised, by Great Britain for sixteen years, until Cass himself as secretary of state took up the old argument of his pamphlet which Webster had deemed inconclusive, and compelled the

English government to recognize its cogency and publicly to abandon her pretensions. What Cass said in these letters to Webster had already been suggested in the debates in the Senate, and events soon proved him "in the right and Mr. Webster in the wrong."[1] The secretary in this correspondence quoted with approbation a passage from the President's message, which intimated that the clause of the treaty providing for cruisers on the coast of Africa had removed "all pretext on the part of others for violating the immunities of the American flag on the seas." But English statesmen at once repelled such an interpretation. "Nor do we understand," said Sir Robert Peel, then prime minister, "that in signing that treaty the United States could suppose that the claim was abandoned." It was undoubtedly unfortunate that, at a time when the statement would have carried peculiar force, Webster did not see fit to announce our unflinching adherence to our rights.

In one particular the ex-minister was wholly at a disadvantage. The treaty as ratified was none of his special business, and he was not called upon to denounce it except as a private citizen. On the other hand Webster was, as Sumner said, as powerful as he was unamiable, and the lack of good humor gave his adversary an opportunity for effective retort which he might otherwise have missed. The quarrel continued until March, 1843, some months after the return of General Cass from

[1] Schuyler's *American Diplomacy*, p. 255.

Paris; but, of course, nothing was accomplished by it. It may be doubted whether this ill-natured controversy was of great assistance in the race for the presidency; probably it did help a little, although the people of the country were, on the whole, pretty well satisfied with the Ashburton settlement, and did not perceive the need of a bolder stand against English presumption.

This matter has heretofore been treated of in a partisan manner. The lives of Webster hold his letters up for admiration. Cass's letters appear without their answers in his biographies. Mr. Peter Harvey has left us a story in his "Personal Reminiscences and Anecdotes of Daniel Webster," which has found credence in the minds of more trustworthy writers. According to this account, Cass was so overwhelmed by the replies of Webster to his attacks that he confessed himself beaten, said his position was unbearable, and begged that he be allowed to write another letter to which the secretary should promise to make no surrejoinder. This tale bears its own refutation on its face, but it has been accepted even by those who have generally placed the correct value on Mr. Harvey's productions.[1] Cass was applauded and toasted for his success in the controversy, and it is perfectly clear that it did not detract from

[1] Mr. Lodge in his life of Webster has declared that "a more untrustworthy book it would be impossible to imagine." Yet his own admirable sketch of Webster's career has given new currency to the tale.

his popularity and the high estimation in which he was held at the time. Moreover in recognizing him as one of their great leaders the Democracy accepted his attacks upon Webster. He had lost his senses, if he whined for pity, as Harvey asserts that he did. I have the explicit denial of this fact from Mr. Charles E. Anderson, who was secretary of the legation at Paris, and who knew Cass with a keener appreciation and with a better judgment than this "loving and devoted Boswell" knew Webster.

"The sage of Marshfield" was mighty in argument, but Cass was well able to hold his own. His ability, of which there cannot be the slightest doubt, his strength in debate, and his power in argument have been greatly under-estimated since his death. The eulogistic biographies which appeared in his lifetime, though not without their merits, lack discrimination and lose the weight belonging to judicious approval. The generation of the Rebellion, naturally enough, is but just emerging from a state of antipathetic criticism of all who were not of the vehement antislavery school. Those still living, who knew Cass in his vigor, are not willing to admit, whatever may have been their political convictions, that in real strength and capacity, in mental virility or acumen, he was overmatched by any save the very greatest of his day. His placid, kindly disposition won for him a lasting affection among those who knew him, and remembrance may have warped judgment; but the name of Cass recalls to an old Michigan Whig a friend to be loved and admired, and a foe to be dreaded. Of the statesmen of his generation, only Webster surpassed him in profundity of argument. Calhoun excelled him in keenness and directness of debate. Clay outstripped him in fiery beauty of eloquence and in power for popular leadership. Although he never tried to imitate the professional tactics of Van Buren, the only Democratic leader comparable to him, he at least equaled the "Little Magician" in all the more graceful and honorable arts of statesmanship.

The American citizens of Paris were loath to bid farewell to the representative of their country, whose constant attention and courtesy they appreciated. His residence was elegant and attractive. "General Cass's hotel is furnished sumptuously," wrote Charles Sumner in his journal. "The table was splendid, and the attendance perfect; servants in small clothes constantly supplying you with some new luxury. . . . Mr. Cass is a man of large private fortune, and is said to live in a style superior to that of any minister ever sent by America."[1] On November 11 a public dinner was given the retiring minister by his resident countrymen. The expressions of regret at his departure were many, and seemingly from the heart. The master of the feast in his address reminded the company that they had come to-

[1] *Memoirs and Letters of Charles Sumner*, by Edward L. Pierce, vol. i. p. 253.

gether, without distinction of party, to testify affectionate respect for their distinguished guest. Making due allowance for the flattering unction of post-prandial phrases, we still see that the news correspondent was right in his message, which announced: "General Cass has won all hearts at Paris. They loved the man; they admired the dauntless envoy of their country."[1] The speech of General Cass in answer to the toast, "Honor to our illustrious fellow citizen, and a happy return to a grateful country," was a finished piece of declamation over the smiling Providence which especially shapes the ends of the United States of America. His eloquence had the old-fashioned sonorous quality. He offered none of "the foam Aphrodite of Bacchus's sea," nor the froth and airy nothingness of modern after-dinner speech-making. There was little to lighten the heavy rhythm of his sentences. His response was, as his addresses usually were, scholarly, philosophic, sensible, and, above all, democratic. He could continually strike the keynote of the democratic anthem, leaving the frivolous overtones for more frolicsome speakers and writers. The peculiar victory of Cass as the champion of American rights was applauded in the toast, "The sovereignty of the seas, common to all nations, but exclusive under every flag."

Another chapter of the career of Cass was ended. He had conducted himself with rare dis-

[1] Communication to *New York Courier and Enquirer.*

cretion as an American minister, and had quite outdone himself as a politician. Diplomatic missions are usually dangerous to political ambition, for absence does not make the voter's heart grow fonder; but his six years' residence abroad had increased his reputation and his popularity.

Wm Hull

James Buchanan

Norvell Cobb

CHAPTER VII

A DEMOCRATIC LEADER. — THE ELECTION OF 1844

General Cass left his son-in-law, Mr. Ledyard, as *chargé d'affaires* at Paris. After a voyage of three weeks, not a slow trip for those times, he arrived in Boston on December 6, 1842. The people of the country were ready to welcome him with enthusiasm. Immediately upon his arrival the "citizens of New England," in a flattering letter, congratulated him on his safe return to his native country, "after faithful and energetic service in an important crisis" of his mission, and asked for a meeting with him in Faneuil Hall, "the spot in which of all others America would desire to welcome her deserving ones." He was obliged by other arrangements to forego the pleasure and the profit of communion with the political spirit of New England, and contented himself with meeting informally at his hotel those who wished to pay their respects to him. In New York even greater honors awaited him. A new luminary had been discovered by the sweeping astrolabe of the political astrologer. Ignorant of his fame and unappreciative of the popular curiosity, he had intended to hurry on to Washington, and thence home, where business matters claimed his immediate attention. But metropolitan democracy has generally obtained what it has sought. The governor's rooms were tendered him, and there he was received with cheers and all the approbation of party and patriotic devotion. Such ceremonies were bearding Van Buren in his very den; but as yet they could be accounted for as admiration for the envoy whose boldness had dignified America.

These evidences of popular approval in Northern States prove that his opposition to the quintuple treaty was not considered truckling to the slave power. Although an abolitionist was still an outcast, if no longer an outlaw, nevertheless open bidding for Southern favor or the use of a diplomatic mission for the defense of slavery would have been promptly resented. The political "bossism" of the Southerner added a sting to what might have been otherwise harmless. Indeed that fact must be remembered through the whole history of the slavery question. Without doubt the immorality of human bondage aroused the slumbering consciences of the people; the shrill cries of the fanatic, the pleading eloquence of Phillips, the wonderful bravery of Giddings and Adams, the incessant agitation of a subject which would not down, were more than mere steps in a progress toward united Northern sentiment; they were productive of a thought which, in the end, led the people, rejecting extravagances, to accept what was politically sound and morally right. But the infamous three fifths compromise gave power to the owner of chattels, and allowed the representation of things; the domineering slave baron, in the halls of Congress, kindled by his insolent orderings the resentment of the "d—d trading Yankee." Without doing injustice, therefore, to the impetus of higher motives, or under-estimating the mighty propelling power of any moral movement, simply because it is moral, we must admit that very often, when the North was animated to special effort, and when Northern representatives showed themselves persistent and energetic, there was some current beside the moral one holding them to their duty, there was an evident dislike of the tactics, methods, and aims of the slave-holder. So, even if hatred of the black sin of the South had as yet found no broad resting-place, jealousy of Southern dictation, as well as national pride and human shame, would have prevented the people of New York and Boston from receiving with acclamations any one who in their opinion had used a diplomatic office to pander to the prejudices of the slave-owner, and had for personal glory sought to shield a piratical traffic behind his country's name and his country's honor.

Cass was welcomed at Washington by the Congressmen and satellite politicians who wished to scan the face of a new prophet. All the way from the capital to his Michigan home there were applause and curiosity sufficient to satisfy the most hungry. He did not reach Detroit until February 14, and his way from Washington was one triumphal march. The legislatures of Pennsylvania and Ohio welcomed and honored him, and the governors and principal officers came out several miles to escort him to their respective capitals, under the firing of artillery, ringing of bells, martial music, and a general turnout of all the volunteer militia. It is interesting to read in Niles an item recounting the popular enthusiasm over Cass, and by its side to see another short paragraph telling how Henry Clay was boisterously applauded at each step of a journey through the South. There were warmth and color in those young days of our country. There were heroes and a hero worship strange to us in these later days. A committee from Detroit met their returning fellow citizen at Ypsilanti, and he was conducted to his home by the route he had taken thirty years before, when he had hoped to escort Brush with his supplies to the assistance of Hull. Nothing speaks so well for Cass as the honor he had at his own home. The city was enthusiastically devoted; he was the political Nestor of the State. Without using the arts of machine politics he retained his hold on the popular confidence and support, until the later spirit of liberty demanded a new leader inspired by the gospel of a new dispensation.

At a banquet given in his honor soon after his return Cass was heartily toasted, with the hope of adding another spark to the kindling enthusiasm of the country. His name was now fairly before the people, and letters began to pour in upon him asking him all conceivable questions and propounding a series of enigmas, with the intention of ascertaining his exact political belief by the Socratic and Yankee method of discovering truth. Before Cass had reached Boston, on his return from France, the Democratic Central Committee of Shelby County, Indiana, summoned a convention of all who were in favor of "the nomination of either General Cass or Richard M. Johnson." In November, almost before the glare of the rockets of the congressional election had faded away, a convention of his friends in Harrisburg announced their preference for Lewis Cass as the next Democratic candidate for the presidency. The "New York Herald," indorsing the action of this convention, demanded new men and a new movement. The congressional election of 1842 had been unusually mild and sensible, and in this sluggish indisposition the "Herald" saw need for the tonic of novelty. None of the old leaders could longer awaken enthusiasm; "but the movement now first made in Pennsylvania looks more like the real spirit of the people than anything we have seen of late. In that State, and in that way, did the name of Jackson and Harrison come up, and carry all before them." Cass was the very man, this paper declared, who could with proper attention and effort be carried into the presidency with a universal shout of acclamation. The "Herald" went at it with a will, issued extra copies, and shouted in leaded lines for another hero of 1812, believing that a new Jackson was found to lead the chosen Democratic seed back from captivity.

The Whig papers, curious and incredulous, doubted the orthodoxy of the new candidate, and the Democrats desired to be sure of him. Hardly had he landed when a letter from Mahlon Dickerson, a fellow member of Jackson's cabinet, was sent asking him for a full confession of faith. The answer was frankly given. "I am a member of the Democratic party, and have been so from my youth. I was called into public life by Mr. Jefferson, thirty-six years ago, and am a firm believer in the principles laid down by him." Two short paragraphs, in addition to this shrewd statement of old Republican affiliation, announced hostility to a national bank and belief in the saving efficacy of specie payment.

Interrogatories to the various candidates before the country were issued by a convention at Indianapolis early in 1843. To these, answers were sent by Calhoun, Buchanan, Johnson, and Cass. All sound the tocsin of faithful partisanship with no uncertain sound. Even Calhoun, long a free lance ready to strike at anything opposed to his cherished state sovereignty and organized anarchy, seemed to have temporarily left his nomadic politics. He replied that he had no reason to doubt that his friends would abide by the decision of a convention fairly summoned to express the wishes of the party. All this looked like happiness and harmony. Cass gave his answers to the questions at some length and with great good sense. Having always entertained a doubt of the constitutionality of a bank, he now condemned it; the proceeds from the sale of public land should not be distributed among the States, because it was simply taking the money out of one pocket to drop it into the other, and sums equal to those distributed must needs be raised again by taxation; a tariff for revenue with incidental protection should be "wisely and moderately established and then left to its own operation, so that the community could calculate on its reasonable duration and thus avoid ruinous fluctuations;" an amendment to the Constitution limiting the veto power seemed at the time unnecessary and therefore inexpedient. All this constituted a sufficiently good platform. As affairs then stood the Democratic party was without doubt lying quietly at good anchorage. Would it be content without the excitement and flurry of new and momentous issues?

On Jefferson's birthday the Democratic citizens of Philadelphia celebrated the occasion, and Cass was invited to be present. His well-worded letter of regret was read amid the enthusiasm of those present, and the following toast was offered: "General Lewis Cass, the soldier, the diplomatist, and the statesman: his correspondence with Webster proves his knowledge of the American character, and his ability to defend it." Lord Brougham's bitter attack on Cass aided his popularity and his chances for nomination. That noble lord accused him of debasing himself to pander to the lowest, meanest feeling of the "groveling and groundling" politician, and asserted that he, an American minister, had appealed to the hatred of England felt by the "rabble." Such charges by a British aristocrat were sweet morsels for the democracy on whom Cass hoped to rely. In various portions of the country wires were pulled for the new Michigan candidate. A friend in New York insisted that the elective offices ought to be divided among the adherents of Cass and Calhoun as well as of Van Buren, "so as to divide the loaves and fishes party." Men in Pennsylvania, in accordance with Cass's desires, deprecated the attacks upon Van Buren, lest such conduct might react and insure the persistent enmity of his followers.[1]

Early in 1843, therefore, eighteen months before the day of election, candidates for the Democratic nomination were fairly before the country with a careful, reserved, and negative policy. The only difficulty seemed to lie in the choice of any one of them as standard bearer. Many felt that Van Buren had been harshly treated in 1840, and hoped that the people, returning to reason, would undo the riot of the last campaign and put the "Little Magician" in the White House again.

[1] Private papers of Lewis Cass.

He had been a brave and consistent leader; and had been beaten rather by the financial distress of the country and the sins which Jackson had visited upon him than because of any errors of his own. But poetic justice is not political justice; and when once a candidate has been defeated there is a natural hesitation about sacrificing party interest on the altar of idealistic honor. Moreover Van Buren had had his turn, and of course had satisfied only a portion of the horde of hungry officeseekers. Those not satisfied with their share of the spoils would naturally seek another leader, from whom they might expect to obtain their desires. If he could not be elected with prestige of success to buoy him up, with the power of the officeholder to aid him, what reason was there to expect his election after he had been defeated, and when the officeholders had nothing to gain and everything to lose by his election? Although the majority of the party were still favorably disposed towards him, therefore, and though many of the politicians still obeyed the customary rein, and did becoming homage to their peerless teacher, there was good reason to believe that, even if no new issue presented itself, there would be a strong effort for a new candidate in whom the people might imagine any and all virtues, and whose unknown quantity might be substituted to solve widely different problems.

Buchanan could rely on the strong support of Pennsylvania, his own State. He belonged to the school of the cautious, judicious politicians, who seek a safe retreat from worry and vexation in a mild policy of indecision and wise delay. Richard M. Johnson of Kentucky was the reputed slayer of Tecumseh. It might be doubted whether this fact of itself qualified him for the presidency; but that was not the point at issue. It unquestionably added to his availability as a nominee. He had been a convenient and obedient cat's paw for Jackson, a harmless and purposeless vice-president under Van Buren, and was now refreshingly frank and coyly open in the expression of his wants; he would take either the presidency or the vice-presidency as the party desired.

There was never any real hope of Calhoun's nomination. His opinions were too dangerously evident, and he was the enemy of the dying sage at the Hermitage. He exhibited unexpected strength, however, even in New York where Van Buren was supposed to dominate matters; for the young men of the party admired the towering ability of the old nullifier, who had now apparently drifted back fairly within the headlands of the Democratic haven. The experienced voter learns to estimate aright the superiority of mediocrity; but the young voter places too high a valuation upon greatness. Beyond all, Calhoun was of Irish descent, and the potent bond of Celtic sympathy held for him the allegiance of a powerful political constituency in the great cities of the Atlantic seaboard, an element which has never been addicted to fair-weather voting, or to off-year epidemics, or to despising the primary meeting. Since the days of Jefferson there has been an intimacy between the aristocratic South and the congested population of Northern cities, — a union based partly, perhaps, on the very name of the favorite party; partly on the fact that Federalists, Whigs, and Republicans have represented the tariff, the bank, internal improvements, and strong government; partly on the fact that the immigrant, who has come to the "land of freedom," gravitates without thought to the party which was born of opposition to centralization, and was the advocate of individualism; partly on the fact that democracy represents what is peculiar to America, and is forcibly distinct from the civilization of trans-Atlantic countries, and is therefore attractive to him who has shaken from his feet the dust of old association. At this time the foreign element, especially the Irish, was strongly Democratic; for the Whigs seem to have repelled them, and driven them to vote "*en masse* against the candidates of the Whig party."[1] For immigration had begun and had awakened the fears of many Americans. In the fourth decade of the century 538,381 emigrants, and in the fifth decade about three times that number, landed on our coast.

The old competitor of the Democracy was in its turn girding itself for the race. There could be

[1] W. H. Seward's *Works*, vol. iii. p. 387.

no doubt who would be its leader. The victory of Harrison and Tyler in 1840 had proved but a defeat for the Whigs. Perhaps it was a just retribution upon a party which had contented itself with declamation and innuendo, and had drawn to itself all the vexed spirits and the homeless malcontents whose teeth had been set on edge by the personal government of Jackson or the panic of 1837. With one accord this conglomerate party, which disappointment had pressed into some degree of coherency, was decided this time upon the nomination of nobody of unknown principles. It was already shouting for "Harry of the West," who was the very impersonation of Whig doctrine and desire. When a party is unwilling to trust its fortunes and its principles to its true leader, and when in the hour of hope it deserts him on whom it relies in the hour of trial and despair, its fortunes are without real value and its principles of no worth. If one were to seek for the secret of the cohesion and the permanence of the Democratic party he would find it largely in its devotion to its leaders and its faith in itself.

There was another party, whose presence in the coming election was to have decisive influence, which remained unnoticed in the early days of this long campaign. Reference has already been made to the Liberty party, composed of voting abolitionists, who had determined upon reaching their ends by political means. Their insignificant vote in 1840 had not discouraged them, and they were again marshaling for the conflict with unsubdued energy and enthusiasm. Northern opposition to the "gag laws" had borne fruit in tolerance for abolitionism. Adams and Giddings, on the floor of Congress, had fought a good fight, which had won the admiration of the people. The "old man eloquent" had lashed the slaveholders till they writhed in mingled anger and chagrin, and the new Ohio representative, censured by the House for presumptuous resolutions concerning slavery as a "municipal" and not an international institution, had resigned his seat, to be reëlected by an overwhelming majority. These men were the prophets crying in the wilderness, making straight the way for final salvation from the curse of slavery. Adams was anticipating the creed of the Republican party by twenty years, devoted to the Union, opposed to the barbarism of the South, prophesying that slavery would be engulfed in the abyss if the Southern States, in the love of their sweet sin, should endeavor to separate themselves from the Union. Although neither of these men can be considered a member in good standing of the Liberty party as a political organization, they blazed the way for constitutional and legal opposition. They attracted the attention of the thoughtful, and won the respect and sympathy of the generous. Yet Birney himself fiercely assaulted Adams in a letter to his party, and in the very district of the old hero coöperated with the Democrats to defeat him. It was one of the best instances of the way in which principle sometimes runs away with reason, and sense is smothered in sentiment.

Of the Tyler faction there is little to be said. With a great estimation of himself and his popularity in the country, the President seems actually to have anticipated the support of the people. He had turned his back on every Whig measure and read every Whig guide-post backward, until at the end of his administration he had passed by even ultra-Democracy, and was hand and glove with John C. Calhoun himself. A free use of the spoils of office had failed to create a party devoted to his interests, and in isolated self-sufficiency his complacency was fed by the flattery of a cunning "kitchen cabinet," which ruled him and moulded his whims to suit themselves. The people absolutely refused to dance to his piping, and his "great country party" proved but a sorry court party of officeholders and officeseekers and political pariahs.

One question was coming ever more prominently before the country — should Texas be annexed? It will not do to go into the early history of the Lone Star Republic and show how it broke away from stagnant Mexico, how it was colonized by slave owners from the Southern States, who were intent from the first on gaining new fields and introducing their system, and by that element of our population which is always ready for excitement and peril. The annexation plan began in conspiracy; it was carried along by the dark and devious machinery of sly diplomacy; it ended in a disgraceful war, waged under false pretenses, and brought by swaggering success to a shameful end.

Tyler thrust the Texas question into the face of the country. Webster retired from the foreign office in May, 1843, and after a short interim, when the duties of the office were performed by Legaré, Upshur was appointed, to be followed on his death by Calhoun. The appointment of the great advocate of slavery meant that annexation would be carried to a conclusion. The plan had for some time been cautiously whispered over in meetings of the President's intimates. Upshur had used a bullying tone to Mexico, and hints of affectionate consideration had been given to Texas. Calhoun, now at the head of a pro-slavery cabinet, and the adviser of a slaveholding president, bent his energies to obtain more territory where the industrial system of the South might have more room and full play. The annexation of Texas is the first great effort on the part of the slave States to get vantage ground for bond labor in its unequal wrestle with the labor of the North. Of course, vainglory and national pride clothed a loathsome plan with patriotism, and blinded the eyes of many people to its real intent. Immediate "re-annexation" was daily becoming more popular as a campaign cry, and it soon became evident that it must be a determining quantity in the coming election. In spite of the fact that the idea had at first shocked and surprised the people, when they were allowed to look behind the curtain, they soon endured it, and at last embraced it. Every day the danger became more imminent that no candidate could expect Southern sympathy and support who was unwilling to adopt as his own this unjustifiable scheme. It did not appear to the whole North in its worst light, for there was a cry that England had her hand in the mess, and that if the United States was not on the watch the Lone Star would be added to the Union Jack. Such artful and revolting deception was enough to awaken the patriotism of the North, although the truth seems to be that all that England desired was to win Texas for abolition and liberty, — at the same time, however, probably desiring that no other power should profit by annexation.

On the same day in April, 1844, two letters appeared opposing the acquisition of Texas. One was from Clay, who believed that he could reconcile friends and foes.[1] The other was from Van Buren, who entered into a full discussion of the matter from its beginning, and expressed his unqualified dissent from annexation. Clay had not materially injured his chances, for the Whig party was never so strong in the South or so bedridden with slavery as was the Democratic; but from the date of this letter Van Buren's prestige began to decline. Hitherto he had bent the suppliant knee

[1] Coleman's *Crittenden*, p. 218.

to the slavocracy; but here was a breach of discipline not to be tolerated, and a search was begun for a candidate who could be relied on. Jackson had already written a letter in favor of annexation, in which he spoke of the necessity of having Texas for military reasons, and called up the horrors of a servile insurrection which might be engendered by a British army, if the territory did not fall to us. A second letter from Old Hickory, wrung from him by Van Buren's friends, disclosed him clinging to both poles, — true to Van Buren and true to annexation, intimating that his past grand *protégé* had spoken in ignorance, and that all would be right when it came to the pinch.

Cass was ready to throw himself into the breach. He had been urged by friends to embrace his opportunity the moment that Van Buren declared against Texas. A letter written from Detroit, May 10, was decidedly for annexation. It was addressed to Hon. E. A. Hannegan, at Washington. Its publication won for him support from the immediate annexationists. It struck the old key, and the only one which could awaken a sympathetic response in the North. Praising the "intuitive sagacity" of Jackson, and appealing to American fear and jealousy of English ambition, Cass put this question, shrewdly adapted to inspire the patriotism of the North and to excite the South to fury: "What more favorable position could be taken for the occupation of English black troops, and for letting them loose upon our Southern

States than is afforded by Texas?" The end of this letter was worthy of the beginning: "Every day satisfies me more and more that a majority of the American people are in favor of annexation. Were they not, the measure ought not to be effected. But as they are, the sooner it is effected the better. I do not touch the details of the negotiation. That must be left to the responsibility of the government." [1] *Vox populi, vox dei.* Into how many slums and sloughs of wickedness did that absurd Democratic shibboleth summon the country! There was to be no virtue in statesmanship except in clairvoyant reading of the popular will. Obedience was the first and greatest commandment, and a regard for it allowed the politician and self-seeker to pose as a ministering angel obeying the divine voice.

Yet one who studies the career of Cass from the beginning will see elements of earnestness and sincerity in this letter, demagogic as it seems at first. It was another instance of his somewhat absurd yet natural antipathy to England. Moreover, his practice had been from the beginning to respect and cherish the whims and fancies of the people; his admiration for Jackson was not feigned. Had he opposed the annexation of Texas he might have had little chance of nomination in 1844, but his reputation for honesty and independence would be higher with this generation. It is nevertheless not fair to brand a man as a "doughface" because

[1] Niles, vol. lxvi. p. 197.

he happens to be desirous of office and to advocate a plan of action to which thousands around him are attracted. Had he not been a candidate for honors in the Democratic convention, his wish for Texas would not seem strange to any one; it would be entirely consistent with his vigorous American nature, with his broad Western enthusiasm for "bigness" and empire. His later championship of our right to "all Oregon" has never been attributed to demagoguery and insincerity, nor could it be. The longing for territory is much the same, whether the land lies toward the equator or the pole. To call a man a "doughface" and a "Northern man with Southern principles," without attempting to show acts inconsistent with character, training, sectional influence, and previous behavior; to denounce him as a hypocrite without stating more than one fact from which to infer hypocrisy, is a practice more fitted to political harangues than to history. We are just recovering from the habit of talking as if every one who was not an abolitionist or directly in favor of the uprooting of slavery was morally weak, if not spiritually and mentally crooked. This condemns nine out of ten men at the North in the fifth decade of the century. It gives no room even for the play of conservatism, for doubt, for mental inertia, for the feeling so common at the beginning of every great moral movement that the agitator is a senseless fanatic.

After the appearance of Clay's letter, there was

short time for discussion before the Whig convention assembled at Baltimore. Of course Clay was nominated by acclamation; a very whirlwind of applause announced the beginning of a campaign with confidence and enthusiasm. Theodore Frelinghuysen was nominated for vice-president. A ratification meeting, one of the greatest pageants in the history of electioneering pomps, was addressed the next day by the orators of the party. Even Webster, leaving his dalliance with "Tylerism," found his way back into the old ranks, and thundered out his approbation of the work of the convention. There was no long and involved statement of principles. The name of Clay was enough. The convention was content with a short creed: "A tariff for revenue to defray the necessary expenses of the government, and discrimination with special reference to the protection of the domestic labor of the country; the distribution of the proceeds of the sales of public lands; a single term for the presidency; a reform of executive usurpations; and generally such an administration of the affairs of the country as shall impart to every branch of the public service the greatest practicable efficiency, controlled by a well-regulated and wise economy."

Upon the publication of Van Buren's letter opposing annexation, the South looked around cautiously for another candidate on whom it could rely, and when the convention met Van Buren did not receive the full vote of a single slaveholding

State except Missouri. Calhoun had withdrawn. The South had fallen away to Cass and Johnson. Except to those who saw how set the wind, the nomination of Van Buren must have seemed predestined. State conventions in all parts of the Union had instructed their delegates to vote for him, and it was certain that he would have a majority on the first ballot. Mutterings and complaints, ominous of disaffection, were heard in the Southern States, and yet no one could have foreseen that opposition to re-annexation had so undermined him. This convention is an interesting one from more than one point of view. The Northern wing of the Democratic party was clipped and crippled, as it was to be so many times in the future. The South, with definite purpose begotten of common material interest, won its way. This convention marks a differentiation between the Democracy, with its Southern proclivities, and the Whig party, which was hourly drifting farther from such moorings. The Democracy was going over to the South; the Whig party was getting entangled in the skein of "free soil and free men." In spite of the fact that the Van Buren men had a majority of the convention, and indeed because of that fact, a motion was adopted requiring that a vote of two thirds was necessary for a choice, a plan used in two previous conventions. That the motion could be carried amid much argument for its democracy and other absurd falsehoods, proves that delegates instructed to vote for Van

Buren were ready to defeat him and to vote for Cass or any other available Texas candidate. Butler of New York and others argued against the adoption of that rule, which has more than once muzzled a Democratic convention, but it was adopted by a vote of 148 to 118, almost every one of the Southern States voting solidly for the resolution.

The convention met on May 27. The first ballot was taken on the afternoon of Tuesday, giving 151 for Van Buren, 83 for Cass, 24 for Johnson, and scattering votes for other candidates. This showed a clear majority of 31 for Van Buren. Seven ballots were taken in succession. In the second Cass's vote increased to 94, aided especially by votes from the New England States. The seventh gave Van Buren 99, and Cass 123. Every ballot showed the Michigan man steadily gaining, and no other candidate holding his own. But after an ineffectual effort to have the two thirds rule rescinded, the convention adjourned until the next morning. During the night the wire-pullers set their machine in motion. Amid a great deal of confusion and display of ill-temper an eighth vote was taken, in which Cass fell to 114, and James K. Polk of Tennessee received 44. The trap had been sprung. A stampede, that well-known phenomenon of these latter days, was begun. The States swung slowly over to the new man, and before the ninth ballot was finished the convention was in an uproar. States changed their votes from Cass, and Polk was unanimously nominated. Cass had directed the delegates from Michigan to withdraw his name at any time in the interest of harmony. Texas annexation had won the day. The Democratic party, shorn of its manhood, was wooing the infamous policy of Tyler, Calhoun, and slavery extension. George M. Dallas of Pennsylvania was chosen for second place on the ticket, to mollify the protectionists of the home-market State.

Polk was the first "dark horse" of the political race-course. "The nomination was a surprise and a marvel to the country."[1] Benton could find but two small occurrences which might have served as a warning of what was coming. These were well calculated to deceive the people, and the consequence was that the result of the convention bewildered the common voter. "Who the devil is Polk?" was an inquiry constantly made, furnishing the Whigs with unlimited glee. The idea of putting an unknown fledgeling against their peerless Clay seemed ridiculous, and Whig success from the outset was believed to be assured. The convention is an early example of the efficiency of such a tool in the hands of the skillful politician, who has room for his work from the primary caucus up to the final nomination.

Had Cass been nominated, inasmuch as he was pledged for annexation, he would without doubt have been elected, and the canvass would have

[1] Benton's *Thirty Years' View*, vol. ii. p. 594.

been a fair combat with equal weapons; but as Polk was nominated by underhand methods, and against the wishes of the bulk of the party, so the campaign was one of falsehood and intrigue. The Democrats were at first capable only of sad jollity in the presence of the excitement and confidence of the Whigs, but as the months went on this unknown chieftain aroused unexpected enthusiasm, and it became apparent that Polk, with the added cubit of annexation, was not the pigmy which he had been first considered by his supercilious opponents. "Polk, Dallas, and the Tariff of 1842" was a mighty battle-cry. Never has there been anything more shameful in political warfare than the brazen charge in the North that Polk was more friendly to the tariff than was Henry Clay himself. With magnificent effrontery the Whigs were dared to repeal their pet tariff. But Texas, not the tariff, was the question of the campaign, and had Clay been guided to the end by his earlier and better motives, he might have won the day. Texas was destined to be an American State, — its annexation meant more territory for slavery; and it can hardly be claimed that Clay seriously objected because such would have been the result of its acquisition. Nevertheless, had the Whigs been victorious, the Mexican war might have been averted; Texas perhaps might have been secured without a shameless disregard of constitutional law and common national courtesy.

Clay, however, was uneasy. Trustful in his own tact and his knowledge of the popular feelings, his ready pen flowed smoothly on in letter after letter, until at last appeared his famous Alabama letter: "Far from having any personal objection to the annexation of Texas, I should be glad to see it annexed without dishonor, without war, with the common consent of the Union, and upon just and fair terms." The letters, written to win Southern voters, did not win them, but simply weakened his support at the North. For the Liberty party was again in the field, with Birney at its head for the second time, and the "Alabama letter" was an efficient weapon in many of the Northern States. In the North Clay was attacked as a friend to annexation, and in the South as a foe to it. One Whig afterwards wittily remarked that "the only qualification he should ask of a candidate in the future would be that he could neither read nor write."[1] It has been positively asserted recently that Birney's vote was greatly decreased by the "Garland forgery," concocted by the Whig central committee of Michigan;[2] but without doubt Clay's letter added more to the Liberty vote than was lost by any other means. How deeply that shaft struck home is apparent in reading the autobiography of Thurlow Weed, where he exposes the inmost recesses of

[1] Quoted in Schouler's *History of the United States*, vol. iv. p. 478.

[2] *James G. Birney and His Times*, p. 354.

his political soul; he sighs and mourns over that fatal blunder years after it had dealt its destruction. The vote of the Liberty party was greater in New York than the Democratic majority, and if they had united against Polk and annexation, Clay, who represented the better elements of the political life of the time, would have been elected. Birney's home was now in Michigan, and here, too, his party held the balance of power. It was ominous. The free Northwest was becoming imbued with the abolition feeling. Cass's own State was drifting away from pro-slavery Democracy. It will be seen later how his fortunes were influenced by the growth of this sentiment. "The abolitionists deserve to be damned, and they will be," was a usual expression of a common feeling. But only four years later the Whigs of the Northwest were dangerously near the principles of the party so forcibly condemned in 1844.

Cass took an active part in the campaign, not traveling over the whole country to speak for Polk and Texas, but using his influence steadily for the ticket, and not sulking in his tent because of his own failure. A grand Democratic mass meeting at Nashville, where Polk himself was present, was one of the monster meetings so frequent during that summer when men, dropping ordinary pursuits, gave themselves up to the joyful excitement so dear to the politics-loving people of the country. Cass was one of the orators of the occasion, and on his way back to Detroit addressed "immense multitudes" at various places in Ohio and Indiana on the issues of the campaign. All audiences were then "huge concourses" or "immense multitudes," if we are to believe the head-lines of the times; and without doubt the Northwest was alive and interested. Cass returned to Detroit, prophesying that the Northwest would give its suffrages for the Democratic ticket. All but Ohio answered his expectations, and in that State Clay received about 20,000 less votes than Harrison had received four years before. The Northwest, in spite of the fact that it had begun to lean toward free soil, was evidently still clinging to the idol of its youth. If Cass was in favor of annexation so was his section, so were his friends and companions in business and politics. This is not complete justification. A statesman should be a leader, and should create sound public sentiment. But we must remember that a belief in the sacredness of popular clamor was a living faith with the true Democratic statesman of that time; we must remember that Cass was a Western man, and filled with the Western spirit; national grandeur and boldness in action, so much admired by the Western settler, had their charms for him. It is just to take into account atmosphere and environment.

The "dark horse" and his black policy, sped by fraud and political trickery, won the day. The nation seemed hushed and dumbfounded at its own act. There was little rejoicing among the successful, and no glorification; for many had voted for Polk only in reluctant obedience to the party whip. "It is hardly possible at this day," says an observer, "to conceive the distress which pervaded the city of Philadelphia the night following the news, and for many days after. It was as if the firstborn of every family had been stricken down. The city next day was clothed in gloom; thousands of women were weeping, but none exulting."[1] The election of Polk meant the immediate annexation of Texas, war with Mexico, the consequent purchase of California, Nevada, and Arizona; it meant that the golden sands of that western wilderness would be sifted and its quartz crushed, that a magnificent city of American industry and American liberty would stretch itself along the windy heights within the Golden Gate; it meant that American civilization was to penetrate into the nooks and corners of a country which might not have given its blessings to the world for centuries if held by the nerveless hand of Mexico. But one is led to query whether wealth and national grandeur are fairly purchased by dishonor. Even before the great apostle of annexation reached the presidential chair, Tyler and Calhoun had made the last proposition, and only the finishing touches were needed to bring Texas within the fold.

[1] Sargent, *Public Men and Events*, vol. ii. p. 250.

CHAPTER VIII

SENATOR. — CANDIDATE FOR THE PRESIDENCY. — SQUATTER SOVEREIGNTY

On February 4, 1845, Cass was elected to the United States Senate from Michigan, and he was present at the special session in March. He was appointed to the second place on the Committee on Foreign Relations, and during the remainder of his public life was greatly interested in matters of international concern. He at once took a prominent and influential position, and was recognized as one of the leaders of the Senate. His speeches were often too learned and too long to be convincing; his cumbersome sentences were not always enlivening; but when he rose to speak on a subject in which he was much interested he was always impressive. His large figure, his finely shaped head, his firm mouth, and intelligent features bespoke earnestness, thoughtfulness, and intellectual integrity. Through the rest of his life he was the great champion of Americanism and national honor; and though his continual guardianship of our country sometimes caused a laugh at his expense in the few merry days which the Senate enjoyed during these troublous times, his true patriotic fervor and his serious appreciation of our needs and our dangers won respect, while his courteous demeanor and his frank friendliness, which knew not jealousy or envy, endeared him to political foes, and disarmed factious opposition.

The Democratic convention of the preceding campaign had mollified Northern resentment by coupling the "re-occupation" of Oregon with the "re-annexation" of Texas. Care for Oregon had long been a favorite Northwestern policy, and no doubt the proclamation of these unexpected bans by the Democratic party contributed largely to its success in that portion of the country. Cass entered the Senate bent on re-occupation, filled as usual with the aggressive, hastening spirit of his ambitious section. Polk, in his inaugural, had declared the undoubted right of the United States to the whole of Oregon, and now the country rang with another artful alliteration, which was intended to drown all feeble appeals to sense. Russia had receded into the rains of Alaska north of 54° 40′, and America now claimed all the country intervening between the northern boundary of California, then Mexican territory, and the southern line of the Russian possessions. "Fifty-four forty or fight!" was well calculated to tickle the brains of the thoughtless and to arouse the ambition of the West. There has always been an uneasy element in our country preferring the adventure of new settlement to the restriction and comfort of existence in older communities. The rough Northwest was already getting too crowded for these restless spirits. People started in long caravans on their tiresome journey over the dry and dreary plains of the West in search of new homes on the Columbia River, encouraged by the burning hope of the adventurer and by patriotic devotion, fully persuaded of a duty to wrest Oregon, as well as Texas, from the clutch of England.

But Polk was only half-hearted. Texas was made ours, and afterward Oregon seemed not of so much consequence to him. Buchanan, the new secretary of state, offered to accept the line of 49°, which already bounded our possessions as far as the Rocky Mountains. The proposition was immediately rejected by the British minister; and our government, piqued at the refusal of a fair compromise, presented claims to the whole region. Such was the state of affairs when Congress assembled in December, 1845. Although a new member, Cass was not a stranger to national affairs, and the Oregon matter came near to Northwestern feeling and appealed peculiarly to personal prejudices. On December 9 he introduced a resolution on the defenses of the country, and a few days later supported it in an able speech, in which he held up the spectre of war, and insisted that nothing but sensible precautions would avoid armed collision with Great Britain. This was the beginning of the "exciting and at times inflammatory debates on the Oregon question, which lasted, with intervals, for months."[1] In January he

[1] Sargent, *Public Men and Events*, vol. ii. p. 271.

delivered a long and eloquent address on European interference in American affairs, and until the determination of the controversy he was the leader of the "fifty-four forties" in the Senate. His continual reference to an "inevitable" war came to be a source of amusement to the senators; but in the midst of all the heat and anger of a discussion, which almost equaled in acerbity the fiercest debates on the slavery question, Cass never forgot his courtesy or lowered his dignity by personal abuse. The good humor of his intense earnestness is illustrated by the story of his rising to speak with the statement that he was not going to make a war speech nor use the word "inevitable." He had not proceeded far, however, before the use of the familiar word put the Senate into roars of laughter at his expense, in which he joined as heartily as any.[1] It was during these debates that Crittenden castigated Allen of Ohio so severely for his superciliousness and invective, and that Hannegan of Indiana made use of an expression often appropriated since in political screeds: if Polk, he said, had, during election, advocated the occupation of Oregon for mere buncombe and claptrap, he would be doomed "to an infamy so profound, a damnation so deep, that the hand of resurrection will never be able to drag him forth."[2]

It is impossible to go into the whole discussion

[1] Sargent, *Public Men and Events*, vol. ii. p. 273. Newspaper clippings in private papers of Cass.

[2] Benton, vol. ii. p. 665.

of the Oregon question. Such controversies, which find their origin and arguments in the diplomacy of long-past days, or in the uncertainties of discovery and exploration, can be ended by compromise alone, unless the stern hand of war interferes. America had a color of title to the territory as far as the possessions of Russia; but that is about all that can be said of it. Claims were traced back to the early Spanish discoveries on the one hand, and to the voyage of the buccaneer Drake on the other. For Spain by the treaty of 1819 had ceded all her claims to the United States. In spite, therefore, of a number of long orations from Cass, who showed a depth of historical knowledge and a power of arrangement and argument which made him the equal of Webster and of Benton in these debates, the controversy ended in compromise. Seldom does a senator in his first session step forward into leadership; but Cass seemed in a moment to be at home, and was recognized immediately as chief opponent or ally. He was of course struggling to keep himself so before the public that his nomination in 1848 might be certain. His speeches were carefully printed, and a judicious circulation of them kept him prominent as the patriotic champion of American privileges. Although attached to party, he absolutely refused to be identified with the administration on this issue. It was a movement of his own. He could count on the sympathy of the West, at least, and upon the common jealousy of England; and in so far as the Oregon question assumed serious form, or in so far as threats and precautionary preparations for hostility brought England to less arrogant consideration of the case, the credit is largely due to Cass.

England was not pleased at all this. The President, in a special message in March, advised an increase of the army and navy. On the receipt in London of the news that the House had passed a joint resolution to give the one year notice for terminating the joint occupancy of Oregon, stocks fell one per cent. and consols more than two per cent.[1] Both countries, however, soon softened down for amicable settlement. The forty-ninth parallel was taken as the boundary as far west as its intersection with the channel "which separates the continent from Vancouver's Island." Cass and thirteen other extremists voted against ratification in vain. Compromise was sensible; but had it not been for the "bluff" of the "fifty-four forties" a fair bargain would have been reached only with difficulty, if at all. Had every one been as ready to renounce all claims as were Webster and others from the beginning, the outcome would have been doubtful.

Even more serious matters were holding the attention of the President and the country. The annexation of Texas had not driven Mexico to immediate war, but every day made hostilities more certain. Slowly and craftily Polk proceeded

[1] Niles, vol. lxx. p. 65.

to win the coveted prize of California, to bully and to bribe until poor Mexico should satisfy the unjust ambition of a people who boasted of their liberty and enlightenment. The events of Polk's administration show us how slavery had poisoned the whole national system. After failure in secret negotiations, which relied on a craven and abject spirit in the Mexicans, General Taylor was ordered to occupy the territory between the Nueces and the Rio Grande, a portion of Mexico to which Texas had not the slightest claim, except a paper one unsupported by successful adverse occupation. His position threatened Matamoras. An engagement ensued. The President proclaimed that American blood had been spilled on American soil, and Congress declared that war existed by act of Mexico.

The legislation which carried on this war, begun with these specious falsehoods, cannot here be reviewed; but in these Democratic straits Cass came forward once more as the champion of national rights, and was the main stay of the President and his party. The Machiavellian methods of the administration have been fully made known only recently, and we cannot charge that every supporter of the war countenanced the whole procedure, and was *particeps criminis* to the whole extent of the crime. Cass's speech on the Ten Regiment Bill was good campaign powder. Not that his defense of the measure was disingenuous or insincere; for no one can say that when once the war was begun it ought not to have been carried on effectually. The conduct of Cass as a Democrat is open to little criticism at this juncture; and possibly it would not be fair to expect him to see so clearly as those Whigs whose party interests made their very prejudices incline towards the right course, or as the younger men of the North, who were growing restive under the saddle and bridle of slavocratic masters.

Considerable space has been given to Texas and the piratical assault on Mexico because the most prominent fact of the later career of Cass is connected with this acquisition of new territory. On August 8, 1846, a resolution was offered in the House to appropriate $2,000,000 "for the purpose of defraying any extraordinary expenses which may be incurred in the intercourse between the United States and foreign nations." This signified that land was to be acquired from Mexico by purchase, and in the course of the discussion David Wilmot, a representative from Pennsylvania, offered an amendment providing that the fundamental condition to the acquisition of any territory from Mexico should be that slavery should never exist in any portion of it. The bill with the amendment was passed by the House. But in the confusion at the end of the session it was talked to death in the Senate by Senator Davis of Massachusetts, who was effusively defending the proviso when Congress adjourned until the next session. Immediately after the adjournment of the Senate

Cass said that he was sorry that the proviso had been lost. His later acts were inconsistent with the inference drawn from this remark, and great political capital was manufactured in consequence.

At the next session of Congress, 1847, the proviso came up again as a rider to the appropriation by the House of $3,000,000 for the purposes mentioned before. But the Senate would not be thus circumvented, and forced the House to agree to the appropriation, riderless. During the session Cass spoke often on the general proposition of voting money to the government. On March 1, 1847, he came out directly in opposition to the proviso. His reasons were six: 1. The present was not the time to introduce a sectional topic. 2. It would be quite in season to provide for the government of a Territory after it was obtained. 3. Any such proviso expressed too much confidence in the outcome of the war. 4. Legislation at that time would be inoperative, and not binding on succeeding Congresses. 5. The adoption of the proviso might bring the war to an untimely issue. 6. It would prevent the acquisition of a single foot of territory, and thus disappoint a vast majority of the American people. He attempted to show by a course of very hollow reasoning that the Northern legislatures which had passed resolutions deprecating the spread of slavery would not be satisfied by the adoption of the proviso. Vermont, New Hampshire, Rhode Island, New York, New Jersey, Pennsylvania, Ohio, and Michigan had already passed such measures. The Democratic legislature of Cass's own State had advocated the extension of the Ordinance of 1787 over any new territory acquired.

This speech is the beginning of another chapter in the career of Cass. He had been the leader and the prophet of his State and the Northwest. His political life from this time on illustrates Northwestern development from the reverse side. His energetic constituents, breathing the free air of the West, their eyes open to national needs and to the immorality of slavery, however much it might be supported by constitutional props, have now outstripped their leader, and erelong he will be looked upon as the representative of their past beliefs and their bygone acquiescence in a corroding sin. This is the true interpretation of Cass's political life. This is what makes him the best centre from which to study the development of the Northwest as a portion of the nation. The great movement against slavery, it must be remembered, came from new men. The old statesmen, who had grown used to the pollution, were unable to take a stand in opposition; not Webster or Cass, but Seward and Lincoln and Chase put the proper estimate upon the institution. Yet the remarks of Senator Miller, after Cass's objection to the proviso, are worth recording: "He was connected in many honorable ways, in war and in peace, with the history of the Northwest, and he is now one of its brightest ornaments, commanding a position so high and so influential, it was hoped, nay expected by all the free North, that he would on this occasion have given all the talent and influence within his control to extend and secure to other Territories that great ordinance of free labor, the practical advantages of which, social and political, he was so fully aware [of], and no doubt highly appreciated."[1]

As the campaign of 1848 approached, it became apparent that Cass was to be the favorite of the Democratic party. His views on various subjects were in consequence sought with care, and in the course of the catechism he promulgated a doctrine which furnished material for discussion until debate was silenced by the more eloquent bombardment of Sumter. This was the doctrine of popular sovereignty in the Territories. It was first fairly announced by Cass; he first introduced it as an active principle in the political life of the time; he first marshaled arguments in its defense. It will not do to say that he created it. No great thought influencing the career of a free nation is begotten in the brain of a single man, to spring into existence at once endowed with full vigor. Senator Dickinson of New York had already suggested the idea. But Cass took the wandering, tentative suggestions of statesmen and people, and combined them and arranged them in a clear, succinct statement of a great political principle. He first struck the clear note, for which others had

[1] *Congressional Record*, vol. xvii. p. 551.

been unconsciously or furtively feeling. In that sense he was the author of the doctrine of which Stephen A. Douglas afterwards became godfather and fiercest defender. So intimately did the later debates between Douglas and Lincoln associate this theory with the name of the former, that an explicit statement of its true origin is needed here. The "Little Giant," a ready and active debater in years when Cass was beginning to feel the burdens of age, leveled his lance in agile defense of this proposition so often and so valiantly, that to him has been attributed a paternity to which he has no right.

In answer to queries from Mr. A. O. P. Nicholson of Nashville, Tennessee, Cass wrote a letter, December 24, 1847, which was the first embodiment of the doctrine of "squatter sovereignty." The Wilmot proviso, he said, had been long before the people, and he was impressed with the belief that a change had been going on in the public mind, and in his own as well as in the minds of others; doubts were resolving themselves into convictions that the principle involved should be kept out of the national legislature. He went on to argue that the central government did not have the authority to govern the Territories under those provisions of the Constitution which grant "the power to dispose of and make all needful rules and regulations respecting the territory and other property belonging to the United States;" that the lives and possessions of citizens could not be controlled by an authority which was merely "called into existence for the purpose of making rules and regulations for the disposition and management of property." "If the relation of master and servant may be regulated or annihilated . . . so may the relation of husband and wife, of parent and child, and of any other condition which our institutions and the habits of our society recognize." The internal concerns of the Territories ought, he maintained, to be regulated by the people inhabiting them, without molestation or direction from Congress. "They are just as capable of doing so as the people of the States; and they can do so at any rate as soon as their political independence is recognized by their admission into the Union." Even if the central government could interfere with the internal affairs of the Territories, a proposition which he denied, it would be inexpedient to exercise a doubtful and invidious authority that statehood would soon brush away.

The Ordinance of 1787, under which Cass had acted as governor, and which bestows upon the appointees of the central government almost despotic power, did not furnish good material for his arguments. But he succeeded in presenting with great ability his belief that the Territories ought to decide for themselves whether or not slavery should exist within their limits. It was not such an easy task as it might seem at first to prove the unreasonableness of this doctrine. It was afterwards so ably defended as to win the favor of the

Northern Democracy until the outbreak of the war. Nevertheless, the author of a principle which half the North accepted has, without fact or testimony, been charged with selfish insincerity in its inception and advocacy. We can judge of animus and motive only from acts. The rest of the life and conduct of Cass furnish no evidence to sustain the charge of inconsistency or insincerity in the Nicholson letter. While governor he had encouraged popular participation in the affairs of the Territory, had aided and promoted local self-government, had obeyed the wishes of the people without regard to his own official right of appointment, and had yielded other high prerogatives. His Democracy was orthodox, and his practice cannot be shown to have varied from his fundamental theory. His article on the removal of the Indians, published twenty years before this, contains an exact parity of reasoning. Moreover, if in drafting this letter he was hollow and insincere, hoping by dodging an issue to win Southern support without losing Northern favor, the same indictment must be brought against many others in whom the people of Michigan have had the utmost confidence. He was warned by the most influential of his colleagues from his State of the danger of writing letters, but when this letter was shown them before its publication they accepted its principles.[1] From the information I have been able

[1] Conversation with Governor Alpheus Felch, senator from Michigan, 1847.

to obtain by conversation with those who were intimate with General Cass at the time, I have been induced to draw the conclusion that his Nicholson letter was a frank statement of his conscientious belief, not an avoidance of a dreaded issue nor an attempt to devise new interpretations.[1]

Within three years after the appearance of Cass's letter four distinct solutions of the problems arising from the acquisition of new territory were presented and found their advocates: first, the principle of the Wilmot proviso: that slavery should be entirely excluded; second, the doctrine of Calhoun: that slaves were property, and that it was the bounden duty of Congress to protect the rights of the Southerner to his slaves within territory of the United States, just as the law protected property in sheep and oxen; third, that the line of 36° 30′, extended to the Pacific, would be an equitable division; fourth, that the people of the Territories ought to be allowed to decide the question for themselves. This last was nicely calculated to take its skillful way between the two extremes. It is not unreasonable to think that Cass hoped and believed that popular sovereignty would show the advantage of freedom over slavery, and that the Territories would be won naturally for and by free labor. Thus his action is interpreted by men who were his political opponents at the time.[2] In February, 1848, the treaty of

[1] See, also, Judge Cooley's *Michigan*, p. 205.

[2] Private correspondence with the author.

Guadalupe Hidalgo added to the United States a half million of square miles. Whether or not this territory, stretching away from the western boundary of Texas to the Pacific, was to be inundated by the black tide of slavery or consecrated to freedom, was the question which awakened the people of the country; and all the hushing cries of the conservatives, who cried down and frowned down "agitation," could not lull the men of the North to sleep.

Cass received from various quarters recommendations and nominations for the presidency in 1848. His only serious competitor was Buchanan, and when Pennsylvania announced in convention that Cass was her second choice, the people of the country saw that she had practically given way before the popular demands for the Northwestern candidate. But the party was not without its schisms. New York was torn by conflicting factions, separated largely on personal issues. The fond personal attachment for Van Buren, which argues more strongly than words that he was not all a political juggler, held many old stalwarts of the party in faithful adherence to him. His rejection by the convention of 1844 because of his opposition to annexation had won a semi-trustful respect from the haters of slavery who were not of his party, and had kindled an unexpected spark in the hearts of his old friends, who had seen no wrong in human bondage till their chief was repudiated by the slave owners. Silas Wright, a Van Buren Democrat, had accepted the nomination for governor in 1844, and his name was invoked in behalf of Polk and the straight ticket. In spite of this, the "wheelhorses" of the party were not rewarded for their labors; after some offers to give what the Van Buren faction did not want, the spoils were turned over to the other faction by the President, who was thrown into an agony of jealousy when it was asserted that Wright had elected him. Hunger for office, therefore, and disappointment put the disaffected ever more at variance with the orthodox Democrats who supported the administration. The supporters of Wright and Van Buren were sneered at as "Barnburners," a name borrowed from the recent disturbances in Rhode Island, where the defeated Dorrites, it was alleged, had sought revenge by burning the barns of the law-and-order party.[1] Their tampering with anti-slavery suggested that the name was an allusion to an "anti-Radical story of a thick-skulled Dutchman who had burnt his barn to clear it of rats and mice."[2] Marcy's faction, representing the conservative men of the party, who were ready to abide by the pro-slavery acts of the administration, were dubbed "Old Hunkers," the name referring to their "hankering" for office, or perhaps simply to their heavy, plodding conservatism in matters of state policy. As the slavery question came more prominently

[1] *Autobiography of Thurlow Weed*, vol. i. p. 534.
[2] *Whig Almanac*, 1849, p. 11.

before the country, the Barnburners and the Whigs in New York coöperated to discountenance slavery extension, and the two factions of the Democracy became more widely separated. Many, of course, were not so much friends of freedom as foes to those who had disappointed their own fond hopes for their chief; and longings for revenge were at the bottom of many of their aspirations for free soil. Such persons ultimately dropped back into the pro-slavery, non-interference wing of the party, so soon as personal disputes again gave place to vital political principles. A moral reform gets no real life blood from pique.

After the Democratic convention of Syracuse, September, 1847, the warring cliques were so widely separated by questions of policy, as well as by jealousy, that they can scarcely be considered portions of one party. At that time a resolution was offered on the part of the Barnburners, declaring "uncompromising hostility" to the extension of slavery into the Territories then free. The refusal of the convention, which was plainly in the hands of the Hunkers, to accept this caused the secession of their opponents, who thereupon organized for themselves, and prepared to contest the seats of the delegates chosen for the national Democratic convention. The Van Buren men announced the severance of all bonds which would bind them to vote for a presidential candidate who was pledged against the Wilmot proviso. Thus the fall elections of 1847 in New York showed how utterly demoralized the party was in that State; the Whigs elected their ticket by over thirty thousand majority, and unless these grievous wounds could be healed there was little hope for the candidates presented by the Baltimore convention.

But the healing art is quite beyond the intelligence of a popular gathering, and when the national convention met, in May, 1848, it attempted a simple cure by offering to admit both factions to active participation in its proceedings. The committee on credentials first tried to bind both delegations to abide by the decision of the convention. This the Barnburners refused to consent to, and in consequence New York had no further share in the proceedings. Cass was nominated on the fourth ballot. General William O. Butler of Tennessee was presented for vice-president. These nominations were received with satisfaction by the party. Independent newspapers acknowledged the upright character and ability of General Cass, and prophesied his election unless the Whigs should present a man who possessed the popular confidence and respect. Success was, however, far from certain. The Hunkers acquiesced quite readily, and were thus fairly installed as the "regular" Democratic party of New York. But the Barnburners were now more fierce than ever, for the Van Buren men had never forgiven Cass for his candidacy in 1844; and, moreover, he now stood out conspicuously as the opponent of the Wilmot proviso. Those who were Free-

Soilers for personal considerations, as well as those who had conscientious scruples, were held by this nomination in political affinity.

The Baltimore convention handled the slavery question with that masterly caution which was to characterize its action until the Rebellion. The Southern wing must be kept true to its work by statements which were also shrewdly calculated not to turn away Northern adherents. From this time forward the regular programme was to deprecate discussion, and to beseech the people of the North to rest in security on the bosom of the Constitution. A platform of platitudes declared that Congress had no authority to interfere with slavery in the States, — a very safe proposition, — and then condemned all efforts to induce it to interfere with questions of slavery, or to take "incipient steps thereto." Yancey of Alabama offered a resolution so cleverly worded that Benton himself seems to have misunderstood the meaning of its rejection: "The doctrine of non-interference with the rights of property of any portion of this confederation, be it in the States or in the Territories, by any other than the parties interested in them, is the true republican doctrine recognized by this body." This article of faith was rejected by a vote of 246 against 36. The non-interference advocated by Yancey was apparently the absolute "non-interference" of Calhoun. The refusal of the convention to accept the resolution may have come merely from a wish not to publish its sentiments; but, on the other hand, it may have been a tacit declaration of a belief in the right of States and Territories to "interfere" and to settle the question of slavery within their limits, which was the Cass doctrine of popular sovereignty.

Upon receiving the news of his nomination, General Cass wrote a brief letter of acceptance, acquiescing in the platform of the convention. He stated his determination, if elected, not to be a candidate for reëlection, a pledge that seems to have had a certain popularity in those days. He believed that the real difference between the two great parties was the difference between Hamiltonism and Jeffersonism. With a "sacred regard to 'the principles and compromises of the Constitution,'" he earnestly desired their maintenance "in a spirit of moderation and brotherly love so vitally essential to the perpetuity of the Union." He at once resigned his seat in the Senate as inconsistent with his presidential candidacy, and prepared for the active work of the campaign.

The Whig party had no principle it dared to avow. It had been so long toying with its better self that a serious regard for its own high aims seemed lost in the frivolity of the excited hunt for office. At the best the party was moribund; but it was determined now upon one frantic effort for success; for the dragon of Democracy seemed to sit as perpetual guardian of the golden apples of the public patronage. Yet its course for the past few years had been its greatest. Its leaders had constantly objected to the crimes of "Polk the Mendacious;" and had it now dared to utter the thought which arose in it, a new lease of life would have been given to it; nay, more, the very fountain of youth was at its lips, offering a vigor which it had never yet possessed in the vital elixir of a great moral principle. Clay, still at the head of the party, held the deep affection of its members. His many defeats, however, had tempered their admiration with discretion, and though he was hopeful and bright under the lengthening shadows of age, and felt his heart beat as quickly at the prospect of success as it had done twenty years before, even some of his personal friends and devotees searched for some one who would win more votes and appeal to the people with the enthusiasm of novelty. Webster never had any chance for nomination to the presidency, as indeed no New England man of principle and vigor could have. Scott had won his spurs in the war of 1812, and had since that time been kept before the people because of his military position. The Mexican war gave him opportunities to attract attention, but he was from the first overshadowed by Taylor, whose rough energy had caught the popular fancy, ever ready to clothe with heroic ornaments and to endow with heroic spirit the image of its own worshiped self. Such has been the history of the Democratic spirit. Not even Jefferson, who taught and led, became the perfect popular hero; but Jackson, who certainly did not pose above the people to influence or instruct them, became the one real dictator whom the country has had. Taylor, therefore, from the first was sure of strong support in opposition to the other three possible candidates, if he could be brought before the people with adroitness, and could be shown in politics, as well as in war, to be possessed of a rough, hearty devotion to his country's interests. He must, of course, have slight predilections to Whiggery to keep the party in countenance. But the country was for the moment weary of this ceaseless conflict of old party principles, of questions about national banks and internal improvements; the Whigs desired above all to shun any true issue brought up by the war and the new territory; and the candidate who has no gospel to preach is sure of the support of those who would rather talk than listen.

Thurlow Weed takes to himself the credit of first proposing the name of General Taylor. Soon after the battle of Resaca de la Palma, in May, 1846, this cunning prophet, who in the past had often played the Cassandra in Whig councils, met the brother of Zachary Taylor, and after asking him of the general's health and inquiring as to his political "prejudices," remarked quietly, "Your brother is to be our next president." Weed thought it advisable to send the "rough and ready" soldier some suggestions concerning his conduct, and they admirably illustrate the nature of this whole campaign from the Whig standpoint. The general was warned that if he kept "his eyes toward Mexico, closing them and his ears to all that was passing behind him, the presidential question would take care of itself and of him; . . . and that, finally, if General Taylor himself left the question entirely to the people they would certainly elect him." At the start Taylor was probably quite in earnest in his short letter, which said that he had enough on hand in Mexico without paying any attention to presidential prospects. Until the convention he was fairly circumspect and silent. In the beginning surprised at his own prominence and distrusting his own ability, he soon came to look with the eyes of others, and to entertain an ambition which bade fair to make him dangerously restless. But he consistently proclaimed himself a candidate of the whole people rather than a straitened party man, and finally said he would not withdraw even if Clay were nominated, for no nomination, he said, would occasion a change of principles or make him the creature of party prejudices.

The Whig convention assembled in Philadelphia June 7, 1848. An exciting contest followed. While the majority of the party still clung fondly to the idol of their past, the chief engineers of the machine had determined that sentiment must make way for availability. On the first ballot Taylor received 111 votes, Clay 97, Scott 43, Webster 22. On the fourth Taylor had 171 and Scott 63. Clay had but 32 and Webster 13. Millard Fillmore of New York was nominated for vice-president. Such was the result of the convention, which was branded as the "slaughter-house of Whig principles."

There was only one issue before the country, and that was whether or not the new territory of the West was to be given to slavery or dedicated to freedom. But the convention retained its self-possession with regard to this matter as patiently as had its opponent, and was content to push on to the hustings a man who stood for no policy, whose ideas were not known on a single great problem of government, who had no experience in civil life, who had never so much as exercised the right of suffrage, whose knowledge of public men and events was confined to the information he might desultorily gather at a frontier post from the newspapers and periodicals of the day. But there were many members of this assembly who would not be bound by its insolent indifference to the sentiment animating the great mass of the party, especially in New England and the Northwest. In Massachusetts there was a division into "Cotton Whigs" and "Conscience Whigs," and in the Northwest not only did the Liberty party have strength, but the Whigs also in various ways had proclaimed opposition to slavery extension. In the convention, immediately after the announcement that Taylor had received the nomination, a series of declarations were made by delegates from Massachusetts and Ohio which caused the wildest excitement, and showed clearly enough the disorganization of the old party. Allen of Massachusetts pronounced the Whig party disbanded, uttering the prophetic words that "under the providence of God its dissolution may be for the benefit of humanity." Henry Wilson proclaimed that he would not recognize the nomination. "We have nominated a candidate who has said to the nation that he will not be bound by the principles of any party. Sir, I will go home, and, so help me God, I will do all I can to defeat the election of that candidate." Many complained because "free soil and free territory" had yielded to the discipline of the selfish heavily laden South, and because machine politics and chicanery had overborne the real wishes of the people. "That great moral principle," said Campbell of Ohio, "which has fastened itself so firmly on the free Whigs of Ohio, will arouse to action, in all the majesty of her strength, the young giant of the West." How true this was the speaker himself could not have known; the whole gigantic power of the West was to arise in a righteous fury in defense of this great moral idea; caution and old-fashioned regard for order and organization might still keep many within the old lines; but the recreancy of the Whig party to the fondest hopes of the free Northwest must sooner or later occasion the conception of a new and overshadowing party, untrammeled by a past, unburdened by dead issues, pressing forward to the goal of a high calling.

If the two great parties were satisfied to shut their eyes to danger, and to pretend that there was none, simply because they would not see it, such voluntary blindness was intolerable for many whose vision had been touched by the entering light of truth. In the evening after the nomination of Taylor, fifteen of the dissatisfied delegates met to consider plans for the future. A mass convention of the citizens of Ohio in favor of "free territory" had been summoned to meet in Columbus in June, and these fifteen conspirators for liberty decided to use their efforts to persuade this convention to issue a call for a national gathering at Buffalo. The Ohio convention issued such a summons for August 9. About the same time the Barnburners met in Utica. A letter was read from Martin Van Buren, expressing his determination not to accept a nomination, declaring his inability to vote for either Taylor or Cass, and branding the extension of slavery as a "moral curse." In spite of this declaration he was chosen by the convention. Henry Dodge, United States Senator from Wisconsin, was selected as the candidate for vice-president. Van Buren accepted. Dodge concluded to support Cass. In November, 1847, the Liberty party had nominated John P. Hale of New Hampshire for president, but there was definite hope that the action of the Buffalo convention would be ratified. All waited, therefore, with some anxiety for that meeting. Already the Democratic papers were furious because the

"Little Magician" had forgotten his past "greatness," and revealed the truth of the "federal charges" that "Mr. Van Buren's distinguished characteristics are selfishness and a propensity for intrigue."[1] Even if there were no confluence of the different anti-slavery streams, Cass's chances in New York were greatly lessened by the Barnburner discontent, and party hatred of the "renegades" was proportionately increased.

On August 9 there assembled at Buffalo a strange company. The Barnburners, who had been orthodox Democrats, supporters of Jackson and Van Buren in the palmy days of the party, met with delegates of the Liberty party, who not long before had been hated as crazy fanatics; the "Conscience Whigs" of Massachusetts, the free-territory men from Ohio, the disappointed Clay Whigs, who had cursed the supporters of Birney four years before, the "Land Reformers" and "Workingmen of New York," and the advocates of cheap postage, came together as strange bedfellows in the misery of an eventful crisis. This Free-Soil movement has often been denominated a Democratic movement. The enumeration of the elements given above shows us that no old established party name can be applied to it. The party was composed of various elements now united for a common purpose. Some of the men of this convention were to drop back into the old Democratic ranks; others were to be charter mem-

[1] *New York Sun.*

bers of the Republican party. Samuel J. Tilden was there as well as Charles Francis Adams and Salmon P. Chase.

The platform, chiefly the work of Mr. Chase,[1] was a masterpiece, filled with ringing sentences, and charged with enthusiasm. "Congress," it declared in a forcible aphorism, "has no more power to make a slave than to make a king." "Thunders of applause" followed the reading of such clarion-toned sentences as this: "Resolved, that we inscribe on our banner free soil, free speech, free labor, and free men, and under it we will fight on and fight ever, until a triumphant victory shall reward our exertions." The convention from the first seemed impressed with the solemnity of the occasion and the weight of its responsibility. And yet one must confess that there was a very mundane alloy in this heavenly sentiment; for many longed for revenge on Cass and the Hunkers, and were willing to obtain it by shouting for free soil. Van Buren was nominated amid acclamations of enthusiasm. The conscientious Free-Soilers were willing to take the bitter portion in humble hope that good would result. The name of Charles Francis Adams, the son of John Quincy Adams, was placed below that of the old chief of the Albany Regency, the calm and gentle man to whom "the old man eloquent" had once ascribed "fawning servility" and "profound dissimulation and duplicity." How strangely in 1837 would

[1] G. W. Julian, *Political Recollections*, p. 58.

have sounded the war-cry of 1848, "Van Buren and Free Soil — Adams and Liberty."

This Buffalo convention was a prominent event in the life of Cass. The nomination of Van Buren, this combination of dissatisfied Democrats and Liberty men, assured his defeat, unless his party, in spite of its distressed condition in New York, should work with a rare courage and vehemence. But Cass's career is peculiarly connected with the development of the Free-Soil movement from the point of view of principle. He was hailed throughout this campaign as the candidate of the vigorous West. He was rightly called the "Father of the West." "The history of the Western States forms a part of his biography," the "Detroit Free Press" said with truth. But a calm scrutiny of the forces at work in the old Northwest, for which he had done so much, shows that its vigor was no longer his. Its strong and characteristic sections, which had formed its very pith and marrow, were no longer in sympathy with their great leader and representative. Already the Western Reserve had shown its parentage by sending Giddings to Congress to labor by the side of Adams. The Puritan stock of Ohio, awakened to the existence of a new crusade for liberty, brought forward its hard sense, sound morality, and obstinate adherence to principle. "Beware! the blood of the Roundheads is aroused," shouted a delegate in the Buffalo Convention. This is not mere metaphor, it is sober statement of fact. The counties of the Northwest first settled by New Englanders furnished early supporters of the Liberty party, active advocates of free soil. There the Republican party had its strength in the days of its youth, when all the vigor of its new life was given to assailing the aggressions of a national sin. Political affiliations are not soon forgotten, and to-day Republican strength lies in this old robust region of Ohio. A political party could gerrymander the State successfully if its managers were acquainted with the genealogy of its counties. The New Connecticut has given us Giddings and Garfield. It has given us many pathfinders in unexplored regions of culture, education, and liberal citizenship. We must not omit, however, the influence of that milder Puritan of mysticism, the Quaker; his kind and gentle influence is traceable through the Northwest. The inhabitants of Pennsylvania pushed their way westward through the middle of Ohio across the Indiana line.

Speaking generally, the New England township system has most effectually made its way westward along the parallels of latitude. Michigan and Wisconsin adopted the township nearly in its primitive simplicity. There was the same tendency in northern Ohio; and wherever we see the self-governing spirit of New England, there we see in the field of national affairs a relationship with the politics of the same stalwart section. The early settlers of Michigan were in a marked degree from Massachusetts or from New York, to which latter State many of them had moved from homes east of the Hudson. The political and educational history of Michigan has its individuality, but the influence of inherited tendencies is apparent. Of course in early days the popular creed of Jacksonian Democracy made itself felt among the people of a new country. But it is fair to assume that Michigan would have swung into the Whig column much sooner if it had not been for the personal admiration and respect which its people felt for Lewis Cass.

An examination of the vote of Ohio in 1844 will exhibit the truth of these general statements. There were seventy-nine counties in Ohio in 1844, but Trumbull County alone, the heart of this western New England, gave one eleventh of all the votes cast for the Liberty ticket in Ohio. Five counties of this same region, containing one eleventh of the total vote of the State, gave more than one fourth of the Liberty vote. And if one examines more closely he will see even more definite proof of the assertion. The Whigs, of course, had their strength largely in the districts where the Liberty and Free-Soil movement manifested itself. In 1848 the twentieth Congressional district, including the counties of Ashtabula, Cuyahoga, Geauga, and Lake, cast 7338 Free-Soil votes, only 700 less than the whole Liberty vote of Ohio in 1844. That district gave Van Buren three fourths as many votes as were received by both Cass and Taylor. In this election the Free-Soilers held the balance of power in the State, casting 35,354 votes; but of these nearly one half were cast by the three districts of the Western Reserve, although there were twenty-one districts in the State.

But northeastern Ohio, the peculiar centre of western New Englandism, has not simply followed and reproduced. Modern Puritanism and the spirit of the latter-day Ironsides have here deeply cut their lines. The saying is not uncommon that the Western Reserve is more New England than New England herself.[1] Here the Yankee character developed under new and inspiring conditions, and furnished brain and conscience, sincerity and moral enthusiasm to the whole country. Its earlier inhabitants were, it is true, rough in their manners and "stupid" in religion;[2] most of its first settlers perhaps hurried to the West to escape the iron-clad theology and the stilted social régime of old,. dogmatic, straight-laced Connecticut, and there in the freer air of a new country, unburdened by prescription, there grew a more liberal theology, a more generous citizenship, and a more human idea of liberty. Slipping their old cables, these thoughtful people drifted off occasionally into "isms" and fanaticisms. But this was the natural revolt from a sad theology and acrid Federalism, and with this personal freedom of thought was a

[1] *The Old Northwest*, Hinsdale, p. 388.
[2] Robbins's *Diary*, p. 225.

sound Puritan principle and a guiding common sense. President Storrs of Western Reserve College preached anti-slavery doctrines as early as 1832,[1] and planted the humanizing seed in youthful minds of northeastern Ohio. The result was that the Western Reserve had a definitely formulated anti-slavery sentiment before any other section of the country. John Quincy Adams led his district and showed it the way. But Giddings was the child of his surroundings, the voice and expression of the will of his constituents.

Ohio has been taken to illustrate the energy of New England in the West, because, the early settlers coming into the State within well-known geographical lines, their influence is easily traceable and capable of definite description and comparison. The compact New Englandism of the Western Reserve has made itself conspicuous, but the same general statements of tendencies and influences will hold true of the whole Northwest. When once Michigan was aroused to a sense of the real state of things she too fell in beside Ohio, and has remained her political sister.

Cass was admired and respected by his State. Even those who disagreed with him in politics found it hard to oppose him at the polls. Upon the appearance of the Nicholson letter, many of his old admirers felt constrained to turn against him. Yet they still had faith in him as a man. "From the time of the publication of this letter," writes

[1] *The Old Northwest*, Hinsdale, p. 392.

one of his friendly enemies, who used every effort to defeat him, "I opposed the election of General Cass to the presidency, though it cost me a pang as keen as to have set myself against my own father."[1] It was believed by those who knew the liberal character of the general that he thought his theory of "popular sovereignty" would assure in the end free Territories. And so it would, if the slave power had allowed a fair application of it, and not simply used it until it was no longer serviceable. The consistency of Cass was unquestioned by all who knew his previous career; his sterling character, his honesty, his uprightness in political affairs, the purity and charm of his private life were admired by all who were not blinded by party animosity. So in spite of differences and these Free-Soil antipathies, in spite of the most malignant attacks upon Cass by the Whig newspaper of his own city, which denied him credit even for his masterly governorship, Cass carried Michigan by a good plurality. Yet Van Buren received over 10,000 votes,—more than Cass's majority over Taylor. Cass also received the support of Ohio, a rare tribute to the personal admiration and respect for the man. He received 16,415 votes more than Taylor, whereas Clay had defeated Polk by 5940. The Northwestern candidate received the electoral vote of every Northwestern State, but in each one the Whigs and the Free-Soilers together outnumbered the Democrats.

[1] Private and confidential letter to the author.

Even young Wisconsin gave 10,418 votes for Van Buren, more than one fourth of the total vote of the State. A prophet was not needed to trace the future political development of the Northwest.

Cass was bitterly attacked in some portions of the country, particularly in his own section, because he had not accepted an invitation to attend a convention at Chicago, called to discuss the subject of internal improvements. The New West needed the aid of the general government in developing its resources, especially in opening its harbors for commerce. The Democrats, never lenient toward such hopes, had recently been charged with "salt-water" interpretation of the Constitution, and the residents on the fresh water of the Great Lakes wanted a recognition of their claims. Cass always disclaimed hostility to national improvements, and afterwards, in a speech in the Senate in 1851, proved that his course had been in favor of such assistance from the government. But he was now running on a platform which denied the constitutionality of a general improvement system, and the severe and continuous attacks upon him in the Whig papers on this ground probably reduced his vote to some extent.

The slavery question was, however, the prominent if not the determining factor of the campaign of 1848. Taylor was a Southern man, a plantation owner and a slave owner. The South felt that it could trust him, that a Southern man with Southern interests was preferable to a Northern man, however Southern might be his principles. A mass Democratic convention of the citizens of Charleston selected Taylor as their candidate. The "Richmond Times" said that he was "thoroughly identified with the South in feeling and interest." He was represented in Alabama as one who loved "the South and her cherished institutions;" and so, while the Free-Soilers were designating Cass and Taylor as "the Devil and Beelzebub," and the Northern man was being castigated in the North for his apostasy to slavery, he was marked by Southern Democrats as an unsafe candidate because he was not, as Taylor was, a slaveholder. Polk carried Georgia in 1844. Cass lost it. The same is true of Louisiana. Everywhere south of Mason and Dixon's line the Democracy lost ground. Yet the Democratic support of Van Buren in New York was decisive. This cannot be attributed to anti-slavery sentiment. The Barnburners, fighting for political existence and revenge, and aided by opponents of slavery, polled more votes than the "regular" faction. This fact proves that personal pique was the great motive in that State of politicians.

CHAPTER IX

SENATOR. — THE COMPROMISE OF 1850

THE Buffalo convention and the evident uneasiness of the North had perhaps influenced Congress, as it droned along far into the summer of 1848. A territorial government was given to Oregon, by an act approved August 14, which extended over that territory the Ordinance of 1787 with its "restrictions and prohibitions." But in the meantime new complications had arisen, for California was even more in need of organization and government than Oregon had been a year before. Although it was known when California was acquired that gold had been found there by the Mexicans, the idea of a New Eldorado did not immediately take hold of the people. An accidental discovery by workmen of the yellow grains of gold in January, 1848, soon set the country afire, and a perfect exodus from the East began in the early summer. Business men and school-teachers, lawyers and clergymen, forsook their callings to hasten to the gold fields; the restless and unemployed class of every community begged or borrowed money for the journey. The young men especially were overcome with anxiety to make a fortune in a moment, and quickly broke all ties which bound them to the humdrum life of the plodding East. The "New York Tribune" estimated that 8098 persons had set sail for California between December 7, 1848, and February 8, 1849. The very crews of the vessels deserted to dig for gold when once they had reached the fabled coast. "Nothing, sir," wrote Commodore Jones from Monterey, "can exceed the deplorable state of things in all Upper California at this time, growing out of the maddening effects of the gold mania."[1] He described the country as in a very "whirlwind of anarchy and confusion confounded," where life and property were everywhere in great jeopardy.

When Congress met, in December, 1848, it had to face a stormy and unsatisfactory session. None of the real problems before the country had been solved. On the contrary, there were feelings of greater bitterness than ever. All were uncertain about the meaning of the election, except that it had disclosed great opposition in the North to the extension of slavery and an unexpected defection from the ranks of the old parties. No one knew where the President-elect would stand on the momentous issues which were agitating the country. Had Cass been elected, every one would have known his position, his belief in the absolute unconstitutionality of excluding slavery from the Territories by act of Congress. Yet even an admirer of him, with confidence in his sincerity, his up-

[1] October, 1848. Niles, vol. lxxv. p. 113.

rightness and honor, would hesitate to assert that under such circumstances his election would have been for the best interests of the country. Possibly the election of Taylor showed much more clearly than anything else could have done the utter futility of the Whig organization and the folly of dodging principles. The only thing that the Whigs gained by the election was a redistribution of the spoils. Inwardly, the party knew not itself. One of its greatest men, William H. Seward, who, faithful to his party, was faithful also to freedom and free territory, who had shown many times before his readiness to withstand the slave power with boldness, was to take his place in the Senate on the same day that a slaveholder, a member of the same party, took the oath as president. Under such circumstances it was impossible to foretell the future, or to see even so far as to the end of this thirtieth Congress. In Ohio politics were in such a condition that Chase, the author of the Buffalo platform, was during the winter elected to the Senate. He had been a Democrat, and perhaps never entirely freed himself from the fundamental ideas of the Democracy, but his clear vision led him away from the fold of the old party, and his election was an era in the progress of Free-Soil ideas in the free Northwest.

Measures were at once introduced into the House which tested its sentiment and disclosed unusual harmony among Northern members. From this time the part which the Democracy had played since 1844 began to react against it. Contrary to its inherited belief that such issues were not proper material for political discussion, it had allowed the slavery question to become an active political principle. By its energetic advocacy Texas and the vast territory to the west had been acquired, and now the Nemesis was upon it. The party must either divide into two opposing wings incapable of working together, or the Northern wing must make itself subservient to the interests of the slaveholders. To such action we can trace its ultimate loss of power in the agricultural States of the North, which by all the traditions of the past were the natural allies of the planting South. For the free Northern farmer, whatever might be his economic interests, was unable to remain in a party which was devoted to slave labor.

President Polk, in his annual message, called the attention of Congress to the anomalous condition of New Mexico and California, and advised that they be given territorial governments at once, and that the Missouri line be extended to the Pacific. But it was not easy to do anything in this short session, and it wore away to its close without any decision of the great question.

Although Cass had shown, on the whole, remarkable strength in the Northwest and had carried every State in the election, there was considerable dissatisfaction in Michigan with the principles for which he stood, and there was strong evidence that the anti-slavery sentiment had obtained a hold upon many members of his own party. When the legislature assembled in January, 1849, it was apparent that he was to have difficulty in securing reëlection to the Senate. Resolutions favoring the Wilmot proviso and instructing senators to vote for it were passed by both Houses by substantial majorities, and it did not seem possible that he could win the requisite support. But he was still the leader of his party and had great personal influence, while party discipline could be relied upon to overcome a portion of the opposition and to force some of the wavering members into line. On January 23 he was reëlected by a vote of 44 to 38. Plainly enough Cass no longer represented as he had done the growing sentiment of the Northwest. The day of defeat might be postponed by dint of energy and party management, and if for any reason a conservative spirit gained ground, he as its conspicuous exponent would gain new support; but in the end the controlling sympathy of Michigan was sure to be with the principle of Free Soil, and the growth of this sentiment meant his ultimate overthrow.[1] Cass

[1] Mr. T. C. Smith, in discussing the condition of the Free Soil party in 1849–50, points out the fact mentioned in the text at various times, viz., that the personal influence of Cass was very marked in Michigan, doubtless retarding the growth or at least delaying the full expression of the anti-slavery sentiment. "In Michigan," says Mr. Smith, "the one great difference at the outset was that the State, unlike its neighbors, was in the hands of a 'boss.' Lewis Cass, though an honest, able man, was a thorough politician and partisan, and kept a controlling hand over every

presented his credentials and was sworn in on March 3. He was a member of the Senate during the famous debate on the appropriation bill, which lasted well on into the morning of the 4th. But he refused to take any part in the discussion, on the ground that the Senate was adjourned by lapse of time at midnight between the 3d and 4th.

Taylor took the oath of office on Monday, the 5th of March. His cabinet did not stand for a distinct principle; it contained four Southern representatives, one of whom was an avowed pro-slavery man, and three Northern men, of whom one had an anti-slavery record. The President himself was unquestionably determined to do what seemed to him right, and he proved himself singularly fair and candid. That the South should be robbed of its property seemed to him wrong; on the other hand, he could see no justice in the demand that the western territories should be admitted with slavery, if the people themselves did not want it. He was able to make the non-interference rule work both ways. The South was furious. The idea that the domain for which it had plotted and fought was to be lost to slavery, after all, was simply maddening. California, however, was in need of some government at once. The existing military rule was inappropriate and inadequate, and it seemed unjust that the people should be

movement of his party in the State." Smith, *The Liberty and Free Soil Parties in the Northwest*, p. 198. (N. Y. 1898.) This judgment confirms the result of my own studies.

left in anarchy till Congress could come to some conclusion on slavery, a question which little troubled the average gold-hunter of the Pacific slope. The President was ready to protect the people if they took steps to organize a state government.

The people of California now gave a remarkable example of the wonderful institutional instinct of the Anglo-Saxon. Of their own accord they adopted a constitution, October, 1849, established a government, and applied for admittance to the Union as a State, without having passed through the stage of territorial pupilage. This step was entirely in accord with the wishes of President Taylor, who had already sent an agent to suggest this very move, which was begun, however, before he arrived. A clause prohibiting slavery was adopted unanimously in the convention, and the constitution was ratified by the people with only 811 dissenting votes. This was a severe blow to the South. It brought the slaveholders face to face with the weakness of their peculiar institution; they saw the need of the artificial aid of the national government if slavery was to maintain itself against the power of free labor and the mighty energy of the North. Hence came the bitter vehemence of despair and the instinctive fierceness of a struggle for self-preservation. From this time forward the thought of dissolution of the Union gradually grew into a confirmed belief of its necessity, and continually became more familiar to the Southern people.

In January, 1849, the legislature of Michigan passed a joint resolution concerning the extension of slavery to the new Territories. It repudiated squatter sovereignty, and asserted that Congress had the power, and that it was its duty, to prohibit by enactment the introduction of slavery into the West. The senators were "instructed" and the representatives requested to use their efforts to accomplish such an object. Cass was elected to the Senate but a few days after these resolutions were approved, and he therefore began his second term with the knowledge on both sides that his own beliefs on the great question were different from those of a majority of the legislature and of his constituents. His election under these circumstances shows that he was still trusted, even if he did hold disagreeable theories concerning slavery. Strong opposition to him had appeared in the nomination by the separate houses; and in the joint election the vote was close. The first ballot, which actually tested his strength, gave him 44 votes and to all others 38. This indicated quite a change in feeling when compared with the action of the legislature in 1845, when the opposition was scarcely worthy of consideration. To vote against General Cass was a severe trial to some of his old friends, who loved him personally and admired him as a statesman; but Michigan was on the high road to its later Republican beliefs, and in reëlecting its trusted leader it was simply postponing the day of separation from him.

Some hoped that the resolution of the legislature would be binding on him; others expected that the difficulty would blow over, and that Cass would thus avoid without disobeying the instructions. How clear and firm his opinions were, however, is illustrated by his correspondence during the following autumn. In November he received a letter from prominent Democrats of New York, among them Daniel E. Sickles and Charles O'Conor, asking him to name a day for a public dinner in his honor. "Even amid the fierce contests of party," they said, "all men have awarded to you the praise and admiration due to one who has so highly distinguished himself as the father of the West, a soldier in war, a statesman in peace, an eloquent advocate and defender of the honor of his country both in councils at home and in her representation abroad; and therefore you cannot be surprised to learn that the Democracy of this city, whose leader and champion you are, regard you with an affection almost filial." He declined the invitation in a vigorous letter, in which he discussed at some length the topics of the day. His strong Western spirit plainly forms part of his robust nature still; and though growing out of harmony with his section in some particulars, he has not lost his sense of its desires or tendencies. "An emigrant to the West in early youth, the better portion of my life has been passed in that great contest with nature in which the forest has given way and an empire has arisen, already among the most magnificent creations of human industry and enterprise. Placed in a geographical position to exert a powerful influence upon the duration of the confederacy of republics, attached to the Union, and to the whole Union, and attached equally to the principles of freedom, and to the Constitution by which these are guarded and secured, should the time ever come,—as I trust it will not,—and come whence and why it may, when dissolution shall find advocates, and the hand of violence shall attempt to sever the bond that holds us together, the West will rise up as one man to stay a deed so fatal to the cause of liberty here and throughout the world,—aye, and it will be stayed. Success can never hallow the effort." He clearly foresaw the meaning of the coming contest, and appreciated the loyal Union spirit of his constituents. This statement comes from the leader of the Democratic party who has been accused of weak-kneed subserviency to the South,—from the leader of a party whose Northern members ten years later too often decried "a Union founded on force." This is one of the first frank announcements from a Democratic politician of the North that peaceful dissolution is impossible,—aye more, that dissolution can and will be prevented. Such gift of prophecy lay in his sympathetic appreciation of popular feeling, in his clear perception of actual facts.

The thirty-first Congress was very able, and one of the most famous in our history. The session lasted nearly ten months, dragging its weary length through the summer of 1850. Nearly the whole of the first month was consumed by the House in an endeavor to elect a speaker, a difficult task, inasmuch as the balance of power was held by the "immortal nine," dogged opponents of slavery. But the territorial contest, once fairly begun, continued with unflagging energy for months. The President's message told of the action of California, recommended its admittance should its "constitution be conformable to the Constitution of the United States," and advised Congress to abstain from the discussion of "those exciting topics which have hitherto produced painful impressions on the public mind." So mild an exhortation to temperance sounded almost ludicrous in the midst of the intense excitement.

On December 27 Foote of Mississippi offered a resolution that it was the duty of Congress to establish suitable territorial governments for California, Deseret (Utah), and New Mexico. Cass spoke on this resolution January 21 and 22. He desired to make a complete exposition of his views, and, if possible, to influence his own State; for he felt that if the legislature persisted in its instructions he must resign. He spoke for the greater portion of two days with great clearness and force, and this speech stands to-day the most complete defense of the doctrine of "squatter sovereignty" that has ever been given. He argued that the people of the Territories were capable of governing themselves, and that the exercise of powers of government by Congress would be an act of unwarranted tyranny, contrary to the great principles of American liberty. Moreover there was, he contended, no clause in the Constitution which gives to Congress express power to pass any law respecting slavery in the Territories. Such power was not contained in the clause which gave Congress power to make "all needful rules and regulations respecting the territory or other property belonging to the United States," for that was a power over property and not persons; a misconception had arisen because of a confusion between "territory" and "Territory," which latter was not land, but a political community organized as a territorial government. This proposition he discussed at length, and with great keenness. He then denied that the authority of Congress could be deduced from the war or treaty-making power; for that would not account for congressional control over territory not acquired by war or treaty, and no agreement with the individual States could enlarge the competence of Congress under the Constitution. The right to admit new States was equally ineffectual; the reasoning on this clause was simply analogical, and not convincing; though the Territories might be likened to boys in pupilage, the analogy was not perfect, nor could such suppositions bestow authority upon a body possessed of enumerated powers. The right to sell, the right of ownership, and the right or duty of settlement were equally insufficient privileges from which to deduce a right to govern persons; for every implied power ought to bear a fair relation to the specific one. The right of sovereignty, the nature of government, nationality, and the principles of agency and trust had all been summoned to do battle in opposition to "squatter sovereignty;" but these principles overlooked the character of the Constitution itself, and lost sight of the doctrines of that "noble state paper," the Virginia Resolutions of 1799.

Other more technical reasons for claiming that this power was inherent in Congress he brought up and combated. The right of self-government by the people of the Territories was given by no earthly potentate or people. "They got it from Almighty God; from the same omnipotent and beneficent Being who gave us our rights, and who gave to our fathers the power and the will to assert and maintain them." He ended by asking those who could think that there was any constitutional basis for the Wilmot proviso to consider the circumstances of the times and the inexpediency of the measure. His closing sentences were as follows: "I will endeavor to discharge my duty, as an American senator, to the country and to the whole country, agreeably to the convictions of my own duty and of the obligations of the Constitution, and when I cannot do this I shall cease to have any duty here to perform. My sentiments upon the Wilmot proviso are now before the Senate, and will soon be before my constituents and the country. I am precluded from voting in conformity with them. I have been instructed by the legislature of Michigan to vote in favor of this measure. I am a believer in the right of instruction when fairly exercised, and under proper circumstances. There are limitations upon this exercise; but I need not seek to ascertain their extent or application, for they do not concern my present position. I acknowledge the obligation of the instructions I have received, and cannot act in opposition to them. Nor can I act in opposition to my own convictions of the true meaning of the Constitution. When the time comes, and I am required to vote upon this measure as a practical one, in a bill providing for a territorial government, I shall know how to reconcile my duty to the legislature with my duty to myself, by surrendering a trust I can no longer fulfill."[1]

The modern student, thinking calmly on these great questions, soon finds common sense a sufficient rebuttal of "squatter sovereignty." If the Constitution is to be strictly construed, then Congress has no power to acquire territory. But if such a power is admitted, government is essential to complete acquisition, and follows as a natural consequent upon the very heels of possession, if it is not actually a part of it. Such authority has been exercised by the national government from the beginning of its history. It throws a strong

[1] *Appendix to the Congressional Globe*, vol. xxii. pt. 1, p. 74.

light on the confusion of the times that such self-evident propositions were rejected by a large portion of the people, and that "squatter sovereignty" was accepted as logically sound and conclusive; but we must remember that the Rebellion has cleared the air for us, and we now see plainly what was befogged forty years ago.

On January 29 Clay introduced a series of eight resolutions, the intent of which was to compromise the conflicting claims of North and South. The first proposed the admission of California without any restriction by Congress; the second, that, inasmuch as slavery was not likely to exist in any of the Territories obtained from Mexico, governments ought to be established there without restriction or condition on the subject of slavery; the third, that the boundary between Texas and New Mexico should be agreed upon; the fourth, that Texas be paid a sum of money in consideration of giving up in large part her claims to land in New Mexico; the fifth, that the abolition of slavery in the District of Columbia under present circumstances was inexpedient; the sixth, that it was expedient to prevent the slave trade in the District of Columbia; the seventh, that a more effectual fugitive slave law ought to be passed; the eighth, that Congress had no power to prohibit the slave trade between slave States. Clay begged the senators to refrain from discussing this measure until they had taken time to consider it; but debate immediately ensued, and continued for months. Cass was on his feet often during these debates, a steady and consistent advocate for putting an end to an unnecessary agitation. In addition to his arguments on unconstitutionality, he insisted that the law of nature had banished slavery forever from California, and that the proviso discussion was one of selfish sentiment.

The presentation of a petition by Senator Hale of New Hampshire for the peaceable dissolution of the Union called forth (February 12) an eloquent and forcible address from Cass. "To dissolve this Union peaceably!" he exclaimed. "He who believes that such a government as this, with its traditions, its institutions, its promises of the past, its performances of the present, and its hopes of the future, living in the heart's core of almost every American, can be broken up without bloodshed, has read human nature and human history to little purpose." February 20 he frankly outlined his course in regard to the proviso. He confessed his inconsistency. The "retailing of conversations in railroad cars" was not needed to prove that at first he was ready to vote for the measure. A calm investigation and unimpassioned consideration of expediency had led him to change his mind. With unusual vehemence he repelled the insinuation that he was a "doughface" because he was not ready to "cover the country with blood and conflagration to abolish slavery." On the conclusion of his speech Clay thanked him, and agreed with him that the country was in danger because of "ultraism," which made calm discussion an impossibility. No one can read these fervid speeches without being convinced of Cass's thorough sincerity and intense moral earnestness. He believed slavery was a misfortune to the South; yet that only the passing ages could bring about emancipation without the destruction of both races; but that "God in his providence" might bring it about. Only one who is intent upon finding chicanery and low ambition in this period of his life will fail to sympathize with his intense, however mistaken, eagerness for compromise.

Webster's famous 7th of March speech, in which he deplored unnecessary agitation, advocated compromise, and lamented sentiment, had direct effect at the North. It was itself the expression of reaction and conservatism. It aided the growing desire to settle the question and to restore harmony, and seems to have influenced the legislature of Michigan to reconsider its instructions and requests to the congressmen of the State.[1] April 11 Cass exultingly read to the Senate resolutions freeing him from any obligation to vote contrary to his judgment, and heartily approving the patriotic stand taken by those who had "united their efforts to preserve the Union one and indivisible."

This was a session of great speeches. On March 4 Calhoun's views were read to the Senate by a fellow-senator. He himself was too weak to speak.

[1] Private correspondence between the author and a member of the legislature at that time.

The old nullifier was dying. But his last energies were devoted to the South and to slavery, to a cause that was doomed and to a system that had cast its blight on the State which he had loved so well and served so faithfully. His argument was simple — equilibrium must be maintained; the encroachments of the North must be prevented; only by a zealous care for Southern interests, by a maintenance of political equality, could harmony be secured and the Southern States remain in the Union consistently with their honor and safety. "The cry of 'Union, Union, the glorious Union!' can no more prevent disunion than the cry of 'Health, health, glorious health!' on the part of a physician can save a patient lying dangerously ill." The South, he said, must be protected by some constitutional provision, which there would be no difficulty in devising. He referred, doubtless, to his plan of electing two presidents, one from each section, who should protect their respective interests, a plan he had already worked out in his "Discourse on the Constitution and Government of the United States."

As Webster's 7th of March speech expressed the longing for peace and the growing weariness at the North of the endless discussion, and was a manifestation of conservatism and reaction, so on the other hand Seward's and Chase's words declared the unwavering zeal of the earnest and serious, who were content with no temporizing compromise, and demanded principles in accord with the "higher law." Seward's speech was one of the greatest in the annals of American oratory; he saw so clearly, he felt so keenly, he argued so calmly and logically. "I feel assured that slavery must give way, and will give way, to the salutary instructions of economy, and to the ripening influences of humanity; that emancipation is inevitable, and is near; that it may be hastened or hindered; and that, whether it be peaceful or violent, depends on the question whether it be hastened or hindered; . . . that all measures which fortify slavery, or extend it, tend to the consummation of violence; . . . all that check its extension and abate its strength tend to its peaceful extirpation." Webster and Clay and Cass saw through the glass of past prejudices but darkly. Seward and Chase read the present and the future face to face. Cass in an elaborate address on March 13 and 14 sharply rebuked Seward for accepting office under a Constitution which recognized the necessity of an "immoral" fugitive slave law, and criticised the "equilibrium" propositions of Calhoun.

There was great disagreement concerning the various proposals of Clay's compromise measure. One objected to one clause and another to another clause, and finally the whole subject was on April 13 referred to a select committee of thirteen, of which Clay was chairman, and Cass was a member. On May 8 this committee reported, and recommended three bills. The first provided for three distinct objects: the immediate admittance of California, the establishment of territorial governments for New Mexico and Utah, with the stipulation that the territorial legislature should pass no law with reference to slavery, the settlement of the boundary of Texas, and the payment to that State of a sum of money, as a recompense for her giving up her claim to part of New Mexico. The second bill provided for the return of fugitive slaves; the third for the discontinuance of the slave trade in the District of Columbia. This report had been agreed upon by the committee after long discussions and debates. Its reception by the Senate was not flattering. Some of the radical Southern members demanded that California should not be admitted. Others from the North, on the other hand, asserted that the admission of California should not be made conditional upon the formation of territorial governments, and desired that the principle of the Wilmot proviso should be applied to the Territories. It seemed absolutely impossible to harmonize differences. The debate went on day after day with mechanical regularity, but with unfailing vehemence and bitterness. Cass was continually on his feet, the able and persistent ally of Clay and a champion of the compromise.

President Taylor had been drawn into obstinate opposition to the committee's plans, partly because his loyal heart was stirred to resentment by the treasonable threats of the South, and partly because he had from the first been in favor of admitting California with her constitution as adopted. On July 9 he died. Presidential duties had worried and annoyed him, and had told severely upon him. His last words tell the tale of an unpretentious life, whose late ambition had not brought peace or happiness: "I have always done my duty; I am ready to die; my only regret is for the friends I leave behind me." Fillmore became president, and the weight of executive influence was thrown in favor of the compromise measure.

On June 11 and August 12 the doctrine of non-interference, of the absolute and divine right of the people of the Territories to govern themselves, was ably discussed and defended by Cass. He fondly believed that the compromise would still the raging tempest. "There can be no Wilmot proviso, and no one proposes to interfere with the claims of Texas. Then why not terminate this whole controversy, and thus banish its remembrances from our councils and country. . . . That done, we should enter again upon a glorious career, with none to trouble us or to make us *afraid.* God grant that the denunciation contained in the command to the prophet may not already have gone out against us. Say ye not a confederacy, to all them to whom this people shall say a confederacy; neither fear ye their fear, nor be afraid."

He was winning his State to a temporary faith in his beliefs. A Democratic convention of Michigan in June passed resolutions in favor of the compromise, and eulogized the "patriotic efforts" of General Cass. "Placing himself in the breach, and stemming a current of popular prejudice and fanaticism as relentless and proscriptive in its character as it is sectional and destructive in its objects, he has achieved a moral triumph no less creditable to himself than it is salutary in its results upon the permanency of our republican form of government." The convention also advocated congressional non-intervention as the only sound basis for the Democratic party.

The different provisions of the compromise bill were finally passed piecemeal. Territorial governments were given to Utah and to New Mexico. California was admitted. Texas was given $10,000,000 in lieu of all title to land organized as part of New Mexico. The slave trade in the District of Columbia was abolished. An infamous fugitive slave law was passed, providing for summary proceedings and a shameful disregard for the rights of free blacks. Undoubtedly the country breathed more easily when the compromise was adopted, and many deceived themselves into believing that strife was forever stifled. But the act contained the seeds of its own destruction. Slave-hunting in the North began at once, and in earnest. Greeley[1] estimated that within the first year of the existence of these new regulations more persons were seized as fugitive slaves than during the preceding sixty years. Cass had been in favor of making the original slave law of 1793 more

[1] *The American Conflict*, p. 216.

effective by adequate amendments. He was willing to do "justice" to the South. But the South on its part did not, and could not, appreciate Northern hatred of slave-hunting; and the consequent result of this strict law was to bring the evils of slavery, in its most revolting and inhuman aspects, home to the consciences of a people whose moral sense was not blunted. The compromise of 1850, which was hailed as the final settlement of sectional differences, in fact precipitated the Rebellion, and hastened the destruction of the "institution" of the South. Strange does it seem now that a representative of the free Northwest could not see more clearly, could have thus lost moral insight into the first principles of respectable republican liberty. He desired, it is true, that provision should be made for a jury trial in the State to which the alleged runaway might be transported, but he voted against allowing such a safeguard of liberty in the North, because that would be doing "injustice" to the South. He refused to favor an amendment to this infamous law, which would have permitted the issue of a writ of habeas corpus. A dark complexion was a crime which freed the nation from all consideration.

Those who had worked so strongly through the long oppressive weeks of summer for a compromise which would save the Union were terribly disappointed and goaded to a pitch of anger because there was still agitation and opposition. The strong and uncompromising adherents of free soil were thought to be nursing "in their bosoms the feelings of disappointment and hate,"— and to have shut their eyes to the fruits of a happy Union "which compromise ushered into existence."[1] Yet unquestionably there was on the whole a feeling of rest and relief because the crisis had passed without destruction. A great reaction toward conservatism had made itself felt among the mercantile classes of the North, who began to realize how much the industries of the country would be disturbed by disunion. Trade is always timid. The steady compromisers were therefore honored at the marts of trade and commerce. A number of citizens of New York gave Cass a public reception November 28, 1850, just before the opening of Congress. His "eloquent address" was received with "vehement applause."[2] It was an earnest appeal for contentment, and for a recognition of the finality of the compromise. A member of the Congress which had just passed one of the most shameful acts that ever sullied a statute book, depriving a man with a black skin of all security in liberty or in the pursuit of happiness, talked about the "precious heritage of liberty. . . . And where in the long annals of mankind do we find a people so highly favored as we are at this moment, when we seem to be struck with judicial blindness — almost ready, I may say, in the language of Scripture, to rush upon the thick bosses

[1] Smith, *Life and Times of Lewis Cass*, p. 710.
[2] Newspaper article.

of Jehovah's buckler? The sun never shone upon a country as free and prosperous as this, where human freedom finds less oppression, the human intellect less restraint, or human industry less opposition."

There was a vigorous desire on the part of the people to reason themselves to sleep, and to make use of all sorts of devices to rid themselves of this horrid insomnia; but it was a hard task, although there was an evident backsliding after the high excitement of 1850. Cass was elected senator in February, 1851, by a handsome majority. This is a clear indication of the acquiescence in the "finality" of the compromise. Many people of the North were prepared to assert that they would take no thought for the morrow. The appalling cases of cruelty were too frequent, however; and action was bound sooner or later to follow reaction. Orators might depict the beauties of patriarchal slavery, but the despair of the captured fugitives, their readiness to die rather than to be taken back to the South, belied all efforts of that kind. The contradictions of pamphleteers and deluded conservatives were daily made more glaring; the sentimentalists of the North were upbraided because they discountenanced the capture of slaves and their return to the blessed and happy bondage, from which ecstatic state they were escaping in hundreds to the ruin of their kind, gentle, and Christian masters.

Other orators and statesmen used words similar

to those of Cass. But all Union-saving speeches and prayers were ineffectual. When Congress met, in December, it was apparent that, although there was a calm after the storm, some would insist on being shocked and horrified at the fugitive slave act. President Fillmore's message indorsed the finality of the compromise. But the indorsement itself called forth a bitter debate. "The farmer of Ohio," said Giddings, "will never turn out to chase the panting fugitive." Petitions against the act came in scores. Cass lamented that sentiment and ultraism had bewitched the people. In a speech in the Senate (February, 1851) he deplored the statement that the law was contrary to public sentiment, and could not be enforced. He read a ringing resolution adopted by a meeting in Springfield, Massachusetts, which hailed the escape of a hunted slave, and avowed the hope that, "law or no law, constitution or no constitution, Union or no Union, the hospitality of Massachusetts will never be violated by the deliverance of any fugitive from oppression to his tyrant again." Such "unpatriotic" resolutions he attributed to the teachings of English emissaries, who were journeying over our land, preaching abolition and the sinfulness of the Constitution.

As the campaign of 1852 approached, it became evident that the Democrats had the advantage of harmony and discipline. Not all Democrats were in favor of the Fugitive Slave Act, but there was no such division in their ranks as in those of the

Whigs, where the anti-slavery sentiment would not down. The conservative reaction was still vigorous during the summer of this year. Those who were crying "Peace, peace," would evidently still cling to the old parties, and many would turn to the one whose history promised no attack upon the "peculiar institution" of the Southern States. The horrors of the slave chase were not yet completely brought home to the Northern conscience and sympathy. The National Democratic Convention met in Baltimore on June 1. On the first ballot Cass was the favorite. He received 116 votes; Buchanan received 93; Marcy, 27; and there were 27 scattering. The contest was long and exciting. Cass was still recognized as the leader of his party; but the practical politician is loath to place in nomination a man once defeated, whose weak points have been brought into view, and who no longer can awaken enthusiasm from novelty. The balloting continued; Cass's vote at one time dropped to 25. Douglas, on the thirtieth ballot, had as many as 92. On the thirty-fifth Cass's vote reached 131. Then the name of Franklin Pierce was introduced. Marcy was still formidable, receiving 97 on the forty-fifth ballot; but on the forty-ninth the New Hampshire man was chosen. The second place on the ticket was given to William R. King of Alabama.

The candidates were suited to the task assigned them. Pierce is not one of the great men of our political history, but belongs in the column of presidential accidents. He had served in Congress for some ten years, and had been a brigadier-general in the Mexican war. He had in no way shown any preëminent ability. What was wanted was precisely such a colorless candidate to carry the standard of the party announcing the "finality" of the compromise of 1850. Resolutions were adopted declaring that Congress had no power to interfere with the domestic institutions of the several States, and that all the efforts of the abolitionists to induce Congress to take such steps were calculated to lead to the most alarming consequences. The party was pledged to resist all attempts at "renewing" the agitation of the slavery question in Congress or out of it. Pierce accepted the nomination, and approved heartily of the platform.

The Whig convention, which met soon afterward, seemed to have as great travail as its rival had suffered in bringing forth a candidate. Its Southern members had already indicated the necessity of agreeing to the compromise, while at the North there was a strong element of the party which was no longer bound to it by principles, but simply by past associations. Scott, Fillmore, and Webster were the candidates. The first was nominated on the fifty-third ballot. Had Webster been nominated the campaign might have taken a different line, for his readiness to accept radical conservatism on the slavery question had already been demonstrated; but he did not receive a single

Southern vote in the convention. The platform, supposed to have been the work of Webster, adopted adjustment and finality, and acquiesced in the Fugitive Slave Law. The party had passed its last resolution. There was truth in the epitaph which the public wrote upon its tomb: "Died of an attempt to swallow the Fugitive Slave Law."

A Free-Soil National Convention in August nominated John P. Hale for president and George W. Julian for vice-president. Both the great parties were pronounced hopelessly corrupt and unworthy of confidence; and were wittily characterized as the "Whig and Democratic wings of the great Compromise party of the Nation." This campaign was conducted with great enthusiasm and with the courage of moral earnestness; but the result seemed to furnish even less encouragement than had been offered four years before. The vote had actually fallen off. It represented, however, the actual strength of the anti-slavery men in politics unaided by any side issue. There was great zeal in the North to lie prostrate in worship before the Constitution, compromise, and conciliation. In New York, where Van Buren had received such a great vote in 1848, the Free-Soilers did not hold even the balance of power. In Michigan there were 3000 less votes cast for Hale than had been cast for Van Buren. The same proportionate falling off appears in the other Northwestern States, including Ohio, and yet this portion of the Union was especially true to the faith. Most of the old Barnburners of New York forgot their Free-Soil aberration, and voted and worked for Pierce. Many of the Northern Whigs found it hard to be reconciled; they were said, in the slang of the day, "to swallow the candidates and to spit upon the platform."

The Democrats had felt great confidence in their success, but no one had anticipated such a victory as they won. Scott received only 42 electoral votes, carrying in the North Massachusetts and Vermont, in the South Kentucky and Tennessee. Not a single State especially interested in slavery deigned to reward the party which had been for years stifling all its better feelings and hopes out of tender consideration for the "rights" of the South. The popular plurality was not so crushing, only 202,008; but Taylor had beaten Cass by a plurality of 138,447. There was no excuse for the Whigs longer to pretend to exist as a party. They had been kept together since 1848 by spoils and the memory of past glory. In the light of this defeat even memory lost its sweetness. Though some were still obstinate and used the old name, the party was gone. Some rude shock was necessary to shake into crystals the different elements held in the solution of uncertainty and doubt. Such a shock soon came, and the study of the next eight years of this sixth decade of our history may be devoted to watching the effect upon the North of blow after blow from the arrogant South. The Democracy, now given up to Southern policy and flushed with victory, scarcely realized the danger of presumption until the free Northwest had brought into being a gigantic young party filled with the enthusiasm of youth, principle, and patriotism. Not till the Whigs were disorganized and thrown into confusion by overwhelming defeat, was there an opportunity for a recombination in opposition to slavery. The triumph of the compromise was all that was needed to destroy it.

CHAPTER X

THE REPEAL OF THE MISSOURI COMPROMISE. — THE NORTHWEST FORMS A NEW PARTY

A STUDY of the popular vote of 1852 might have made the Democratic party somewhat cautious; for its actual majority was very small. But compromise and finality, as represented by Pierce, seemed to be triumphant, and the new president was eager for adjustment and for the enforcement of the law. His message, December, 1853, once more proclaimed that the slavery contest should be considered settled. From its uneasy slumbers the country was suddenly awakened on January 16, 1854, by Senator Dixon of Kentucky. The successor of Henry Clay gave notice that when a bill to establish a territorial government in Nebraska should come up for consideration, he should offer a resolution repealing the Missouri compromise and permitting the citizens of the several States and Territories to take and hold their slaves within any of the Territories of the United States. January 23, Stephen A. Douglas reported from the Committee on Territories a bill for the formation of two Territories, — Kansas and Nebraska, — which provided that all cases involving the title to slaves and questions of personal freedom should be referred to the local tribunals with right of appeal to the Supreme Court of the United States. This, of course, meant the repeal of the Missouri compromise. It was declared to be the intent of the act to carry into practical operation the principles established by the compromise measure of 1850. Non-intervention was now made applicable, not alone to the "broken crests and deep valleys," nor to the mountain tops "capped by perennial snow," nor to the barren mountain sides of New Mexico and Utah, but to the broad rolling prairies west of the Mississippi. The section of the Missouri compromise, excluding slavery north of 36° 30′, was declared inoperative and void, as being inconsistent with the principle of non-intervention recognized by the legislation of 1850. There is ostensible but not real truth, therefore, in the statement of Jefferson Davis that the Missouri line was erased, not in 1854, but by Clay's last effort at mediation.

The act as adopted contained the following statement, afterwards a subject of some discussion: "It being the true intent and meaning of the act not to legislate slavery into any Territory or State, nor to exclude it therefrom, but to leave the people thereof perfectly free to form and regulate their domestic institutions in their own way, subject only to the Constitution of the United States." Jefferson Davis, in his work on the "Rise and Fall of the Confederate Government," maintains that the claim afterwards advanced by Douglas and others, that this declaration was intended to assert the right of the first settlers of the Territory to determine the character of its institutions, led to the dissensions which resulted in a rupture of the Democratic party. He insists that this right to "regulate their domestic institutions" belonged to the people of a Territory only at the moment of forming a constitution for admittance into the Union. The same statements have been made by other writers in behalf of the "Lost Cause." The "Little Giant," who declaimed in his frenzied fashion in favor of the rights of the slaveholder, until he was abused and execrated by the more advanced people of the North, is now slandered and maligned by the advocates of the South. He is described as an "able and eloquent demagogue," whose popular sovereignty was merely "a short cut to all the ends of Black Republicanism." The truth is, however, that the South, finding itself beaten at its own game, thereupon followed the advice of the old lawyer to a member newly admitted to the profession: having neither law nor facts in its favor, it abused the other side. An unprejudiced reading of the speeches of Cass and Douglas on the act of 1854 will show that popular or "squatter sovereignty" meant control over legislation by the people of a Territory. Cass made two eloquent and skillful speeches on the subject, clear as the sun at noonday.[1] The fact is that the

[1] As late as 1855 Cass repeated the argument for popular sov-

remarkable infatuation of the South allowed it, even as late as 1854, to believe that it could compete for the Western prairie with the free North, whose population was far greater, and which was constantly receiving such additions from the old world that it could pour a steady stream of immigrants into the new Territories. Not until the painful truth came home, that competition with the free North in expansion, in power, in vigor, was a hopeless task, did the ordinary slave-owner abuse popular sovereignty and demand the affirmative protection by Congress of all his rights to property in persons. We shall see that in this hopeless contest he at last turned even to the nefarious slave trade, which had been piracy for forty years and illegal for fifty, hoping in spite of defeat that the forests of Africa would give the means to counteract the emigration from the crowded fields and cities of Europe.

Cass, as the inventor of popular sovereignty, has been burdened with abusive epithets, and accused of pernicious intents; but, after all, popular sovereignty, though artificial, and an absurd deduction from general principles, if honestly carried out would have chained slavery within its early limits, wherein it was doomed to destruction by

ereignty in the early sense of that word: "The negation of all power of interference by Congress in the internal government of the Territories is the true constitutional doctrine." From a letter to the *Detroit Free Press*, August, 1855, quoted in Smith's *Cass*, p. 771.

the silent operation of economic and industrial laws. But the South would not live up to the doctrine when the struggle went against it. California was lost; the mountain-passes of New Mexico were forbidding; and the plains beyond the mountains had not yet suggested their beautiful transformation at the touch of irrigation and modern mechanical skill. The Kansas and Nebraska country, stretching away to the Rocky Mountains and north to the British provinces, the remaining portions of the Louisiana purchase, must be won for slavery, or the slave baron could no longer crack his whip in the halls of the Capitol in defiance of Northern sentiment and "sentimentality."

Cass lamented the reopening of the slavery contest by this bill. He regretted that it should be necessary to reconsider a compromise of over thirty years' standing; but he admitted that the line of demarcation was inconsistent with the theory of non-intervention, and he believed that the complete recognition of that theory was the only means of obtaining peace. He therefore announced his adherence to the bill. He did not believe that the South would gain anything by the equality she demanded, for he trusted that the region in dispute was so ill adapted to slave labor that no human power could ever establish it there. Borrowing the famous words of Webster, he exclaimed, "It is excluded by law, superior to that which admits it elsewhere, — the law of nature, of physical geography, the law of the formation of the earth. That law settles forever, with a strength beyond all terms of human enactment, that slavery cannot exist there." Curiously enough, the eloquent historian of our civil war, Dr. Draper, propounded the same opinion as late as 1867;[1] but the learned advocate of the control of nature over man hit upon an unfortunate example. The Great American Desert has bloomed as if touched with the wand of Ceres herself, and the skill of man, by upturning the soil, has brought rain from the clouds; the dry plains of Kansas and Nebraska are dry no longer, and the rough buffalo grass and cactus have given place to more useful and luxuriant crops. It is fortunate that the American people were not willing to trust to the apparent infertility of their wild lands, but aroused themselves to active opposition. For the South was determined that at least one more slave State should be added to the list. The passage of the Kansas-Nebraska bill was the beginning of the end. The advice of Seward had been neglected. The slave States, ignorant of their own inherent weakness, madly began a struggle for equality, demanding an opportunity for the contest.

President Pierce signed the measure May 30, 1854. The day of compromise was past. They who had boasted of final adjustment by the compromise of 1850 now disregarded one which had been considered inviolable. The basis was non-interference. Freedom must be attained, not by

[1] *History of American Civil War*, vol. i. p. 411.

"bargains of equivocal prudence," but by fair legislation, by the vigor of free labor and free thought, now by Southern folly given fair play without let or hindrance. The shifting sands of compromise were gone. "This seems to me," exclaimed Seward, "auspicious of better days and better and wiser legislation. Through all the darkness and gloom of the present hour bright stars are breaking, that inspire me with hope and excite me to perseverance." Cass did not see so clearly nor feel so deeply as the men of the new generation. His companions in thought had gone, and he lingered still, one of the old school who had loved the Union with a tenderness and loyalty which could be known only by those who had seen it rise and prosper, and who had helped make it what it was. He hoped and believed that his doctrine of non-intervention would preserve the Territories for freedom. The violence, the greed, the stern resolve of the leaders of the new South appeared as dire portents to Seward, to Chase, to Sumner; but they were hidden from the patriarch of a generation whose memories recalled Southern hospitality and true chivalry, when as yet embittering topics had not arisen.

His opinions are well expressed in a letter written to a friend in Detroit, June 4: "As you are aware we have passed the Nebraska bill. I believe it was a wise measure, and that it will have the effect of forever withdrawing the slavery contest from Congress. And it is founded on the true American principle of allowing every political community to regulate its own domestic concerns for itself. I am aware that the measure has excited a good deal of opposition in our State, but I believe that the more it is examined and becomes known, the more favor it will meet from reasonable men of both parties."[1]

The repeal of the Missouri compromise came like a whirlwind upon the people of the North. At a time when the Federal Government was giving itself up to the demands of slavery, the sentiment of liberty was growing. The Democratic party had surrendered to the South, but it was called to reckon with true democracy at the North. Many who had not been aroused hitherto now shouted for the sacredness of the bargain of 1820. The awaited shock had come. Indignant Democrats who had voted for Pierce in 1852, thinking that the last word had been said for slavery, joined with Whigs who were half gleeful that their boastful old-time enemies had not found such easy sailing, and half angry that the compromise of their own chieftain had been abandoned. Crystallization into a new party came at once. Emigrant aid societies and private benevolence armed the sturdy New Englander and hurried him off to the new Territory to hold the doubtful ground for liberty with the rifle. Earnest men in all the North, startled by seeing the last barrier broken, demanded an end of irresolution and trifling.

[1] Letter to Mr. J. H. Cleveland, Detroit.

The Whigs and the Democrats who were provoked to opposition wasted too much time and thought on "breach of faith," and lamented with overmuch sorrow the destruction of a geographical line, which had been for many years the bane of our politics. Such persons, however, were soon found hand in glove with the Free-Soilers, who saw in the obnoxious measure only an instance of the perfidy of slavery and the folly of compromises and bargains with sin.

The Republican party was born in the Northwest. It breathed its early life in that virile region which had never felt the enervating influence of colonialism, in a section which was now filled with the power of a highly developed and organized society, and yet had not lost the zeal, vitality, and energy of a primitive and newly settled country. Men of the young West easily free themselves from associations of party and leave the shallow ruts of custom. They do not know the burdening weight of tradition and inheritance, and they readily think for themselves and act as they think. The pioneer who has wrought his own work and fought his own fight has no respect for prescription, and bases superiority on skill and endurance. Yet side by side with this marked individualism and independence, there is a generous altruism and a comprehension of society. Lessons are learned from nature. Her breadth and liberality do not teach the settler selfishness. He may lose opportunities for refinement and culture, but his views are not limited to a narrow horizon. These characteristics display themselves variously; there is a deep, broad, and fervent love of country, an admiration of her greatness and an appreciation of her manifest destiny. Geography teaches patriotism. "Vast prairies covered by the unbroken dome of the sky, and navigable rivers all converging to a common trunk, perpetually suggest to him Unionism."[1] He is proud of the mightiness of the Republic. Without acute susceptibility to criticism, he delights in praise of the grandeur and glory of his country. "The true American is found in the Great Valley." Naturally, therefore, in 1854, old party trammels were soonest cast aside by the people of the Northwest. They most readily bent to the task of forming a party upon the corner-stone of unionism and freedom, a party opposed to state sovereignty and to a sectional constitutional interpretation which would shield wrong. They gave their strength to the party which advocated nationalism. From 1854 until the close of the civil war, the upper part of the Great Valley was the centre of loyalty and Republicanism. Here was the early home of the new union-anti-slavery party, and it has never yet wandered far from its birthplace; every one of its successful candidates for the presidency has come from the old Northwest, and all its nominees, save one, have been Western men.

[1] Draper's *History of the American Civil War*, vol. i. p. 412.

In addition to this natural tendency, there were two other reasons for the appearance of the Republican party in the West, before the East was ready to break old party lines. The South long counted on the influence of commercial conservatism in the North, and it cannot be denied that this operated much more strongly in the mercantile centres of the East than in the farming West, which had few commercial relations with the cotton States. The second reason was an equally potent one. The Northwest was honeycombed by the underground railroad. The fugitives from service found their way to Canada by the shortest road, and the slave chase awakened Northwestern resentment.

Upon the passage of the Nebraska bill there came a demand for a new party. Men who had never voted a Free-Soil ticket now avowed their willingness to support any candidate on a sound anti-slavery platform. The East, with its usual conservatism, hesitated to break old ties and to launch a new party without prestige and traditions. Possibly the very first active suggestion of the new party came from the little town of Ripon, Wisconsin. There, in February, 1854, while the obnoxious act was under discussion in Congress, a local meeting was held, and the principles for the coming emergency were considered. On March 20, in a town meeting, the committees of the Whig and Free-Soil parties were dissolved and a new committee was chosen, composed of three Whigs, one Free-Soiler, and one Democrat.

Thus in miniature were the dissolution of the old and the formation of the new faithfully typified. The "solitary tallow candle" and the "little white schoolhouse" have become immortal in our history. In May, immediately after the passage of the Kansas-Nebraska bill, some thirty congressmen at Washington met and considered the formation of the "Republican" party.

By that time the name was in the air. It was a question as to where and by whom it should be adopted. Horace Greeley, who had fought so valiantly against slavery, was getting disheartened. "I faintly hope the time has come predicted by Dan Webster when he said: 'I think there will be a North.'" The veterans of the East listened to calls from the excited Northwest. Editors "can direct and animate a healthy public indignation, but not create a soul beneath the ribs of Death."[1] Greeley wrote to Jacob M. Howard of Michigan, that Wisconsin on July 13 would adopt the name Republican, and he advised Michigan to anticipate such action in the convention summoned for the 6th.[2] But no such advice was needed; the work of arousing interest in such a plan was already begun, and to Michigan belongs the honor of really conceiving and christening the Republican party. The "Detroit Tribune," June 2, formulated its proposition frankly: "Our proposition is that a

[1] Greeley, quoted in Fowler's *History of the Republican Party*, p. 163.

[2] *Ibid.*, p. 173.

convention be called, irrespective of party organization, for the purpose of agreeing upon some plan of action that shall combine the whole anti-slavery sentiment of the State upon one ticket." The "call" published in that paper, said to be the work of Isaac P. Christiancy, began with the words, "A great wrong has been perpetrated." It invited all, "without reference to former political associations, who think the time has arrived for Union at the North to protect liberty from being overthrown and downtrodden, to assemble in mass convention, Thursday the sixth of July next, at one o'clock, at Jackson, there to take such measures as shall be thought best to concentrate the popular sentiment of this State against the encroachments of the slave power."

On that date, July 6, 1854, the Whigs and Free-Soilers, or the "Free Democracy" of Michigan, met and formed a single party. The name Republican was adopted. A powerful platform, attributed to Jacob M. Howard, was accepted as the basis of the new party. It resolved "That in view of the necessity of battling for the first principles of republican government and against the schemes of aristocracy, the most revolting and oppressive with which the world was ever cursed or man debased, we will coöperate and be known as Republicans until the contest be terminated." The strength of the new party was at once great. Wisconsin took the same position the next week. In the East the Whigs, as a rule, maintained their organization. The Northwest was on its feet and equipped for battle.

Under these circumstances General Cass had a hard campaign in Michigan. The theory of "squatter sovereignty," which he first had amply unfolded to the world, was now made applicable to nearly all the Territories; but his own State had inaugurated an attack upon the doctrine, and in his own city strong men were loathing it. He spoke at length before the Democratic convention of Michigan in September, and took an active part in the campaign, ably defending his theory of the Constitution and the incompetence of Congress in territorial government. In the course of his speech before the convention he denounced slavery as a great social and political evil, asserted that he had said the same thing more than once in the Senate, and that he never entertained any other opinion regarding it. His whole career attests the truth of this. But the slaveholders, now keenly sensitive to unkind allusions, resented such unpleasant truths. The South fondly nursed the viper which was poisoning its life. The "Richmond Enquirer" arraigned Cass before the bar of popular judgment: "If this language be correctly given in the report of his speech, he has severed the last cord which bound him to the Democracy of the South." Cass had tried to do "justice" to both sections, and had fallen into disrepute with each. It is pathetic to see him left naked to his enemies after all his zealous service and honest striving after duty, which in the corrupt currents of the world does not always lie in the trimming consideration of contesting principles. The "Enquirer" ranked him with those "illustrious apostates," Benton and Van Buren, "in the limbo of lost and dishonored politicians," — a trio, one would think, of no mean proportions. On November 4, in a "grand rally" at Detroit, Cass elaborately defended his spoiled child, "squatter sovereignty." He took leave of the South, but avowed his purpose manfully to defend its constitutional rights. He pleaded with friends of the Union to be moderate and forbearing, so far as mere personal interests were concerned, but counseled that they be vigilant for the maintenance of justice and law. It was an able and noble speech. This man, who has been accused of vacillation and skillful legerdemain in politics, knew how to cling amid the abuse of foes, and of old-time friends, to a position which he thought right. The spirit of Henry Clay and of the past generation permeated the speech of the 4th of November. It contained the old calmness, the fairness, and the judicial blindness which would not and could not see that moral enthusiasm was awakened, and that argument could no more lull it to sleep than whistling could calm a tempest.

The result of the elections showed the strength of protest against the violation of the compromise. The Northwest vigorously supported the new party. Michigan elected the whole state ticket, and three out of four congressmen. Cass seemed ill requited for his services to the old party, but a comparison of the figures will prove that, though his influence had waned, it was still of weight. Two of the three congressmen elected in Wisconsin were Republicans. In Illinois, the Nebraska and Douglas Democrats were 18,000 behind in the vote of the State, although two years before Pierce had had a clear majority of more than 5000 over Scott and Hale, the last having received less than 10,000 votes. Even in Indiana the Republicans had a majority of some 14,000. Ohio, of course, came prominently forward. The old Western Reserve district cast two Republican votes for every one cast for Nebraska and "squatter sovereignty." Maine was the only one of the Eastern States that adopted for the campaign the new name or elected a Republican ticket.

The different elements in Northwestern life once more gave evidence of the power of inherited ideas and prejudices. The Southern element, as if in obedience to the famous words of King James's charter, 1609, advanced into the country on a line running "west and northwest,"—its presence is evident in the southern counties of Indiana,—and running northward penetrated as far north as the centre of Illinois. In the northern tier of counties, which were settled from New York and New England, the Republican vote was 8372, and the Nebraska vote 2776; in the ninth district, in the southern point, 2911 votes were cast for the Republican candidate, and 8498 for the Democratic. Possibly the most characteristic and startling exception, which proved the rule, was the vote of Madison County, the former home of Edward Coles, who moved from Virginia to Illinois to free his slaves, and left the impress of his character on the surrounding country. Madison County cast 2220 Republican ballots, and but 393 "for Nebraska."

The great danger to the Republican party seemed to be the American party, — a *sub rosa* organization, which attempted to substitute another question for the slavery question, and to excite the people by holding up the spectre of Rome and the tyranny of Catholicism. This party was not built on the broad foundation of the necessity of preserving a pure ballot and free government by maintaining sound American doctrine and insisting upon good American intelligence as a basis for suffrage. Its platform was not so much its oft-repeated "America for Americans," as it was America for Protestants, and anything to avoid a decision on the real problems of the day. Its secret organization was at once an insult to the people and the assurance of its failure. No "order" having a hierarchy and degrees, and encumbering a political topic with paraphernalia and mystic symbolism, can rise to dignity in a free country and dominate a frank and thoughtful people, the very essence of whose institutions is common participation, common undertaking, and common judgment. So great, however, was the desire of men in those harrowing days to avoid responsibility that this organization assumed alarming proportions, and threatened the success of the party which faced present realities. It served a purpose quite different from the one hoped for or contemplated. Whigs and Democrats too obstinate or proud to transfer their allegiance at once to the Republicans took this secret passage, and finally emerged thence into good standing with the antislavery party, without the shame of having changed their coats in broad daylight.

This organization appeared in 1852. At first it simply interrogated candidates, but in 1854 it masqueraded as a political party, and for a few years played its rôle not without some success. In some of the Eastern States, especially, it held its head high; and in the border States it long lingered, until Western Republicanism with its sense of present duty, sincerity, and actuality shamed it out of sight. The real name adopted by these whispering politicians was as silly as their purpose. "The Sons of '76, or the Order of the Star-Spangled Banner," was the title used in its inner mysterious circles. The sobriquet, "Know-Nothing," arose from the answers of its members, who uniformly replied "I don't know" to all inquiries as to the name and purpose of the organization; only those who had taken the higher degrees knew its more serious intents or how ambitiously it had been christened. No party can hope to succeed in the United States which has but one aim, and that, too, not a political one. The success of the Republican party has often been cited to disprove such a statement and to furnish inspiration for new movements. The historic analogy is deceptive. The Republican party, although inspired with a truly moral purpose, was a political party, with a well-known and well-defined policy in affairs of state, and not simply a combination of enthusiasts burning with zeal for the realization of a single idea. The Know-Nothing party had no political virility. "It would seem," sneered Greeley, "as devoid of the elements of persistence as an anti-cholera or an anti-potato-rot party would be."[1]

Such an unwholesome fungus was specially obnoxious to Cass, who was peculiarly liberal and sympathetic. He was too much of a scholar to be a bigot, and too much a man of affairs to be a pedant. He lamented that such narrow and bitter intolerance could exist. "Mr. President," he said in the Senate, "strange doctrines are abroad, and strange organizations are employed to promulgate and enforce them. Our political history contains no such chapter in the progress of our country as that which is now opening. The grave questions of constitutionality and policy, which have been so long the battle-cry of parties, are contemptuously rejected, and intolerance, religious and political, finds zealous, and it may be

[1] *Whig Almanac*, 1855, p. 23.

they will prove successful, advocates, in this middle of the nineteenth century, boasting with much self-complacency of its intelligence, and, in this free country, founded upon immigration, and grown powerful and prosperous by toleration. It is a system of proscription which would exclude the first general who fell at the head of an organized American army . . . from all political confidence, because he happened to be born on the wrong side of the Atlantic, and would exclude, also, the last surviving signer of the Declaration of Independence from any similar token of regard because he was a Catholic, were those eminent leaders in our revolutionary cause now living to witness this appeal to local and sectarian prejudices."[1] This spirit of fanaticism and intolerance Cass unfortunately considered a part and parcel of that Northern enthusiasm which had begotten the Republican party. He did not see that nativism was merely histrionic. Hamlet called to duty, feigns a silly madness, goes about unkempt, wreaks in sudden wrath unpremeditated vengeance on poor old Polonius, arranges a pretty mimicry of the murder in the garden, all to tickle his imagination, consume time, and delay action.

Resolutions from the legislature of Michigan were presented in the Senate, February 5, 1855, by Mr. Stuart, the colleague of General Cass, instructing these two gentlemen, and requesting the representatives, to vote for an act prohibiting slav-

[1] *Cong. Globe*, vol. xxx. p. 556.

ery in the territories, and for the repeal of the Fugitive Slave Law. Cass replied at length, refusing to obey the dictates of a party which had suddenly and, as he believed, temporarily become possessed of the government of the State. When instructed before, he had acknowledged that such instructions were valid "under proper circumstances," but asserted that there were "limitations upon this exercise." He now thought these limitations in force. He was fully persuaded that the adoption of the measure proposed "would be the signal for the breaking up of the government and the dissolution of the Confederacy." Mr. Stuart followed the example of his senior colleague.

The South was alert in many directions during these years. Its appetite, only whetted by the acquisition of Texas and the West, those pleasing results of Southern "filibustering," craved more for slavery. Cuba, almost touching Florida, was provokingly near, and the South was tantalized by the propinquity. Not to speak of attempts at robbery, more than one attempt had been made in previous years to secure the island honorably. In 1852 England and France suggested to the United States that the three countries pledge themselves not to make any effort to acquire Cuba. Our country refused. In August, 1854, James Buchanan, J. Y. Mason, and Pierre Soulé, ministers to England, France, and Spain, were instructed to meet and to adopt measures for perfect concert of action directed to the end of obtaining Cuba from Spain. From Aix la Chapelle, in October, they issued what is known as the Ostend Manifesto. After outlining how profitable and honorable a sale of the "fair isle" would prove for Spain, this notorious document pointed to the needs of the United States in the premises, and contemplated the possible necessity of "wresting" the treasure from its owner. It was said that we should be "recreant to our duty and unworthy of our gallant forefathers, and commit base treason against our posterity, should we permit Cuba to be Africanized and become a second St. Domingo with all its attendant horrors to the white race, and suffer the flames to extend to our own neighboring shores, seriously to endanger, or actually to consume, the fair fabric of our Union." This shameful proclamation, characterized by the Republican platform of 1856 as "the highwaymen's plea, that might makes right," was at first scarcely credited in its enormity at home or abroad. It was not, however, discountenanced by the Pierce administration. The free American Republic held itself out to the world as the armed champion of slavery, and acknowledged its brutal indifference in the face of Christendom. The countries of Europe, too apt to hide larceny under the cloak of diplomacy, looked upon our avowed greed with a sense of awe, surprise, and shame at the inartistic nudity of our propositions, not covered even by respectable and cunning verbiage.

Such schemes attracted the attention of Cass.

He had a never-failing ambition for his country and a never-ceasing suspicion of England. In February, 1854, he called the attention of the Senate to a speech delivered by Lord Clarendon, in which it was announced that on questions of policy the French and English nations were in entire accord in every part of the world. Cass then declared that this meant opposition to our acquisition of Cuba; and, though Lord Clarendon afterward, in referring to this statement, disclaimed all such agreements or intentions, and was said to be "the most astonished man in Europe at General Cass's construction of his speech," yet circumstantial evidence strongly contradicts his denial. Alluding again in February, 1855, to the general subject of our foreign relations, after the issue of the Ostend Manifesto, Cass in a masterly speech resented the interference of foreign countries. Yet the stealing of Cuba he heartily condemned: "Such a case of rapacity will, I trust, never stain our annals." While condemning all allusions to "filibustering, and the bullying spirit of Democracy," and while irritated by the paternal tone of European nations, he did not forget common decency or advocate robbery in behalf of slavery.

This buccaneering spirit, grown so great by feeding on the coarse meat of slavery, manifested itself in many ways. An attempt was made to conquer and colonize Nicaragua and to give it up to the unique civilization of the South. The Democratic convention which nominated Buchanan actually proclaimed that the people of the United States could but "sympathize with the efforts which are being made by the people of Central America to regenerate that portion of the continent which covers the passage across the inter-oceanic isthmus." A belief in the "positive goodness" of slavery had made the South mad. This "regenerating" process was unsuccessful. Moreover, those who had longed for more territory in the West now asked for more slaves to fill it. "We are losing Kansas," said the "Charleston Standard," in 1856, "because we are lacking in population." The only remedy seemed a reopening of the traffic which had been piracy for thirty years and more.

The attitude of Cass on the questions of international concern from 1850 to 1856 was not far from right. He made a number of very able speeches, all showing his old-time jealousy of interference by foreign powers. The Clayton-Bulwer treaty he had accepted with the hope that it would settle some of our difficulties regarding Central America. But when England, desiring a substantial footing in that reëntrant angle of our continent, began to quibble and demur, he expressed his usual antipathy to what he considered her ambitious duplicity. The last speeches of his active life in the Senate exhibit little decline in vigor of thought and feeling.

In the meantime the contest for the possession of Kansas was waging. Such scenes a modern American would wish to pass by with averted eyes. Missouri poured armed ruffians over the border to hold the Territory for slavery, and for some time this element seemed to have its own way. A pro-slavery territorial government was established early in 1855 by wholesale fraud and intimidation. A series of acts were passed which savored of the blackest of the early laws of South Carolina. Governor Reeder vetoed such bills, but they were passed without hesitation over his veto. At the petition of the pro-slavery men he was removed, and Wilson Shannon of Ohio was named in his stead. At the outset this man apparently showed a zeal for ruffianism and barbarity, and in the end was incompetent. The Free-State men, in October, 1855, formed a constitution and, after the adoption of it by the people, they applied for admittance into the Union. In March, 1856, the House sent a committee, composed of William A. Howard of Michigan, John Sherman of Ohio, and Mordecai Oliver of Missouri, to examine the proceedings in Kansas. The first two members declared in their report that elections were carried by fraud and violence, and that this constitution framed by the convention embodied the will of a majority of the people. A bill to admit Kansas under this free constitution, at first defeated in the House, was afterwards passed by a majority of two. The Senate, however, preferred to pass an act for authorizing the formation of a constitution under which the Territory could be admitted. Cass was selected to propose the memorial of the Topeka legislature asking for the admittance of the State. Yet he was opposed to the recognition of an instrument agreed upon by "one portion" of the people. He was in favor of allowing the citizens of the Territory to vote fairly upon the question; but he did not approve of admitting the State under the Topeka Free State Constitution above referred to, asserting that such a course would simply perpetuate ill feeling and division. On May 12 and 13, 1856, he spoke at length on this topic, severely arraigning Seward and others who tried to heap upon the administration the opprobrium of the anarchy of Kansas.

Sumner followed Cass on the 19th and 20th. This famous speech reached the highest point in the denunciation of slavery and its devotees. The Northern men with Southern principles were denounced as bitterly as the Southern men with no principles. Senator Butler of South Carolina was depicted as the Don Quixote of slavery, accompanied by Douglas as its very Sancho Panza. There was no cowardly mincing of terms, but the crime against Kansas was presented with all the burning eloquence of this classicist among American orators. Because of his tendency to load his speech with overwrought and hyper-cunning phrases, and to burden it with historic allusions and Latin quotations, highly dramatic passages sometimes fell flat before an unappreciative audience. But now he was so much in earnest, so bitter in his intensity, that the galleries and the Senate listened with breathless attention to his daring, scathing attack, and watched him in bewilderment as he tore garment and veil from the foul creature he detested. He ended with an appeal for the purity of the ballot and protection against violence, that free labor might not be blasted by unwelcome association with slave labor. "In dutiful respect for the early Fathers, whose aspirations are now ignobly thwarted; in the name of the Constitution which has been outraged, of the laws trampled down — of justice banished — of humanity degraded — of peace destroyed — of freedom crushed to earth; and in the name of the Heavenly Father, whose service is perfect freedom, I make this last appeal."

When Sumner sat down Cass rose. He had listened, he said, with equal regret and surprise to this speech, "the most un-American and unpatriotic that ever grated on the ears of the members of this high body." Douglas followed with a highly personal and offensive speech, ranting like a common scold, and storming about with wild and uncouth gesticulations. Sumner's reply to these respondents so amply discloses his estimate of the character of each that it merits passing attention. The following reference to Cass shows the respect of this ardent anti-slavery man, and goes far to disprove the groundless attacks upon Cass's conduct and character which became so common at the North in the heat of the slavery discussion: "The senator from Michigan knows full well that nothing can fall from me which can have anything but kindness for him. He has said on the floor to-day that he listened to my speech with regret. I have never avowed on this floor how often, with my heart brimming full of friendship for him, I have listened with regret to what has fallen from his lips." Douglas was treated to a castigation, which must have made the "Little Giant" squirm, bold as he was. "No person with the upright form of a man can be allowed, without violation of all decency, to switch out from his tongue the perpetual stench of offensive personality." These parallel passages illustrate the kindness felt for the sincere, earnest, scholarly, mistaken advocate of "squatter sovereignty," and the dislike for the younger advocate of the same false doctrine.

This speech, too caustic and trenchant to be received with calmness by Southern members, was ground for personal assault. Preston S. Brooks, a member of the House from South Carolina, took it upon himself to avenge the honor of the South and his State. A day or two after the speech was delivered, he entered the senate chamber, and finding Mr. Sumner at his desk he brutally attacked him, striking him over the head with a heavy walking cane, and leaving him bruised and insensible on the floor. It was years before Sumner recovered his health and strength sufficiently to continue his duties, and he was never again the same man; his physical vigor was permanently impaired. His empty chair long stood as a mute appeal to the thoughtful lovers of justice.

Cass was elected by the Senate a member of a committee to investigate the circumstances of the assault. It is to be regretted that he did not find words to denounce such a shameful attack upon free speech. The Senate committee reported lack of jurisdiction, and the House of Representatives was unable to secure the necessary two thirds for the expulsion of Brooks. Because of the implied censure in the resolutions, however, he resigned, and asserted that the House had no jurisdiction over him. He was quickly reëlected by his district, where he was received with enthusiasm and affection. "Hit him again," were the words of admonition from his constituents, and the Southern papers applauded his "elegant and effectual" blows. This assault, as much as any other one thing, opened the eyes of the North to the brutality, the roughness, and the hopeless vulgarity of the "divine institution." "There is no denying the humiliating fact," said the "Springfield Republican," "that this country is under the reign of ruffianism. The remedy for ruffianism is in a united North." The disease begat the remedy.

The campaign of 1856 followed close upon these exciting events. The Democratic National Convention met in Cincinnati in June. Buchanan had the lead from the start, and was nominated. In answer to a letter signed by Andrew F. Webster and others in November of 1855, Cass said that he did not desire to have his name used in the convention; but some of the delegates insisted on voting for him. He received only five votes on the first ballot, and at no time showed great strength, though retaining a few faithful adherents to the end. John C. Breckinridge of Kentucky was nominated as vice-president. The convention adopted a platform on the old lines, repudiating "all sectional parties . . . whose avowed purpose, if consummated, must end in civil war and disunion." "Non-interference" was once more proclaimed the sovereign remedy. The American party put Fillmore in nomination, and he attracted the few Whigs who still answered to the name. The Republicans, holding their first national convention at Philadelphia, selected as their candidates John C. Frémont of California and William L. Dayton of New Jersey. The platform was definite and decided. It recounted the crimes against Kansas, and advocated its immediate admission as a State under a free constitution; it denied "the authority of Congress, of a territorial legislature, of any individual or association of individuals, to give legal existence to slavery in any Territory of the United States," and proclaimed its belief that Congress had "*sovereign* power over the Territories of the United States." The issue between the two great parties was sharply drawn. One announced that Congress had authority over the Territories, and was in duty bound to exercise it for the prevention of slavery. The other advocated the uniform application of the "democratic principle" of non-interference in "the organization of the Territories and the admission of new States."

The campaign was one of the most serious, earnest, and enthusiastic in our history. Frémont, because of his romantic career and personal charms, was easily converted into an ideal champion, strongly appealing to the imagination and the affection of the vigorous young party of freedom. Everywhere in the North went up the rallying cry, "Free soil, free speech, free men, and Frémont." The times were not yet ripe for complete success. The Democratic party gained the day, carrying every Southern State save Maryland, which gave itself up to Know-Nothingism. But such a victory was the victory of Pyrrhus. The Republicans cast more votes in the free States than did the Democrats. In the East only Pennsylvania and New Jersey, in the West only Illinois, Indiana, and California cast their electoral votes for the Democratic candidate. In the first of these alone, Buchanan's own State, did the Democrats outnumber the Republicans and Know-Nothings combined. The "sectional party" exhibited a wonderful vigor. The threat was often heard in the campaign that its success meant the separation of the Union. From the time of this election that was a standing menace.

It was a source of regret to Cass that a party with a "sectional" aim should find support in the country. For above all else he loved the Union, and he hoped against hope that harmony would be restored by the old sedatives with which he was familiar. Michigan, so long faithful to him, now gave Frémont a popular plurality of nearly twenty thousand, and elected a legislature with an overwhelming Republican majority. January 10, 1857, Zachariah Chandler was elected to succeed the great advocate of popular sovereignty, whose doctrine his own State now so vehemently condemned. Of 106 votes cast by both Houses of the legislature, Cass received only 16. His defeat was a great triumph for the Republicans of the nation. Though they had failed to elect their "Pathfinder" president, they felt as if the signal rebuke administered by Michigan was equivalent to a victory.

Meanwhile matters were in a woeful condition in stricken Kansas. Governor Shannon had resigned in despair, feeling, as he afterwards expressed it, as if one might as well attempt "to govern the Devil in hell" as to govern Kansas. John W. Geary of Pennsylvania succeeded to the trust. The Territory was literally in a state of war. While the marching and counter-marching of election parades were exciting the enthusiasm of the people of the States, men in the harassed Territory carried the rifle instead of the campaign torch, and filled their pouches with powder and shot as the most eloquent campaign arguments. Before the opening of the new year the fighting seemed to have ceased, though each party held its breath expectantly. The Free State government still claimed legal and effective existence, while the territorial legislature, described as a "vulgar, illiterate, hiccoughing rout," plotted and planned for slavery. Governor Geary, suspecting the sincerity of the administration, and perceiving that the election of Buchanan meant a victory for pro-slavery partisanship in Kansas, resigned March 4, 1857. The history of the remaining months of the year is quickly told. Robert J. Walker of Mississippi, appointed to succeed Governor Geary, prevailed upon the Free State men to cease dallying longer with their mythical state constitution, and to join in the territorial elections of the autumn. As a consequence, these resulted in the choice of a Free State legislature. In the meantime, however, a convention summoned by the old pro-slavery legislature had met at Lecompton and adopted a constitution recognizing slavery. It was submitted to the people; but instead of being allowed to cast a ballot either for or against the constitution, they were compelled to choose between adopting it "with slavery" or "without slavery." The Free State men refused to vote, and it consequently received a great majority of the ballots cast. The Lecompton constitution, thus adopted by the pro-slavery voters of the Territory, was accepted by the President, and the next year it was actually recognized by the Senate, although meanwhile, on a fair ballot, it had been emphatically rejected by the people. By the early part of 1858 the pro-slavery party was so hopelessly in the minority that the only question was whether Kansas should be admitted as a free State or barred out entirely. In fact, not until the withdrawal of the Southern senators, after the election of Lincoln, did the Senate consent to its admission with a constitution forbidding slavery.

The Kansas trouble is a long and bloody dissertation on the theme of popular sovereignty. The immigrants from the free States had won the day against slavery. Kansas was saved, not by the Republican party, nor by the abolitionists, who talked and agitated, but by the men who went to the spot to express their "sovereignty" and to fight for freedom. It must be confessed that, as far as saving the Territories from becoming slave States is concerned, popular sovereignty had not been unsuccessful. But no one cared to see again the disgraceful scramble and the rough-and-tumble contest for vantage ground. By the beginning of Buchanan's administration many Democrats began to deny that the people of a Territory had a right to regulate the subject of slavery, save by determining, at the moment of their entering the Union, whether they should come in as a free or a slave State. To the people of the South popular sovereignty had become so objectionable, because of its failure for their purposes, that it was openly spurned, and recourse was had to the solid ground of Calhoun's dogmas: that slaves were property, and that the United States government was in duty bound to protect such property everywhere.

Opposed to this was the assertion of the Republicans: that slaves were not property save by the "municipal" law of certain States; that Congress could not and must not, by act or omission to act, allow the Territories of the Union to be sullied by the foot of a slave.

Buchanan, in his inaugural, while reaffirming the right of the people of a Territory to decide for themselves what their constitution should be, took all the pith and marrow from the doctrine of popular sovereignty by doubting their right to such a determination, except at the time of their forming a state constitution. He humbly referred the matter, however, to the Supreme Court, of whose coming decision he seems to have had knowledge.

The Dred Scott decision, March, 1857, did not help matters. The solemn statement, coming from a portion of a divided court, of the great historical falsehood that negroes were not and could not become citizens; the promulgation of an *obiter dictum* calculated to have effect in the domain of politics; the assertion that the Missouri compromise was beyond the competence of Congress, that slaves were property when taken into the Territories, and that all "needful rules and regulations" of Congress must respect the private property of the slave-owner, — all this simply awakened the Republican party to greater effort. Wrong now came clothed in the ermine of justice. Effort must not cease until the disgraceful decision was blotted from the records of the court.

CHAPTER XI

SECRETARY OF STATE. — SECESSION. — THE LAST YEARS

For the sake of as much perspicuity as limited space would allow, the history of "bleeding Kansas" under border ruffians has been thus briefly outlined, and the contest of arguments until the secession of the Southern States has been suggested in advance. It will now be necessary to turn from internal politics and the hurly-burly of the approaching "irrepressible conflict," and to look into the quieter paths of administration and diplomacy. Cass's more active career ended with the 4th of March, 1857. He remained a political mentor to many in his party and took a sad interest in the never-abating struggle; but he was old, the excitement of continual controversy was distasteful, and his new position fortunately gave him employment for which his experience and talents well fitted him. He accepted the office of secretary of state from President Buchanan, and entered upon his duties at once. His companions in the cabinet were Howell Cobb of Georgia, secretary of the treasury; John B. Floyd of Virginia, secretary of war; Isaac Toucey of Connecticut, secretary of the navy;

Aaron V. Brown of Tennessee, postmaster-general; Jacob Thompson of Mississippi, secretary of the interior; and Jeremiah S. Black of Pennsylvania, attorney-general. This cabinet was an able one, but its four Southern members well indicated that the body of the Democratic party was in the South, and that an administration had begun which would treat slavery with tenderness and handle secession with gloves.

A number of interesting diplomatic problems were offered for solution during the years of Cass's secretaryship. The Clayton-Bulwer treaty presented the usual amount of uncertainty and embarrassment, and an even more serious cause of disagreement with Great Britain came up for consideration. By a strange irony of fortune the most important correspondence conducted by the foreign office during Buchanan's administration had to do with the right of search and with the irritating claims put forth by Great Britain of a right to examine our vessels to determine whether they were slavers. In the celebrated controversy between Mr. Webster and Mr. Cass in 1842–43, the latter had contended that our government should have stipulated or at least vigorously asserted that such aggressions were illegal and must be stopped. In the letters with which he so utterly "demolished" the petulant ex-minister, Mr. Webster declared that such a stipulation was needless. Now the question arose anew under more unfortunate circumstances.

It could not be denied that during the years of Buchanan's administration the South was hungry for more slaves. Its woeful defeat in the Territories, and its continual failure to hold its own in wealth and population in comparison with the North, directed its eyes to the only means of competition, the increase of the dead weight of the laboring population. In many portions of the South the reopening of the slave trade was publicly advocated. Governor Adams of South Carolina, in 1857, denounced the laws which forbade the traffic. During the succeeding year the same yearnings were exhibited by remarks in conventions and by paragraphs in the Southern papers. The genial soil of Florida received many new cargoes of inhabitants, and the vessels of the commercial North lent their aid to the infamous trade. But English cruisers, altogether too zealous in hatred of the nefarious commerce, appeared off the coast of Cuba and in the Gulf of Mexico with orders to search merchantmen suspected of carrying slaves. However laudable the object, its execution was exasperating as well as absolutely unjustifiable. In the spring of 1858 the Gulf of Mexico and neighboring waters frequented by American merchantmen were patroled by a police force of British cruisers in a manner calculated to incense all sections of the country and the members of all political parties. American vessels were searched, or "visited," as the English would say in more polite parlance, with an insolence which awakened the animosity of the very haters of slavery.

In April, 1858, in response to a call from the Senate for information concerning the slave trade, the secretaries of state and of the navy furnished dispatches and correspondence. Although our government professed becoming zeal in the matter, it was evident that the efforts of the British and the American cruisers on the coast of Africa were not efficacious. The slave trade was flourishing. In May the President responded to another call from the Senate for information about search or seizure in the Gulf of Mexico. The correspondence sent in by Secretary Cass showed atrocious interference with our commerce by English cruisers; some of our vessels were fired upon, and a number searched after the insulting fashion which marked so much of our treatment from England before 1861. Warlike speeches followed in Congress. At the suggestion of Cass, war vessels were sent into Southern waters, while he prepared to contest the case with the English government in diplomatic dispatches.

He entered gladly into the controversy, for the circumstances seemed powerfully to vindicate his arguments in his correspondence with Webster. On April 10 he wrote to Lord Napier an able letter. He denied that there was any fundamental difference between "visit" and "search." The right to examine and pass upon a vessel's national character and identity he denied. "To permit a foreign officer to board the vessel of another power, to assume command in her, to call for and examine her papers, to pass judgment upon her character, to decide the broad inquiry, whether she is navigated according to law, and to send her in at pleasure for trial, cannot be submitted to by any independent nation without dishonor."[1] He announced the principle, which makes perfectly clear and reasonable the distinction for which he had always contended between searching a real and a spurious American vessel. It had been argued that if American vessels could not be visited and investigated, any foreign ship, even one belonging to a nation which had a treaty with England allowing search for the prevention of the slave trade, might carry on such trade with impunity by merely hoisting the American flag. In the following words the secretary cleared the subject of its fog: "A merchant vessel upon the high seas is protected by her national character. He who forcibly enters her does so upon his own responsibility. Undoubtedly, if a vessel assume a national character to which she is not entitled, and is sailing under false colors, she cannot be protected by the assumption of a nationality to which she has no claim. As the identity of a person must be determined by the officer bearing a process for his arrest, and determined at the risk of such officer, so must the national identity of a vessel be determined, at the like hazard to

[1] *Senate Documents*, vol. xii., 1857–58.

him, who, doubting the flag she displays, searches her to ascertain her true character. There no doubt may be circumstances which may go far to modify the complaints a nation would have a right to make for such a violation of its sovereignty. If the boarding officer had just grounds for suspicion, and deported himself with propriety in the performance of his task, doing no injury, and peaceably retiring when satisfied of his error, no nation would make such an act the subject of serious reclamation." This was much the same as the logic of his pamphlet issued in 1842, and which had been so unjustly condemned as "inconclusive." In fact it was sound, conclusive, and unanswerable. From the early years of his governorship Cass had pondered this subject, and he was now prepared to write the exhaustive dispatch which contained the thought of years in its irrefutable arguments. His quotations from English authorities were so appropriate and his reasoning so true that the English government had perforce to abandon a claim which had been a source of vexation and annoyance since the definitive treaty of 1783. Various communications passed between the two countries after the writing of this important dispatch of April 10. Cass insisted that search and visitation must cease. On June 8, 1858, G. M. Dallas, our minister to the court of St. James, wrote to our foreign office the summary of one of the most important interviews in the diplomatic history of the United States.

Beginning his letter somewhat disconsolately, Mr. Dallas continued: "I had written thus far when I was obliged to hurry off and keep an engagement to meet Lord Malmesbury at his residence in Whitehall Gardens at twelve o'clock, and I returned after an hour's interview with a result little expected when I went.

"Something within the last twelve hours had shifted his lordship's mind to an opposite point of the compass. He talked a great deal and I listened. He was anxious to fix as precisely as possible what the American government wanted on the right of search, and I said, in as gentle a manner as could be distinct: 'Discontinuance, nothing more, nothing less; that, at all events, was my present aim. General Cass had the broad subject between himself and Lord Napier, and I was not authorized to meddle with that.' He recurred to your admirable letter of the 10th of April last, lying before him, and read a number of passages. He expressed his entire assent with your position on international laws on the illegality of visit or search except by conventional agreement, and seemed full of admiration for its ability. . . . In fine, we came to an understanding."[1] A minute of the conference, written by Lord Malmesbury himself, gave proof of the withdrawal of Great Britain from the position she had held so long and so provokingly. "Her Majesty's government recognizes the principle of international

[1] Senate Docs. 2d Sess. 35th Cong., vol. i. p. 34.

law as laid down by General Cass in his note of the 10th of April."[1] In his annual message of December 6, 1858, President Buchanan said: "I am gratified to inform you that the long-pending controversy between the two governments, in relation to the question of visitation and search, has been amicably adjusted."[2] During the succeeding year, correspondence was conducted between Secretary Cass and the English and French governments, which resulted in the agreement upon certain rules and instructions to seamen, concerning the right of visitation. Singular enough does it seem to see the government of Great Britain explicitly telling her naval officers that "no merchant vessel navigating the high seas is subject to any foreign jurisdiction. A vessel of war cannot, therefore, *visit*, *detain*, or *seize* (except under the treaty) any merchant vessel not recognized as belonging to her own nation."[3] The commanders of her ships of war were instructed to treat vessels bearing a foreign flag with the utmost deference; only under cases of the strongest suspicion might they stop a ship and examine her papers for the purpose of ascertaining her real character, and then for such conduct an officer must consider himself as possibly responsible for damages, inasmuch as any unjustifiable inquiry would be basis

[1] Senate Docs. 2d Sess. 35th Cong., vol. i. p. 35. See also, pp. 36–39, *ibid.*

[2] *Ibid.*, p. 12.

[3] Senate Docs. 1st Sess. 36th Cong., p. 78. The italics are my own.

for a claim for indemnity.[1] Our government sent substantially similar instructions to the commanders of our African fleet. Because of other exciting topics, the greatness of this diplomatic victory attracted comparatively little attention. Yet it was one of the most just and most brilliant triumphs of which to this day our diplomacy can boast. The withdrawal of England's claims to extra-territorial jurisdiction has never been associated as it should be with the name and fame of Cass, who pushed his argument so strongly and clinched it so effectively. Unfortunately for him his distinguished success in this business was thrown into obscurity by the lowering clouds of secession and rebellion, portentous of the awful catastrophe of 1861.

Serious difficulties with Mexico during President Buchanan's administration also called forth many dispatches from our foreign office, which are full of dignified American feeling and replete with pithy maxims of sound international law. The governments of Mexico were at this time turning on their axes in a series of well-executed revolutions, performed with such rapidity that our government scarcely knew in whom to recognize the legitimate authority. General Cass's message to Mr. McLane, minister resident to that country, contains an application of the Monroe doctrine very succinctly worded: "While we do not deny the right of any other power to carry on hostile

[1] Senate Docs. 1st Sess. 36th Cong., p. 78.

operations against Mexico, for the redress of its grievances, we firmly object to its holding possession of any part of that country, or endeavoring by force to control its political destiny." Had it been possible for our government to adhere to this policy, the interference of the French and the unhappy fate of Maximilian might have been averted.

The best known and not the least important of Cass's dispatches and instructions is one sent by him to our various representatives in Europe, June 27, 1859, on the outbreak of the Italian war. It outlined the neutral character and policy of the United States, and defined our position on the subject of commercial blockades in such judicious terms that his words have since been frequently quoted by writers on the law of nations. But general rules in such a matter are dangerous. Only two years before the Rebellion, when our government established the most extensive commercial blockade ever made effective and legitimate in the history of the world, and that too under circumstances which go far to shake any *a priori* arguments concerning the right of such action, our secretary of state entered into a long and learned disquisition, asserting the injustice of any but very limited, definite, and effectual restrictions upon commercial intercourse. This same dispatch contained a summary of the attitude of the United States toward the treaty of Paris and the rights of neutrals.

While engaged in the congenial work of diplomacy Cass could not lose sight of the disturbed condition of the country in internal politics. The growth of the Republican party, protesting against the Dred Scott case and the injustice to Kansas, seemed so perilous to the South during the later years of Buchanan's administration, that threats of secession in case of its final success were made with frankness. Cass, more than many of the prominent men of the time, saw and felt the impending danger. The violence of political feeling, the virulence of party action, the antipathy to slavery, and the hatred of Southern bravado, which no State exhibited better than his own, affected the old statesman with misgivings, and filled the last days of his active life with acute grief and foreboding.

Singularly simple in its real meaning, the campaign of 1860 seems, at first sight, unusually intricate and complex. The Democratic party was split into two factions. The first was composed of those who were unwilling to give themselves up entirely to Southern dictation, or to turn their backs on the doctrine of "squatter sovereignty," which had carried them through the last two elections; they clung to old principles, though professing a willingness to abide by the decisions of the Supreme Court. They nominated Stephen A. Douglas for president and Herschel V. Johnson of Georgia for vice-president. The Southern wing of the Democracy, with those Northern men who were willing to accept the Dred Scott case and to see in it a final decision establishing the legality of slavery in the Territories, nominated John C. Breckinridge of Kentucky and Joseph Lane of Oregon. A third ticket was presented by a party styling itself the Constitutional Union party, a mere reminiscence of the days when words were called upon to fill political chasms and to conceal facts. The nominees of this party were John Bell of Tennessee and Edward Everett of Massachusetts. It stood for union under the laws and the Constitution, which could mean nothing when the question was, "What are the laws and the Constitution?" The Republican party, meeting in convention at Chicago, nominated Abraham Lincoln of Illinois and Hannibal Hamlin of Maine. Theirs was a Northern platform, denouncing the spread of slavery and denying the power of Congress or of any territorial legislature to legalize slavery in the Territories. The popular tactics of the managers of the party, and their shrewdness in appealing to the enthusiasm as well as the moral motives of the people, insured success against the quarreling factions of the enemy. The old Northwest was faithful to its party and its principle, even Illinois giving Lincoln a clear majority over all of nearly 5000, while Michigan gave over 20,000, and Ohio a plurality of nearly 45,000. The North was solid, with the exception of New Jersey, which was divided. Lincoln was elected by a popular plurality of 491,654, and by a decided electoral majority.

The Republican victory furnished excuse for putting into active operation the plots for secession which had been long contemplated by the advanced conspirators of the South. On November 10 a bill to raise and equip 10,000 volunteers was introduced into the legislature of South Carolina, and her senators resigned their seats in Congress. The Gulf States fell into line with some hesitation, while the border States held back, deploring the hasty action of the more slave-cursed States of the South. The cabinet, of which General Cass was a member, was the centre if not the source of the conspiracy. From it flowed suggestion and inspiration for the active agitators in the South; into it percolated all the sly schemes and wily devices of the crafty leaders of the Rebellion. Floyd, the secretary of war, Thompson, the secretary of the interior, Cobb, the secretary of the treasury, were engaged in correspondence with the enemies of the Union, furnishing them with munitions of war, treasonably using their authority and the resources of the nation, filling the vacillating mind of the wavering President with gloomy fears and excuses for delay. Buchanan, lacking the courage to follow out any distinct line of policy, contented himself with argument and appeal. The assistant secretary of state was an active conspirator for secession, even before the election.

Cass himself held a fair and consistent position. Lamenting the threatened disruption of the Union, he was not ready to yield every point for the sake of avoiding trouble. "At a cabinet meeting, held November 9, General Cass spoke with much earnestness and feeling about the impending crisis, admitted fully all the great wrongs and outrages which had been committed against the South by Northern fanaticism, and deplored it. But he was emphatic in his condemnation of the doctrine of secession by any State from the Union. He doubted the efficacy of the appeal for a convention, but seemed to think it might be well enough to try it. He spoke warmly in favor of using force to coerce a State that attempted to secede." This is the testimony of Secretary Floyd himself. Though it is doubtful if Cass ever emphatically acknowledged the right to coerce a State as such, his opinions were substantially those here attributed to him. He was decidedly for the Union. The conspiracy widened and deepened. The secretary of war, openly disowning secession, covertly gave secret information to the foes of the government, who knew before it was transmitted to Congress what would be the position of the President in his message to Congress in December.

General Cass seems, at least at first, to have acquiesced in the general tenor of the President's message, so far as the theoretical relation between the national government and the States was concerned. Secretary Floyd tells us that when portions of it were first read to the cabinet for approval Cass heartily commended it; for it then inculcated, it seems, submission to Lincoln's election, and perhaps even intimated the use of force to compel such submission. The document, when finished, presented a combination of power and weakness in the central government which were conditions of complete inertia. After charging the present unpleasantness upon the sectional antipathy of the North, the message gave a detailed argument on the subject of secession and the powers of the national government — secession is illegal, the union is by nature indissoluble, but there is no power in Congress or in any branch of the federal government to compel a State to remain in the Union; it is the duty of the President to enforce the laws; but, if it is impracticable to do so by the ordinary methods, as at present in South Carolina, Congress should determine whether or not existing laws should be amended to carry out effectually the objects of the Constitution; amendments to the Constitution are advisable. The last proposition was absurd. The amendments suggested would have granted all the South had contended for, and would have nullified the voice of the people as expressed in the last election.

The subtle principles of law propounded by the President were too finely spun to be readily accepted by the practical people of the North. That immaterial entity, the State, may be incapable of coercion, may not be within reach of the iron hand of the law; the federal government under the Constitution may not have been expressly given power to wage war upon a recalcitrant State; one of the great instruments of that great sovereignty, the people of the United States, may refuse to perform its functions; but the federal authority comes into contact with individuals, and they can be held to their allegiance; the property of the federal state can and must be protected, and its laws must act and its writs must run within the borders of every State; war upon States is unnecessary, for an indestructible State, though refusing to perform its functions, can never cease to be a member of an indestructible Union. Such sound, practical sense soon found its place in the minds of the sobered people of the North, although not for months were they fully aroused to fight for its logical conclusions and assert in arms that the nation was an organic whole. But argument was unnecessary and entirely beside the mark; it was the duty of the executive to enforce the laws. Even Buchanan admitted that the central government operated directly on persons. There was, as yet, no practical instance of secession, and if the President had held firmly in his hands the reins of government, quickly dismissed the conspiring secessionists from his cabinet, used his power as the executive and commander-in-chief to protect the property and enforce the laws of the United States, there is good reason to think that secession would have meant less in our history.

Though apparently agreeing with the argument of the message, and believing that a State could not be coerced, Cass was not willing to admit that the federal government was impotent.[1] At various cabinet meetings he insisted that the forts in Charleston harbor should be reinforced, and that, in view of the well-known conspiracy to disobey the laws, steps should be taken to strengthen the hand of the government in the Southern States. On December 13 he made a last effort to convince the President of the necessity of such action, but he was rebuffed. "These forts," he said, "must be strengthened. I demand it." "I am sorry to differ from the secretary of state," the President replied. "I have made up my mind. The interests of the country do not demand a reinforcement of the forces in Charleston. I cannot do it, and I take the responsibility on myself." The next day[2] General Cass handed in his resignation as

[1] "Not recognizing any right in a State to secede except as a revolutionary measure, General Cass would have resisted the attempt at the commencement, and, as the sworn officer of the United States, he would have done his utmost to preserve its integrity. 'I speak to Cable,' he would say, 'and he tells me he is a Georgian; to Floyd, and he tells me he is a Virginian; to you, and you tell me you are a Carolinian. I am not a Michigander: I am a citizen of the United States. The laws of the United States bind you, as they bind me, individually; if you, the citizens of Georgia, or Virginia, or Carolina, refuse obedience to them, it is my sworn duty to enforce them.'" Crawford, *The Genesis of the Civil War*, p. 23.

[2] The resignation was dated December 12, and Buchanan's reply three days later. A memorandum made by the President and printed in Curtis's Life of Buchanan is dated December 15, and refers to the resignations being handed in that evening. But it is apparent that this memorandum was written some days

secretary of state. Mr. Cobb had already resigned the treasury portfolio because of what he considered the "paramount" claims of his State. The resignation of the secretary of state, added to the prevailing excitement, was almost universally commended by the papers of the North that were not indissolubly wedded to the inactive policy of the administration. His house was filled for the next few days with congratulating friends, and Zachariah Chandler called to welcome him into the fold of the Republican party. The old statesman was still consistent, however; he was a Democrat, but a Jackson Democrat.

The letter of resignation is worth reading, inasmuch as it gives in short form the position which Cass held. The important clauses are as follows: —

"It has been my decided opinion, which for some time past I have urged at various meetings of the cabinet, that additional troops should be sent to reënforce the forts in the harbor of Charleston, with a view to their better defense, should they be attacked, and that an

after the day on which it was dated. Dispatches sent to the newspapers seem to make it clear that Cass sent in his resignation on the fourteenth. The following is from a dispatch to the *N. Y. Advertiser*, dated Washington, Dec. 15. "During this morning and yesterday afternoon further developments have been made respecting the causes of disagreement, between the President and the secretary of state, which led to the resignation of the latter." A similar dispatch to the *Herald* dated the fourteenth, speaks of the rumor that Cass had resigned and says that on the afternoon of that day "the report was fully confirmed." Other like evidence could be cited to support the statement in the text. The usual statement is that Cass resigned the fifteenth.

armed vessel should likewise be ordered there to aid if necessary in the defense, and also, should it be required, in the collection of the revenue, and it is yet my opinion that these measures should be adopted without the least delay. I have likewise urged the expediency of immediately removing the custom-house at Charleston to one of the forts in the port, and of making arrangements for the collection of the duties there by having a collector and other officers ready to act when necessary, so that when the office may become vacant the proper authority may be there to collect the duties on the part of the United States.

"I continue to think that these arrangements should be immediately made. While the right and the responsibility of deciding belong to you, it is very desirable that at this perilous juncture there should be as far as possible unanimity in your councils with a view to safe and efficient action. I have, therefore, felt it my duty to tender you my resignation of the office of secretary of state and to ask your permission to retire from that official association with yourself and the members of your cabinet which I have enjoyed during almost four years without the occurrence of a single incident to interrupt the personal intercourse which has so happily existed."

The action of General Cass has been criticised by Buchanan's apologists who, now that the whole conspiracy is as clear as noonday, still claim that it was not the President's duty to act until something was done, and until Congress gave further power. That the Southern forts were in danger there could be no doubt; Buchanan's message confessed that South Carolina was on the point of lawless disregard of the behests of the central government; conventions to consider secession had been called throughout the Southern States; the cabinet itself was in conspiracy against the government; the very air was heavy with threats of secession and violence. Mr. Buchanan's most learned and famous apologist has sneered at the prophetic sagacity of Cass. Not clairvoyance or the spirit of prophecy, but decision, observation, and common sense were the attributes of one who saw, not what might be, but what was.

December 20 Washington was electrified by the announcement that South Carolina had at last adopted an ordinance of secession. Mr. Benson J. Lossing, the skillful writer of American history, was at the house of Cass when a bulletin telling of this action was received. "The venerable statesman read the few words that announced the startling fact, and then, throwing up his hands, while tears started from his eyes, he exclaimed with uncommon unction: 'Can it be! can it be! Oh,' he said, 'I had hoped to retire from the public service, and go home to die with the happy thought, that I should leave to my children, as an inheritance from patriotic men, a united and prosperous republic. But it is all over! This is but the beginning of the end. The people in the South are mad; the people in the North are asleep. The President is pale with fear, for his official household is full of traitors, and conspirators control the government. God only knows what is to be the fate of my poor country! to Him alone must we look in this hour of thick darkness.'"[1] It will be seen, however, that he advocated that action be superadded to faith and devotion.

One other topic remains to be considered in connection with Cass's resignation from the cabinet. The letter, dated December 12, assigned as a reason the President's refusal to reinforce the Charleston forts, and his neglect to prepare for the collection of duties at that port. President Buchanan in accepting the resignation, without deigning to argue the question, stated his belief that reinforcements at Charleston were unnecessary, and expressed his regret that anything should occur to disturb the official relations existing between him and his secretary. From memoranda printed in the "Life of James Buchanan,"[2] it appears that Cass announced his purpose to resign as early as the 11th. Newspapers of the time make it evident that nearly a week before the letter was handed in rumors of Cass's resignation were rife. His withdrawal was received with marked gratification by many, even of those who had not become converts to "black Republicanism." In spite of these facts, Buchanan records that, on December 17, Black and Thompson both informed him that Cass desired to withdraw his resignation. It is always hard to prove a nega-

[1] *Pictorial History of the Civil War*, Lossing, vol. i. p. 141.

[2] By George Ticknor Curtis.

tive, but direct and circumstantial evidence contradicts this statement. In the first place, members of his family who were with him at the time, and were well aware of his thoughts and feelings, positively deny the truth of such assertions. This alone might be sufficient. But, moreover, the resignation, as already suggested, was not unpremeditated; all the world knew of his emphatic disapproval of the President's negligence and timidity, and he found himself lionized and applauded by nearly all save the avowed secessionists. Even the "Charleston Mercury" hastened to add its modicum of praise by styling him a "hoary trickster and humbug," and comparing "his present imbecility" with his "past treachery to the South." "The past secretary will survive," remarked the "New York Times," with laconic sarcasm, as it quoted these expressions of Southern rage. That under such circumstances he should contemplate the backward step of seeking reinstatement is simply incredible and ridiculous.

"Oh, for an hour of Andrew Jackson," sighed the "Springfield Republican." That was what was wanted. With Jackson in the White House and Cass as secretary of war the rebel armies would not have been equipped with governmental arms and accoutrements. The fire and vigor of "Old Hickory" had given to Cass his first great inspiration in national politics. All he could do now was to administer a silent rebuke to timidity where hesitation and cowardice were crimes.

"Ain't it too bad," said a prominent senator, "that a man has to break his sword twice in a lifetime, at the beginning and at the end of his eventful career. At the surrender of Hull at Detroit, Cass was so disgusted at the conduct of his commander, and at not having a fight, that he broke his sword. Now he breaks it because his chief won't fight."[1]

The events rapidly following upon one another through the dreadful winter of 1860–61 do not form part of our story. The treachery of the cabinet, the lethargy of the executive, the confusion and dismay, the low-hanging clouds of war and distress, the frenzy of the insane South and its boastful preparations for a grand confederacy on the cornerstone of slavery, left their sorrowful shadows upon the Union-loving people of the North and filled with gloomy forebodings the mind of the old statesman whose life had been given to his country. When the bombardment of Sumter thrilled the continent and fired the popular heart, Cass was ready with his word of encouragement. At an immense Union meeting in Detroit, April 24, he was made chairman and delivered in a few words an eloquent address. Cheer followed cheer, as the old general, with dramatic effect, thanked God that the American flag still floated over his home and his friends. "No American can see its folds spread out to the breeze without feeling a

[1] Quoted in *Life and Public Services of Andrew Johnson*, by John Savage.

thrill of pride at his heart, and without recalling the splendid deeds it has witnessed. . . . You need no one to tell you what are the dangers of your country, nor what are your duties to meet and avert them. There is but one path for every true man to travel, and that is broad and plain. It will conduct us, not indeed without trials and sufferings, to peace and to the restoration of the Union. He who is not *for* his country is *against* her. There is no neutral position to be occupied. It is the duty of all zealously to support the government in its efforts to bring this unhappy civil war to a speedy and satisfactory conclusion, by the restoration, in its integrity, of that great charter of freedom bequeathed to us by Washington and his compatriots." Sorrowing over his country torn by civil war, the old man was not weakened by age into imbecile maunderings about senseless compromise; by word and example he inspired the patriotic hearts of his fellow citizens. If he was occasionally downcast, his desire for union never faltered. Referring at one time to the bonfires with which New Hampshire celebrated the formation of the Republic, "I have loved the Union," he exclaimed, "ever since the light of that bonfire greeted my eyes. I have given fifty-five years of my life and my best efforts to its preservation. I fear I am doomed to see it perish." It was such a spirit as this which had made him the advocate of compromise and consideration, and which now made him zealous for force.

The last public speech of General Cass was delivered at Hillsdale, Michigan, August 13, 1862, at a "war meeting" called for the purpose of arousing enthusiasm and raising volunteers for the service. The address was short and impressive. He spoke for some twenty minutes earnestly and from the heart. He began with a truthful reference to his own patriotism. "I am sufficiently warned by the advance of age that I can have but little participation in public affairs, but if time has diminished my power to be useful to my country, it has left undiminished the deep interest I feel in her destiny, and my love and reverence for our glorious Constitution which we owe to the kindness of Providence and to the wisdom of our fathers." The whole speech breathes forth the broad sympathy and love of Union which marked his life. Age, which is proverbially kind, did not bring with it enervated principles and the sentimentality of moral and mental languor. He referred to the energy of his own State and praised the exertions it was making for the general welfare. He had visited many portions of it before the Indian had given way to the industry and enterprise of the white man. "I have lived to see it rivaling its sister States in the sacred work of defending the Constitution. And now the course of events has rendered it necessary for the government to appeal again to the people. Additional troops are required for the speedy suppression of the Rebellion. Patriotism and policy equally dictate that our force should be such as to enable us to act with vigor and efficiency against our enemies, and promptly to reduce them to unconditional submission to the laws." Of all the statesmen of his generation, Cass has been understood the least. In the eyes of many, he still appears as a "Northern man with Southern principles," a "doughface," as false and untrustworthy; while Henry Clay and Daniel Webster, whose aims were identical with his, have defenders and apologists by the score; while there is condonation for the rankest acts of the "Copperheads," who maligned and vilified and hissed at home while our soldiers were fighting in the field; while men who proved false to their oaths, and gave their energies to the destruction of their country, are given high offices of honor and of public trust.

One more event of importance intruded itself into the sadly quiet life of the old statesman. Throughout his career he had suspected and opposed the cunning designs of England, had resented her effrontery, had vindicated our rights against her. A fitting close of a public life, which had been strangely consistent and direct, was an act of justice toward England in following out the lines of comity for which he had so often contended. In the latter part of 1861, two commissioners from the Confederacy, intended for England and France, were taken on board the English ship Trent. An American steamer, the San Jacinto, stopped the Trent on her voyage, took from her the Confederate commissioners and proceeded with them to Boston. England claimed with justice that this was a direct violation of her sovereignty, an insult for which immediate atonement was demanded. Our government hesitated. England did not, but immediately made arrangements for war and to mobilize her forces; issued a proclamation to prevent the exportation of arms and ammunition; ordered her minister at Washington to withdraw unless the prisoners were released and our government offered apology within a few days. Flaring into unbecoming wrath, she lavished, it is said, not far from £5,000,000 in preparation for a war which, in spite of the vexations of this whole affair, was needless, and which would not have been nearly so imminent had not her blustering hardened our people into obstinacy. While our government delayed, the people were anxious in spite of their dislike of England's haste. General Cass was besought by some of the influential citizens of Detroit to throw the weight of his advice into the scale, with the purpose of inducing our government to surrender the commissioners and to prevent war. He was persuaded, and wrote a long telegraphic dispatch covering the whole ground, and bringing to bear his learning and the experience of fifty years in which he had thought over and discussed the question of search and visitation. The cabinet decided to humble itself, that it might be exalted on the altar of law and honesty. Seward is reported afterwards to have intimated that Cass's dispatch was of determining weight in the cabinet discussions on the question of surrender. The report seems well founded; but, whether it was thus determinant or not, the dispatch is a graceful end of a life of public service which had been devoted to America, and had resented encroachments upon her dignity.

The last years of Cass were spent quietly at his home in Detroit. He lived to see the Union restored, and the black curse of our country wiped out by the war. His love of books and his scholarly tastes helped him to fill his last days with pleasurable occupation. His many friends, whom he had assisted and to whom he had given a true affection during the years of his active life, did not forsake him when the evil days of sorrow and weakness came upon him. Lifted up by an unfaltering trust, he patiently and cheerfully awaited the end. He was sometimes noticed walking the well-known streets, which he had seen develop from the narrow, crooked ways of the rambling French town into the broad avenues of a modern city. But his work was over; he had reached advanced age before his retirement from public life, and all that was left him was the sorrowful pleasure of peaceful waiting. He died June 17, 1866, in the eighty-fourth year of his age. The reports in the public papers, the resolutions of societies, the farewell comments of friends, betoken the esteem in which he was held and the grief at his death. Members of the bar, who had known his faithful service to the State, spoke in loving admiration of his life. Many men in the prime of life, or nearing the easy descent of age, recalled with gratitude the encouragement and aid given them in the uncertain days of their young manhood. There was no one to cavil. Even his political career, ending in patriotic devotion to country and love for his State and the Union, left little room for fault-finding to those who remembered his pure private life, and his generous friendship and high-minded regard for truth and fairness in all matters of daily business and intercourse. The Republican paper of Detroit, not failing in discrimination while discussing the events of his life, showed a hearty respect for the patriot, the citizen, and the man. Private uprightness, sincerity, and rugged stalwartness of character conquered partisan acrimony in days when even the bitterness of politics seemed sweeter than honey in the honeycomb.

If the foregoing sketch is at all adequate, no elaborate assignment of attributes is needed in conclusion. The character of Cass is presented by his acts, by his attitude on great public questions, and by the results of a life given to the service of his country.[1] Scarcely another man in

[1] In the preparation of the general sketch of the character of Cass, I have relied not only on the impressions produced by a careful study of his words and acts, but also upon statements made to me by men who knew him well, and whose candor and

our history was for so many years so closely connected with the rise and progress of the United States. He stands as a representative of the Old Northwest. Taking his life as a centre, we can trace the political, social, and industrial development of this section of the Union, which, in large part because of his efforts, changed in a generation from wildness and stagnation into order and activity. He was the "Father of the West," but his generous patriotism left no room for selfish provincialism. He was a democrat in the general sense of the word, inculcating throughout his career with unflinching zeal the great doctrine of faith in the people, and in the dignity and worth of the common American voter; but his love of individual liberty and his advocacy of personal

intelligent discrimination I could trust. As I have said in my preface, I have neither cared nor dared to reject the estimate of the personality of Cass given me by men of intelligence who knew him as he was, men of affairs who were part of the times of which I write and who could speak, from their own knowledge, concerning the moral worth, integrity and intellectual strength of the subject of my sketch. I have not placed confidence in the random recollections of those who chanced to know him; but have sought the sober judgment of persons of experience who knew the historical circumstance and were able from their knowledge of the man to reach sensible and reasonable conclusions. To give no credence to the statements of such men as I have consulted, and to rely on the opinion of the secondary writers or the prejudiced assertions of contemporaries would be to disregard the most fundamental canon in the preparation of historical narrative. I add this note because I think that it is customary to underestimate the character and the intellectual ability of Cass, and because some fault has been found by critics of the first edition with my general appraisal of his worth and influence.

rights did not blind his eyes to the grand individuality of the nation, and the bright destiny of a Union which was more than a union of States. With an extreme Americanism he indorsed in his life the party doctrine that the "world is too much governed;" but he did not lose himself in silly sentimentalities about the needlessness of government, nor confound lawlessness and liberty. He was a Democrat in the party sense of the word, a strong adherent to the party organization; but he did not let his hunger for success or his thirst for revenge deaden his senses to a perception of justice, nor cause him to see liberty in rebellion and freedom under the manacles of the slave.

He was fair and honest, winning by his frankness the confidence of fellow-partisans and opponents. The Republican party seemed to him at first a sectional party, built upon localism and inconsiderateness, but, when it proved the defender of the Union, although he never forsook his own standard, nor capitulated in dogma, he gave advice and counsel in behalf of the great purpose of those against whom he might have stored up wrath. In his speeches in the Senate, in private conversation, and in correspondence with friends, he always pleaded for the broader sympathy and more charitable interpretation. In spite of the vigor of his utterances and the force of his speech when once aroused to defend a great national principle or to expound party doctrine, the records of

Congress will be searched in vain for a prevailing or even passing feeling of ill-will against him. Those who came in contact with him were disarmed of suspicions by his benignant frankness and the complete good faith which action and word emphasized. Yet his sincerity has been especially stabbed by innuendo, and attacked by open statement, until those who have not known him as he was pass him by as a man who smothered his small principles and traded conscience for applause. That the hope of the presidency did not dazzle his judgment until it could not read in the inner white light of his heart, it would be presumptuous to declare. Blind self-deception, so ready to answer our call for guidance, may have led him into the ditch. But we turn to a full record of his life, and ask that those who cavil at a part may construe with the context before them. The doctrine of popular sovereignty has added its blight to his name, but it was not for him a new doctrine; his more prominent political life was begun in an effort to promote, among the body of the people, interest and action in local affairs. His love of union, his great feeling of nationalism, and his resentment of foreign interference, gave a coherence and consistency to his life, and prove by their continuance his thoroughness, earnestness, and sincerity.

The daily social and family life of General Cass was one of such even courtesy and kindness that mere assertion leaves little room for explanation or addition. To those who came to him for aid or advice he was an interested friend; young men especially attracted him, and he took great pleasure in giving them encouragement, in offering them help in their times of doubt or need. He was not fond of general society; his simple tastes and quiet, abstemious habits held him back from an indulgence in the mere frivolity and formality of Washington life. In his own home, however, he dispensed a large and delightful hospitality. From 1831 until his withdrawal from Buchanan's cabinet, he spent the greater portion of his time away from Detroit; but his old house at that place, filled with curios and interesting relics from the frontiers of America and the gay capitals of Europe, was not infrequently occupied, and he there received his friends with generous, unstinted welcome. He then had the finest library in Michigan, and the room which held his favorite books was his own peculiar home. There he often entertained small companies of more intimate friends and of distinguished men. While agreeable and entertaining in private conversation, showing wide reading and broad comprehension, impressing all who listened to his unpretentious talk with the feeling that they were in the presence of a well-informed and cultured gentleman, he had none of the rarer charms of personal grace or of wit and brilliance; there was no flash of sudden genius or warmth of kindling enthusiasm over a keen or subtle argument. On the contrary, in public and in private speech, his face generally maintained a certain immobility. His features were heavy, only occasionally lighted up when unusual circumstances called for the determination, boldness, and vigor of the man. Even then he was impressive, ponderous, sternly dominant. Yet a customary look of benignity softened the severity of his face; in hours of political success or defeat he maintained his serenity and hopefulness; he habitually, in his private conversations, refrained from rancor or trenchant criticism and imputation.

Before the public, General Cass was a man who carried weight by the density and compactness of his arguments, by the vigor of his language, and the gravity of his sense. He was not always right; his earlier vigor and fire were tempered into boldness and decision in middle age, and became unbending, consistent conservatism in the days of his later public service, a conservatism which often led him to adopt political inexpedients and did not restrain him from error. But his public utterances always made an impression, and doubtless served to dampen a too ardent impetuosity. He often, perhaps usually, read his speeches from manuscript. They were skillfully and elaborately prepared. His large figure and his erect bearing aided the dignity of his words; and often where a man of less significant appearance would escape attention, or leave an audience unaffected by his appeals, the physical poise and stateliness of Cass would arrest the attention of the heedless, and compel conviction in the doubting. So universally thoughtful and well-considered, however, were his public addresses, that mere physical greatness was not needed to make them worthy of notice. What was worth doing at all seemed worth doing well; his orations at agricultural meetings and at great industrial celebrations show the customary breadth of scholarship and careful preparation. He was not an orator in the sense that Henry Clay and Patrick Henry were orators. He belonged rather to the unimpassioned school of steady thinkers and not too ready speakers, whose words come for a purpose and with the stored-up energy of conviction. An opponent was rather crushed by the dead weight of argument than taken captive by blandishments of rhetoric.

He was a scholar and a man of books as well as a politician and a statesman. His essays were often even graceful, and always bore the same marks of care which his speeches presented. When starting on one of his long voyages in his bark canoe in the days of his governorship, he used to supply himself with a number of books; and, as he journeyed, he read them thoughtfully, or he listened while one of his companions read them to him. The information, thus stored away in his mind, often in later years showed itself in some rare and unexpected piece of knowledge. He never was enticed by the excitement of politics entirely to forsake his books. He could not become a profound scholar in the midst of his active life, but his learning was unusually wide, often surprising by its scope even those who knew him well and had reason to respect his studies. To an intimate acquaintance with the great facts of history he added no meagre knowledge of science and literature. In 1827 he read before the Detroit Historical Society an essay on the Early History of Detroit and the Conspiracy of Pontiac, a valuable contribution to historical literature. This essay and three others by fellow-members of the society have been published under the title "Sketches of Michigan." In 1830 he delivered a scholarly address before the Association of Alumni of Hamilton College, and in 1836, as first president of the American Historical Association, he read an article which bears the marks of thoughtful preparation, as well as knowledge and appreciation of the great truths of history and of political philosophy. His articles in the "North American Review" treat generally of Indian and Western subjects, and show his great acquaintance with Indian character and of the problems which affect our country's progress. These essays are long and discursive, written at a time when our important magazines invited profound and exhaustive treatment of interesting and serious topics. While secretary of war he prepared for the "American Quarterly Review" an account of the siege of New Orleans. The article, covering some sixty pages of the magazine, is of lasting historic value, inasmuch as it was based upon papers and information intrusted to him by General Jackson. His most valuable literary work was in connection with the history of New France. Dr. Francis Parkman acknowledges his indebtedness to "Hon. Lewis Cass for a curious collection of papers relating to the siege of Detroit by the Indians."[1] While minister in France, he collected and examined documentary evidence relating to the French power in America, and procured important papers which were published by the Wisconsin Historical Society. He not only gave material and inspiration to Mrs. Sheldon for her "Early History of Michigan," but aided and encouraged M. Pierre Margry to begin the studies which have resulted in such valuable additions to historical information. His own studies of contemporary France, while representing our own government, were embodied in a book already mentioned, "France, its King, Court, and Government," a book of 190 closely printed octavo pages. About the same time he published "Three Hours at Saint Cloud," and an article of no little worth in the "Democratic Review" on "The Modern French Judicature." All the contributions to periodicals were more than mere trivialities dashed off in haste for a penny a line; they are real additions to knowledge.

In public and private life he was honest. About 1815 he bought, with funds received from the sale of lands in Ohio, a large tract of land near Detroit. As the city grew, this property came into

[1] *Conspiracy of Pontiac*, Preface.

demand, and its sale in lots made him wealthy. He had no temptation to be dishonest in public dealings, or, as is sometimes charged, to be a "money-maker." He was completely free from the taints of financial corruption. To honesty he added temperance. He seldom tasted wine of any kind, though not refusing to provide his guests with the best. His public work in behalf of temperance has been spoken of; when secretary of war he called attention to the subject of intemperance in the army, and advocated that other rations be substituted for whiskey. He also spoke publicly of the evils of drink. His moderation reached beyond the limits of meat and drink, and showed itself in a life strangely regular and methodical, prolonged, in consequence, to an advanced age, unimpaired by disease, or weakened by aught save the attacks of time.

The name of Lewis Cass will not be written in the future with those of the few men whose influence is everywhere discernible, and who perpetuate themselves in institutions and in national tendencies. He was not a Washington, nor a Lincoln, nor a Hamilton, nor a Jefferson, nor a John Quincy Adams. But he was a great American statesman, building up and Americanizing an important section of his country, struggling in places of trust for the recognition of American dignity and for the development of generous nationalism. With the great slavery contest his name is inseparably connected; he stood with Webster and Clay for Union, for conciliation, for the Constitution as it seemed to be established. He was one of those men whose broad love of country and pride in her greatness, however exaggerated, however absurd it may seem in these days of cynical self-restraint, lifted her from colonialism to national dignity, and imbued the people with a sense of their power.

INDEX

INDEX

A native of Illinois, ANDREW C. MCLAUGHLIN (1861-1947) began teaching at the University of Michigan in 1891. He then moved to the University of Chicago, where he taught for twenty-three years and established a reputation as one of the foremost historical scholars of his era. Winner of the Pulitzer Prize in history, McLaughlin also served as president of the American Historical Association. In addition to his biography of Cass, he authored many books on the Constitution, including *The Courts, the Constitution and Parties*, *Foundations of American Constitutionalism*, and *A Constitutional History of the United States*.

HOLMAN HAMILTON was History Professor Emeritus at the University of Kentucky at Lexington. He served as president of the Southern Historical Association in 1979 and was a member of numerous other historical societies, including the Organization of American Historians and the Kentucky Historic Preservation Commission. Author of many distinguished books on American history, Hamilton is best known for *Zachary Taylor: Soldier in the White House*, *White House Images and Realities*, and *Prologue to Conflict: The Crisis and Conflict of 1850*.